Bombay, Meri Jaan

'Vibrant, engaging and provocative...an anthology that is emblematic of the richly endowed city it celebrates.' —*Business India*

'A delightful addition to the collection of those who love Bombay.'—*Hindustan Times*

'A wonderful collection of writing—poetry, fiction, theatre, social history, memoirs, journalism—on India's most cosmopolitan city.'—*The Telegraph*

'Organizing an anthology on a city like Mumbai is a bit like making the perfect bhelpuri—not too hot, not too bland...on the whole the mix (in *Bombay, Meri Jaan*) is entirely palatable, even delicious.'—*The Hindu*

'A tribute to the undying spirit of the city...This compilation of essays, poems, illustrations, photographs, a play and a sing-along song... encapsulates the hope and the despair, the grime and the glamour...of this maddening, soulless but often self-fulfilling metropolis.'—*The Statesman*

'The word "addiction" stays in your mind as you begin with the first writing...By the time you are onto the second chapter—an exhaustive piece by Pico Iyer...you not only begin to fathom what this addiction is all about but also find yourself getting ensnared to read more and more about this "richest and most corrupt" metropolis in the subcontinent...There is never a dull moment.' —*The Tribune*

'This is truly a bhelpuri of a book, where diverse elements come together to make a mouth-watering and enlightening whole...Even if you are not a regular reader, you will love this book.'—*Business Standard*

Bombay, Meri Jaan

Writings on Mumbai

Edited by Jerry Pinto and Naresh Fernandes

PENGUIN BOOKS

PENGUIN BOOKS
Published by the Penguin Group
Penguin Books India Pvt Ltd, 11 Community Centre, Panchsheel Park, New Delhi
110 017, India
Penguin Group (USA) Inc., 375 Hudson Street, New York, New York 10014, USA
Penguin Group (Canada), 90 Eglinton Avenue East, Suite 700, Toronto, Ontario,
M4P 2Y3, Canada (a division of Pearson Penguin Canada Inc.)
Penguin Books Ltd, 80 Strand, London WC2R 0RL, England
Penguin Ireland, 25 St Stephen's Green, Dublin 2, Ireland (a division of Penguin
Books Ltd)
Penguin Group (Australia), 250 Camberwell Road, Camberwell, Victoria 3124,
Australia (a division of Pearson Australia Group Pty Ltd)
Penguin Group (NZ), cnr Airborne and Rosedale Road, Albany, Auckland 1310,
New Zealand (a division of Pearson New Zealand Ltd)
Penguin Group (South Africa) (Pty) Ltd, 24 Sturdee Avenue, Rosebank, Johannesburg
2196, South Africa

Penguin Books Ltd, Registered Offices: 80 Strand, London WC2R 0RL, England

First published by Penguin Books India 2003

This anthology copyright © Penguin Books India 2003
Introduction copyright © Naresh Fernandes and Jerry Pinto 2003
Cartoons copyright © Harish Morparia
The copyright for individual pieces and photographs vests with the respective authors/
photographers or their estates.

Pages 347–348 are an extension of the copyright page.

All rights reserved

10 9 8 7

For sale in the Indian Subcontinent and Singapore only

Typeset in Ehrhard MT by Mantra Virtual Services, New Delhi
Printed at Chaman Offset Printers, New Delhi

Contents

Zara hatke, zara bachke
Yeh hai Bambai, meri jaan.

Duck a little, save yourself—
This is Bombay, my love.

—Lyrics by Majrooh Sultanpuri from the film *CID* (1954)

Dangerlok, she says, all dangerlok.

—*Dangerlok* by Eunice de Souza

Introduction: The Lived City

Jerry Pinto and Naresh Fernandes

Once Bombay lodges itself in your eye, you're doomed to a lifetime of tunnel vision. Exploring the damp delights of Brussels one morning not so long ago, we made our way to the Cinquantenaire, a triumphal arch erected to commemorate Belgium's golden jubilee. We peered at its drizzly outlines for a few seconds and almost simultaneously reached the same conclusion: it was merely a bombastic version of the Gateway of India.

We already shared another conviction. We'd both lived in other cities, but it was clear that Bombay is home. Our roots had fed off the putrefied ballast of palm fronds and fish entrails that was used to reclaim the seven islands from ocean and iniquity. Unfortunately, it's scarcely that simple. Roots don't hold easily in a metropolis built on ever-shifting flood plains and tremulous marsh. Bombay's always a struggle, but we're hooked on the thrill of daily combat.

Bombay has none of the imperium of Delhi, the self-conscious stasis of Calcutta or the provincial self-satisfaction of Madras. It is the ugly stepdaughter city but Prince Charming must cut his heels off to win her hand. It is a city in which no one dies of starvation but the vast majority are forced to endure living conditions that no enlightened zookeeper would allow for his animals. Yet the exiles and arrivistes keep flooding into the City Imagined, to the Bombay they see as siren and saviour. They never leave.

Why would you do that? Why would you live in a matchbox, breathe bad air, drink foul water, offer yourself as mosquito-fodder and roadkill? Because Bombay is an addiction. It isn't good for you but you need the high of neon and insomnia, concrete and opportunity.

While putting together an anthology such as this one is not rocket science, it tends to have its own challenges. What you exclude becomes as much of a statement as what you include. Then there is always a streak of guilt. Friends become repositories of wisdom and talk about the ancient *hamam* in South Bombay where you can still have a Turkish bath; others ask if you are including anything on the black sand beach from which one of Emperor Ashoka's progeny is supposed to have set out to proselytise for the Buddha; others suggest impossible photo-essays on the interiors of the Governor's bungalow or a dog's eye-view of the city. Everyone has a Bombay story, a Bombay they want represented. And everyone's Bombay is not the Bombay we thought we knew.

When we started on this project, we were clear: we wanted to serve up the taste of the Lived Bombay rather than the more exotic flavours of the Visited Bombay. This is a vision of Bombay, stereoscopic, multiple, fuzzy, alienated, integrated, all of the above.

The inside back flap is blank. That's where you should write your Bombay story or put in the piece you would have written had you the time or the one you wrote and we didn't know about.

Island

Nissim Ezekiel

Unsuitable for song as well as sense
the island flowers into slums
and skyscrapers, reflecting
precisely the growth of my mind.
I am here to find my way in it.

Sometimes I cry for help
but mostly keep my own counsel.
I hear distorted echoes
of my own ambiguous voice
and of dragons claiming to be human.

Bright and tempting breezes
flow across the island,
separating past from future;
then the air is still again
as I sleep the sleep of ignorance.

How delight the soul with absolute
sense of salvation, how
hold to a single willed direction?
I cannot leave the island
I was born here and belong.

Even now a host of miracles
hurries me to daily business,
minding the ways of the island
as a good native should,
taking calm and clamour in my stride.

From *Collected Poems* (1989).

Bombay: Hobson-Jobson on the Streets

Pico Iyer

All cities are best seen in the dawn, but in Bombay this is especially the case, for only when the day is fresh and young, and the city still uncrowded, can you see what this swampy spit of land is, what it was, what it will be. Go to Sassoon Dock at break of day, and there before you are the two unchanging forces of Bombay—commerce and the sea—in jostling, clangorous, Technicolour profusion. As the sun rises behind rows of multicoloured fishing boats, blue and orange and aqua, and as birds begin circling the pinkening sky, the small, slippery, partly covered area becomes almost unimaginably crowded with women carrying baskets on their heads, baskets piled high with the night's silver catch, and people slipping coins from palm to palm.

Shacks on all sides advertise 'Fish Industries' and 'Batteries for Launching Boats,' and the area stinks of fish, and as you make your way through a courtyard full of trucks, with people clinging to their sides, you can see nuns urging themselves forward, tiny, pinch-cheeked women pushing them aside, flirty-eyed girls barking numbers back and forth and determined matrons flinging themselves into the crush like battering rams, hands on the shoulders of the person in front of them. The fishermen stand in their holds, watching the yelling chaos on shore, and the noisy fishwives in their tropicoloured saris bustle around with their tattoos and jangling bracelets and tiny mirrors at their wrists, and a whole babel of shouts and invective rises up as the day's cut-throat business begins. And as the baskets float across a sea of bobbing black heads, you can see that Bombay is a place where good cheer collides with enterprise, in a raucous defiance of every notion of

From *Tropical Classical* (1997).

propriety and order and a woman's place being in the home.

At such moments, I always feel I can see a Bombay that existed long before the Portuguese, the British or the latest invasion of Coke and Colonel Sanders: a Bombay changeless as the sea, and one that still betrays its origins in its weatherworn surfaces, its skinny palm trees, the balconied apartments along the sweeping corniche of Marine Drive that is still known at night as the 'Queen's Necklace'. Like its kindred spirits, Hong Kong and Manhattan, Bombay is a street-smart, cash register-quick, anomalous hive—and an island; but for many Indians it has always been an island in a deeper sense, a beachhead for the modern, a multi-cultured port, and a haven of tolerance in a country too often torn apart by 1652 dialects, more than 2000 castes, several major religions and all the extra divisions imposed by the East India Company and their successors.

Culturally, then, Bombay has always been a money-minded mix, where Christians called Coutinho, da Cunha, and de Souza have mingled with Parsis (from Iran) called Merchant and Engineer, in the company of Muslims, Sikhs, Jains and an odd variety of cross-breeds (the hero of Salman Rushdie's last novel, *The Moor's Last Sigh,* is Bombay itself—depicted as a half-Catholic, half-Jewish Moor not unlike his creator, a Christian-educated, Hindu-surrounded, Muslim-apostate Englishman). Socially, the centre of the subcontinent's bright-lights, big-city dreams—home to the strenuous fantasies of 'Bollywood' and hunting-ground of mobsters and their molls—is at once the 'Capital of Hope', to which hundreds of thousands of newcomers flock each year, dreaming of making their fortunes, and a decidedly ruthless place, where more visitors find jobs than homes. And economically, the country's capital of capital, responsible for nearly half of India's foreign trade, has always been no less extreme, as five million of its people live in slums or on the streets, while those above them recline in apartments more expensive per square foot than anything in Tokyo or New York.

In the nineties, however, all these quickening divisions have been intensified as all India has suddenly been released from forty years of socialist policies, and Bombay has suddenly found itself more than ever like some mythic creature in a Rushdie novel, experiencing dawn and dusk at the same time. On the one hand, the masala melting pot—India's Hollywood and Wall Street combined—has become the natural nerve centre for a new 'wired' free-market India, a time-worn Manhattan of the eighties, with its own insider scandals, runaway fortunes, and slightly precarious, self-exhilarated sense of being at the centre of the universe. Yet even as—and largely because—it has been launching itself so eagerly into the future, some of its loyalists have been trying to tug it back into the past, and while Benetton and web sites and long-banned multinationals have streamed into the 'City by the Sea', the nervous right-wingers of the Shiv Sena Party, led by their cartoonist-turned-demagogue Bal Thackeray, have gone about setting off riots, bombing international buildings and threatening to smash every Coke bottle in the country. Just over a year ago, they even managed to change the city's official name to 'Mumbai', a way of telling the world that Bombay belongs to its original Maharashtrian settlers, and the outsiders who have helped to make it prosper—Parsis and Muslims and Gujaratis and Jews—should stay out.

Yet for me, the most recent agitations were set against a background even deeper, and marked by the mingled origins that define the city at its heart. For it was in Bombay that my mother and father (coming from North India and South India, respectively) both grew up, and it is in Bombay that most of my family still lives. It was in Bombay, on my first visit, at the age of two, that I learned to walk. Yet Bombay remains as alien to me as the street signs I cannot read and the names I can't pronounce. It is common these days to hear the city spoken of as a pressure point for an archetypal global struggle between a multicultural future and a tribal past, a place (like Hong Kong) where one kind of empire—economic and postnational—is running up against another (Bombay is, after all, the birthplace of Kipling as well as of Rushdie). But for me it had a more complicated meaning, as the place where my parents imbibed the eminent Victorians that sent them to an Oxford where I was born (with the luxury of taking Victorians for granted).

When I returned to Bombay, therefore, on the eve of the country's

Golden Jubilee—its fiftieth year of independence—it was partly to see the forces of nationalism and internationalism in collision. But it was, no less, to look in on what I regard as my hometown once removed, in my virtual stepmotherland. And it did not take me long to recall that some things—especially in India—never change. On the flight coming in, the man on my right, with typical Bombay pluralism, extended his cup for coffee when the cabin attendant came around with that beverage, gulped it down in a second, and then extended it again for tea when the next woman came around. The man on my left, in equally typical Bombay fashion, remained buried throughout in Leviticus.

As soon as we stepped out into the terminal, we were greeted by a list of 'Dos and Don'ts for Security Officials' (beginning with 'Be Courteous to Passengers', but quickly moving on to 'Do Not Accept Any Gift') and a crush of signs for 'Car Hailer', 'Liquor Permit' and even one 'Miss Rainbow'. Ignoring a board that said: 'Please Ensure that Your Drawers Are Locked Properly,' I pushed my way to a 'Pre-Paid Taxi' desk, and as soon as they saw me, the cashiers turned around and began eating dinner. I got into the pre-paid taxi, and the driver closed the door on me and walked away. I gave him a pre-paid taxi chit, and a fight broke out. India's maddening charm was all around.

When at last we started up and began coughing into town, at a pace only slightly slower than that of the passing autorickshaws, I had a chance to take in all the signs of a bright new city. The last time I had been here, ten years before, nearly all the few cars I'd seen were aging, look-alike Indian Ambassadors (copied from Morris Oxfords); now the streets were swarming with cars, and they were Sumos and Marutis and Zens. The last time I was here, I had come upon exactly one Western-style coffee shop in all of India; now I saw ads for Pizza Hut, Baskin-Robbins, even a Mexican restaurant. And the last time I'd come, Indian television had consisted of precisely one government-run channel, broadcasting a few hours a day in black-and-white; now, as I checked into my hotel, I found seventeen different channels, blasting out *Batman* in Hindi, 'The Top Ten Arabic Countdown' (from Dubai), and *Hard Copy*.

Yet my hotel, the celestial Taj, built almost a hundred years ago as a response to British rule, was a tonic reminder that India trumps everything—especially the normal, the foreign and the new. The luxury hotel still offers an astrologer, and its bookstore (with *Jughead's Double Digest* on sale next to *The 99 Names of God* at the cash register) has a large section devoted entirely to 'Erotica'. Outside its ceremonial entrance, horse-drawn victorias still clop towards the ocean. And when I weighed myself on the scale in my room, it said I had gained fifteen pounds since the morning.

The next day, I set off to explore the city in earnest, a place that was originally so far from England's sights that Lord Clarendon, upon its purchase, had pronounced it 'within a very little distance of Brazil'. Though the shrewd entrepreneurs of the East India Company had been the first to see the potential of the largest deepwater harbour on India's west coast, Bombay is essentially a product of the nineteenth century, when the British built a national railway network around it and local shipbuilders developed its position as India's chief port and link to the world. Bombay has long been a fragrant souvenir of the shotgun marriage of mercantile greed and imperial dreams.

I decided my first stop, therefore, should be a British cemetery marked on a map in my recent guidebook. I took a taxi down to Moscow Lane, at the very tip of Colaba Causeway, and began walking, past cannons and Connaught Barracks, past an 'officers' mess' and 'Single Officers Accommodation' bungalows—all the way down to an abandoned light-house. Not seeing any sign of English tombstones, I turned in to the Indian Institute or Geomagnetism, and asked a passing geomagnetist where they might be. He asked a passing nongeomagnetist, found out the cemetery was now a high school, and said, rather gallantly, 'Goodbye, my dear', as I trooped off. Behind us, in the back of the old army school, a man was standing solemnly in khaki shorts, in the middle of a huge patch of empty grass, practising 'Reveille' on his trumpet.

Thus was I introduced to the first great rule of Bombay life, which is that everything goes wrong, and everything's all right. I never did locate the British cemetery, but when I turned around, there—as if by magic—was an Afghan War Memorial, complete with small weathered cross and plaques inscribed to 'My Beloved Wife Lily Meek' and 'Sarah Chandy'. In the church behind the memorial, the reverend was sending birthday greetings this month to Mr Christopherson Ebenezer and Bishop S.B. Joshua. (Names have always told the history of Bombay—or Mumbai—and the map is still a lexicon of bittersweet hybrids—Apollo Bunder, Cross Maidan, the J.J. Parsi Benevolent Institution. Mahatma Gandhi Road crosses Wellington Circle here, and the figure of Sir Dinshaw Maneckjee Petit looks nobly out amidst a sea of Kemps and Wellingtons. Though the independent government tried to rename all the great British sites when the last imperial regiment sailed away, it was as quixotic a gesture as most things here: no one ever talks of Netaji Subhash Road when she's off to Marine Drive.)

For me, too, growing up half a universe away, the grand complications of Bombay had always been softened in my parents' reminiscences by the euphonious sound of their studies in Elphinstone College and their excited discoveries at the Royal Asiatic Library. Phrases that had long since lost their currency in England—'once in a way' or 'alpha mind'—came down to me as the latest thing. And even now, when I asked my aunt how to get to her house, she told me to look out for V.J.T.I. (Victoria Jubilee Technical Institute), somewhere in the general vicinity of King's Circle.

The cathedral of this mildewed classicism—and a pounding reminder of the days when Bombay was the second-largest city in the Empire (after London)—is Victoria Terminus, the one-of-a-kind world-within-a-world railway station where the daily Indian madness plays out amidst the undecayed pillars of the Empire. Outside it, you will find a Palgrave's treasury of styles—stained-glass elephants, Progress atop its central dome, a British lion next to an Indian tiger, sculpted by students of John Lockwood Kipling, the father of the poet (and once principal of Bombay's school of art).

Inside, however, is a world even more polymorphously perverse. When I passed through the first door I saw, I found myself within a whirl devised by Lewis Carroll, and then translated by Jorge Luis Borges into Esperanto: booth after booth after incomprehensible booth, in room after room after hangarlike room, some offering 'Manual Booking Refund on Pre-bought Ticket', some promising 'Refund on Reserved Tickets for Trains Leaving on Same Day and the Following Day up to 0900 hours', some dealing only with 'Freedom Fighters', others only with 'Blind Persons', or those who might qualify for the 'Military Quota'. And all of them governed by a hundred rules both courtly ('Kindly Tender Exact Amount of Fare') and relentless (when informed of a seat's availability, you must say yes or no 'in twenty seconds'). I imagined teams of men in tatty uniforms with stopwatches in hand, timing the responses of those who had so patiently observed the injunction to 'Please Stand in Q.'

Upstairs was a 'Ladies Waiting Room', a 'General Waiting Room' (which was, in fact, full of ladies), a sign for a 'Housekeeper', and a pair of shower stalls. There was a 'Superviser' on one floor, a 'Supervisor' on another, and a set of rather gloomy rooms under the title 'V.I.P. Suites'. The second rule of Bombay life, I was reminded, is that anything one person can do, ten can do better—or, at least, more slowly.

Yet the biggest shock of all in VT is that somehow, amidst all the chaos, something works. Every morning, a small army of dabbawalas—couriers in Nehru caps and khaki shorts—scatters around the city, collecting cylindrical stainless-steel lunch boxes, or dabbas, from housewives in the suburbs. They then bring the virtually identical containers to VT—more than 1,00,000 of them in all—and, with the help of nothing more than a simple colour coding, deliver the right one to the right man at the right desk in the city. The third rule of Bombay is that its wonders are as beyond reason as its horrors.

Around VT and the General Post Office (a comparable labyrinth of 101 booths, with extra options—'Sattelite Money-Order Service' and 'Speed-Post Complaints'—scrawled up on a blackboard), the city blithely continues to inhabit several different cultures all at once, so that past seems indistinguishable from present and future: the Catholic Syrian Bank is at the same circular intersection as the National Hindu Hotel here, and the Aladin restaurant nearby offers 'Moghlai, Punjabi, Chinese, Singapore Fried Rice, Chicken American Chop Suey and Szechwan Fried Rice'. Even the city aquarium has a fish with a line from the Koran on its back, and a crab with a Christian cross on it.

The epicentre of this eclecticism is in many ways the Oval—the stretch of grass built by the British at the centre of the area still called 'Fort'. Along one side stand the proud buildings of the University of Bombay, and in its library, the card catalogues are still made up of handwritten index cards (the signs on the drawers saying, 'Dictator', 'Dynastic', 'Economic Conflict', and 'Family Saga', as if every book were about the Gandhi family). When I was seventeen, I spent a whole summer amidst its cobwebs, reading a small-print edition of the collected works of Shakespeare, and newly interested in India because Krishna and psychedelic posters were all the rage at my English high school. Now, when I returned, it was as if I had never left—and the British certainly hadn't. I walked through its beautifully landscaped gardens, of temple trees and royal palms and noble Amherstia, past doors that said 'Backward Class Cell' and 'Institute of Distance Education'—and, more typically, 'No Enquiries, Please'—and up into the library. As I picked out a 1969 copy of the *'Vogue' Book of Etiquette*, near a statue of Sir George Birdwood, and read about how best to say goodbye to my hostess, birds flapped above me in the rafters, and passed in and out of stained-glass windows held together with rags and bits of cardboard.

Nearby, the Rajabai Clock Tower, which used to chime the sounds of 'Rule Britannia' on the hour, was closed now (too many disappointed examinees having thrown themselves to their deaths here), but Matthew Thomas Titus had been awarded a First Class degree, I read, and there were still signs for an 'Intercollegiate On-the-Spot Fruit-Flower-Vegetable Arrangement Competition' up on the bulletin board. Immediately outside the university gates, a palmist addressed such questions as 'Do I fall in love too easily?'

Across the street, the sidewalks teemed with bookstalls (selling *Time* capsules from after the war, and dog-eared copies of *I'm O.K. You're O.K.*), and in their midst sat ear cleaners and men selling free in-flight magazines and coconuts, and another man, sitting calmly in the middle of a busy sidewalk, typing out applications for Transit Visas to Kuwait. A thousand cricket games were exploding all at once along the grass, and sometimes the batsmen were facing two bowlers (cricket pitchers) all at once, or a player in a soccer game turned around and made a cricket catch. Everything was happening on every side, and loudly, and the sheer energy and innocence of it all recalled to me that, more than a sage or an old woman, Bombay most resembles a mischievous boy—irritating, engaging, quick-witted and eager to make good. Things were collapsing all around him, yet still he could not keep a smile from his face.

What the pandemonium also brings home, with a vengeance, is that the real sights of Bombay are the streets themselves, and though there is not much formally to see here, you can have a great time not seeing it. For it is—this metropolis as populous as Denmark and Costa Rica and Iceland and Mongolia combined—all over the place, in every sense, and though the buildings so carefully re-create Manchester, the life around them contradicts it at every turn. When you drive through the shopping streets in the suburbs, for example, at 7 p.m. on a weekday night, past Lady Diana Tailors and Dreamers' Delight, threading your way between the Eros Hair-Cutting Salon and the Clip Joint Beauty Clinic and School, you may feel as if you're nosing through a rally or a parade. But the rally in Bombay is perpetual, and the parade is held every day, in a celebration of surprise and serendipity. There are few straight lines in Bombay, and even intersections are often roundabouts, so that A gets to B via Z.

Flavouring your steps still further is the fact that nothing ever stops talking along the Bombay streets, and a trip down any sidewalk is like a journey through a bubble-filled cartoon strip, in which every building and car and little shop chatters away at you with the slightly too-confident volume of a man who's drunk too much at the office Christmas party. 'Dark Glasses Make You Attractive to the Police,' one hoarding cried at me. 'You Can't Score with a Bat Resting on Your Shoulder,' advised a large sign in front of the Virgin Mary. 'Stress Is Coming Soon,' piped the sticker on the back of a so-called Tourist Vehicle.

What this constant, compendious eventfulness also means is that rules are religiously observed only in the breach, and the charm of the city lies in its curlicues, its contretemps, the doodles that swallow up its main text: in the 'Free Foot Service' at the tranquil Jain Temple at the base of Malabar Hill; in the trash cans like openmouthed penguins in the landscaped Hanging Gardens; in the door at Balbunath Temple that advertises the Jayash Trading Company; or even in the little boy who comes up to you at a stoplight, flashes you a copy of *Naughty Boy* through the window, and, when you say no, comes back with a copy of *Chastity.*

Faced with a mass of such incongruities—all in a spiced version of English that might be called Bombastic—I decided just to surrender to the streets, and took to going each day, at sunset, to the clamorous riot that forms around the Gateway of India, where everyone assembles just to chat and gawk. Whirring toy helicopters skittered across the sky, groups of homesick Africans gathered where the sun burned the fishing boars golden, and old men paraded around with bags that said: 'Smile. It Increases your Face Value.'

After night began to fall, I continued on to Chowpatty Beach, where once the 'Quit India' movement had held its rallies, and where now you can see flashing robots, flimsy merry-go-rounds, four-foot Ferris wheels, and men setting up shooting galleries made of balloons that spell the names of the latest hit movies. All around, at the Radio Club, along Marine Drive, and within the Indian Education Society, there were society weddings, and huge pavilions of orange garlands, the trees aglitter with fairy lights, and women in gold-brocade saris padding out from under lit-up tents. Such occasions, an uncle of mine told me at a cousin's nuptials, were increasingly like international cricket matches: they lasted five days, they were full of antiquated ceremony, and they generally ended (in all senses) in a tie. ·

In Hare Krishna Land at Juhu Beach—a whole minicity of the spiritual (appointed with its own six-storey hotel, brand-new temple, and, as soon as you enter, branch of the Indian Overseas Bank)—I round myself in what could have passed for a pleasant tourist bungalow anywhere in India (though an electronic ticker-tape display beside the registration desk did flash unceasingly, 'Hare Krishna Hare Krishna ...' and among the young searchers in Gap T-shirts, there were ash-besmirched New Yorkers in orange robes and top knots). Behind it, in the shady compound where devotees live, billboards teach children the two Golden Rules ('Always Remember Krishna/Never Forget

Krishna'), and a board depicts the history of basketball, just under one on 'The Origin of All Culture' (in other words, Krishna consciousness). Another board offers tips on 'Blooming Manners'. Yet this curious tribute to the love affair of East and West is still renowned among canny locals as one of the finest places to stay, or eat, in the entire city.

Even when I went to visit the house where Mahatma Gandhi had lived for seventeen years, and first fashioned his campaign for satyagraha, or passive resistance, what struck me most, to my surprise, was what I saw outside: a 'Suicide Prevention Centre' across the street, and, next to it, a poster for 'Fun 'n' Fair with Funky Games'. All Bombay, in some respects, resembles a suicide prevention centre, and for all the extraordinary difficulties of life here—for all the 6,00,000 people squeezed into less than a square mile in Dharavi, the largest slum in Asia, and the infamous Falkland Road red-light district, where as many as 1,00,000 'cage girls' work in horrifying circumstances, Bombay is not a disheartening place; it has too much gusto for that, and too much crooked sweetness, and when you see the local stores called 'Reliable' or 'Honesty', or hear the tiny drinks stalls playing 'Things Go Better with Coke' (in Hindi), you feel that something is invincible here.

Some of this is changing of course, as the city speeds into a multinational future that brings with it new expectations and foreign hopes. When I opened the antique-seeming *Times of India* (which fills its editorial page with allusions to Bertram Wooster and quotations from G.B. Shaw, and offers, on its cover, 'Invitation Price: Two Rupees'), I found that page 2 was still given over to traditional 'Matrimonial Notices'—but now these included some highly untraditional categories ('Multinational', 'Green Card' and 'Cosmopolitan'). One potential bride listed as a qualification that she 'knows computer language', another was billed as 'Girl with best of Indian and Western values having eight-figure personal assets, seven-figure personal income from property/shares. Heiress to large fortune.' Nearby, a Mr Iyer was advertising his detective services for cases involving 'Data Leakage, White Collar Crime, Debugging and Matrimonial Disunity' (the link between data and dates becoming even more inscrutable!).

Still more vivid a sign of the coming times was the pub to which two recent MBAs took me one lively Saturday night. Five minutes away, the illuminated buildings along the Esplanade looked like pieces of Oxford airlifted through the heavens. Inside the neon-lit boîte, however, Bombay's affluent young were sipping frozen banana daiquiris and cocktails called 'Sexual Delight' that cost them 200 rupees a shot (traditionally equivalent for most Indians to $200). On TV screens around the place, they were watching Vanessa Mae, the teenage sex-kitten violinist, on MTV, and the Charlotte Hornets creaming the Denver Nuggets. Girls in University of Miami T-shirts, boys in tight 501s, sang along to Lionel Richie as they sipped their Long Island Teas, and took their leave of Victorian formalities.

A little later, on Valentine's Day, I got an even stronger dose of the new cutting-edge Bombay when I went out with Shobha Dé, the highly glamorous former movie-magazine editor and fashion model who has become the best-selling novelist in the country. Dé, a fountain of soigné energy and a mine of sex-and-shopping wisdom, moves through the city like its uncrowned queen, her white Mercedes (with its '3000' licence plate) edging through backstreets and past bullock carts, with restaurateurs racing out to bow and salaam as soon as she appears and finding for her, out of nowhere, an empty table (or a fulsome compliment).

'Bombay is an evil city,' the mother of *Sultry Days* and *Starry Nights* said to me over curried crabs, 'but in a glamorous, romantic way. It's a ferocious city, but that's its charm.' Around us, in the fashionable new Italian Trattoria, men were lugging in a twenty-nine-inch Trinitron, and stylish college kids were making plans for the evening— Valentine's Day being the latest commercial craze in this fashion-mad city. Tossing back her long, thick hair, Dé favoured me with a whole anthology of rags-to-riches stories that commemorate the city's promise: about the former scrap merchant from Aden who's now perhaps the richest man in India; about the former fire-eater she recalls performing with Tomoko the Tomato (a professional ecdysiast) and now the boss of the chicest Chinese joint in town ('He has a thousand criminal cases against him,' she purred approvingly); about the twenty-three-year-old villager who came to Bombay in his underwear and now owns stores all over the city and has 'eight or ten' passports that he shuffles judiciously to facilitate his shopping trips to Hong Kong, Europe, the Gulf (the queen knows him because she goes in now and then to 'bless his Levi's, his Giordanos, the lot').

Now, she said, slipping off her denim jacket, 'the big thing is food criticism. And fashion. These saris today cost $6000—who's going to buy them? I mean, here we are in Bombay, where there are only two seasons—summer and monsoon, hot and hotter—and these girls are modelling minks. Who's got the money? But that's the fashion.' Some beautiful young things looked over at her and she threw a few kisses in their direction. A typical wedding, she went on, 'costs $3,00,000. Even the trousseau, you're talking $1,00,000.' But where, I asked meekly, did such money come from? 'Oh, it's all funny money,' she said negligently. 'Smuggling and real estate.'

Yet even as she kept talking, about 'uppers' and audio books and 'the ladies who booze,' not to mention the 524-episode soap opera she was writing (at her kitchen table, surrounded by six children, working a hundred episodes ahead), the 524-episode megadrama of Bombay was continuing, unstoppably, all around us. I walked into the high court buildings nearby, after lunch and instantly I was back inside the crazy, multifarious, completely unmanageable Bombay of old. Rows of ill-lit corridors stretched out in front of me, filled with petitioners sitting in the dark, or crowding into ancient courtrooms. Clerks clicked and clacked away on typewriters older than Lloyd George, like nothing so much as summa cum laude graduates of the University of Busywork. On every wall and bulletin board, lists and papers and requests and regulations fluttered hopelessly. Even in the parking lot there was a list of eight rules.

'Advocates' in tattered black blazers and white ties got up and talked and talked. The figures of Justice and Mercy presided immemorially from on high. Cases snailed ahead like badly translated versions of the opening chapter of *Bleak House*. And as I watched the Bombay free-for-all go on, tomorrow and tomorrow without end, I thought to myself, not sadly: Victoria really had not lived in vain.

Where I Live

(For Anders, Who Wants to Know)

Arundhathi Subramaniam

I live on a wedge of land
reclaimed from a tired ocean
somewhere at the edge of the universe.

Greetings from this city
of L'Oreal sunsets
and diesel afternoons,
deciduous with concrete,
Botoxed with vanity.

City of septic magenta hair-clips,
of garrulous sewers and tight-lipped taps,
of '80s film tunes buzzing near the left temple,
of ranting TV soaps and monsoon melodramas.

City wracked by hope and bulimia.
City uncontained
by movie screen and epigram.
City condemned to unspool
in an eternal hysteria
of lurid nylon dream.

City where you can drop off
a swollen local
and never be noticed.
City where you're a part
of every imli-soaked bhelpuri.

City of the Mahalaxmi beggar
peering up through a
gorse-bush of splayed limbs.

City of dark alleys,
city of mistrust,
city of forsaken tube-lit rooms.

City that coats the lungs
stiffens the spine
chills the gut
with memory.

City suspended between
flesh and mortar and foam leather
and delirium

where it is perfectly historical
to be looking out
on a sooty handkerchief of ocean,

searching for God.

A Very Young Person

1865-1878

Rudyard Kipling

Give me the first six years of a child's life and you can have the rest.

Looking back from this my seventieth year, it seems to me that every card in my working life has been dealt to me in such a manner that I had but to play it as it came. Therefore, ascribing all good fortune to Allah the Dispenser of Events, I begin:-

My first impression is of daybreak, light and colour and golden and purple fruits at the level of my shoulder. This would be the memory of early morning walks to the Bombay fruit market with my ayah and later with my sister in her perambulator, and of our returns with our purchases piled high on the bows of it. Our ayah was a Portuguese Roman Catholic who would pray—I beside her—at a wayside Cross. Meeta, my Hindu bearer, would sometimes go into little Hindu temples where, being below the age of caste, I held his hand and looked at the dimly-seen, friendly Gods.

Our evening walks were by the sea in the shadow of palm-groves, which, I think, were called the Mahim Woods. When the wind blew the great nuts would tumble, and we fled—my ayah, and my sister in her perambulator—to the safety of the open. I have always felt the menacing darkness of tropical eventides, as I have loved the voices of night-winds through palm or banana leaves, and the song of the tree-frogs. There were far-going Arab dhows on the pearly waters, and gaily clad Parsis wading out to worship the sunset. Of their creed I knew nothing, nor did I know that near our little house on the Bombay Esplanade were the Towers of Silence, where their Dead are exposed to the waiting vultures on the rim of the towers, who scuffle and

---

From *Something of Myself*.

spread wings when they see the bearers of the Dead below. I did not understand my Mother's distress when she found 'a little child's hand' in our garden, and said I was not to ask questions about it. I wanted to see that child's hand.

In the afternoon heats before we took our sleep, she or Meeta would tell us stories and Indian nursery songs all unforgotten, and we were sent into the dining-room after we had been dressed, with the caution, 'Speak English now to Papa and Mamma.' So one spoke 'English' haltingly translated out of the vernacular idiom that one thought and dreamt in. The Mother sang wonderful songs at a black piano and would go out to Big Dinners. Once she came back, very quickly, and told me, still awake, that 'the big Lord Sahib' had been killed and there was to be no Big Dinner. This was Lord Mayo, assassinated by a native. Meeta explained afterwards that he had been 'hit with a knife'. Meeta unconsciously saved me from any night terrors or dread of the dark. Our ayah, with a servant's curious mixture of deep affection and shallow device, had told me that a stuffed leopard's head on the nursery wall was there to see that I went to sleep. But Meeta spoke of it scornfully as 'the head of an animal' and I took it off my mind as a fetish, good or bad, for it was only some unspecified 'animal'.

Far across green spaces around the house was a marvellous place filled with smells of paints and oils, and lumps of clay with which I played. That was the atelier of my Father's School of Art, and a Mr 'Terry Sahib' his assistant, to whom my small sister was devoted, was our great friend. Once, on the way there alone, I passed by a huge ravine a foot deep, where a winged monster as big as myself attacked me, and I fled and wept. My Father drew for me a picture of the tragedy with a rhyme beneath:-

> There was a small boy in Bombay
> Who once from a hen ran away.
> When they said: 'You're a baby,'
> He replied, 'Well, I may be:
> But I don't like these hens of Bombay.'

This consoled me. I have thought well of hens ever since.

Paris, India

J. Gerson da Cunha

The Mahim Creek is not the Seine and though the Gateway of India may have a family resemblance to the Arc de Triomphe, the former wasn't even built when da Cunha wrote this comparison.

—Eds

'The great events,' I then said, 'that have materially contributed to the making of modern Bombay, are the Treaty of Bassein, which destroyed the Maratha confederacy, the annexation of the Dekkan, and the opening of the Suez Canal, which helped considerably to raise this city to the proud position of the gateway of India. On the ruins of the Peishwa's dominion, just a decade before the arrival of the French missionary here, was thus rising the edifice of a snug little island on the Konkan Coast, destined to rule over a great part of a vast continent. Since then it has passed through critical phases of growth and development, through years of joy and sorrow, periods of unnatural inflation alternating with those of apparently hopeless depression, but, in spite of all this, Bombay, like Paris, *fluctuat nec mergitur.*' And like Paris, Bombay has grown, due allowance being made for the boldness of the comparison, slowly at first, but rapidly during the last quarter of this century. From Charlamagne to Napoleon, Paris took nearly ten centuries to become a populous city, and Bombay, from Humphrey Cooke to Jonathan Duncan, has spent about 150 years to develop from a mere hamlet into a fair town.

In 1811 Paris contained 6,00,000 inhabitants. From that time to 1846, the population increased by the yearly addition of 11,000 heads, the number of houses increasing in proportion to shelter one million

From *The Origin of Bombay*, a special number of the journal of the Royal Asiatic Society, 1900 of souls. From 1869 to 1895, 41,000 new houses were built, and the population had grown to 25,00,000. The Parisian statistics do not furnish figures anterior to the last years of the Empire; but for the last twenty-five years the city has been enriched by the annual immigration of 25,00,000 souls. The density of the population, which, during the first Republic, was represented by fifty-five *metres carres* per head, is now thirty-three.

This density is, moreover, enhanced by the piling of floors, families *grimpant sur les epaules des occupants primitives*.

Thus Bombay resembles Paris, as some other cities, in the rapidity of its expansion within the last quarter of a century. In 1814 the population of Bombay was about 2,00,000, and the tenements 20,000. Now the population has quadrupled, and the number of buildings has nearly doubled. While in 1814 most of the houses consisted of ground floors, and a few of two floors, there are now hundreds, if not thousands of buildings, of more than five floors. The density of the population has in the meantime become enormous.

The minimum of house population by sections is now higher in Bombay than the maximum in London. In France, even, including the urban population, there are only 187 persons to the square mile, and in England, also including the large towns, a little over 500. There is more concentration and pressure of the populace in Bombay than in Calcutta. Like the Adriatic tribes who took refuge in the city of the Lagoons, all tribes in western India flock to Bombay, and from traditional beliefs, social instincts and tribal affinities are drawn to certain areas in the town, where their tendency is to agglomerate rather than to disperse. Within the memory of many of us fields which were once open and cultivated have now been built over with houses of all shapes and sizes.

Another feature common to both Paris and Bombay is the prestige and the influence, which each of them exercises over all the country, far beyond the limits of their own administrative spheres. Bombay draws, as the metropolis, the best talent from provinces and districts around, and dictates laws and fashions to India as Paris does to France.

It is said that Bombay is the Alexandria of India. Its geographical position and commercial relations bear evidently some resemblance to the great eastern entrepôt of the Mediterranean. As the swampy Rhakotis, a mere fishing village, which Alexander the Great transformed into the splendid city of Alexandria, the desolate islet of the Bombay Koli fisherman was changed into the present capital of western India. Like Alexandria, it is, moreover, on the highway to other cities. As the visitor hurries from steamer to rail on the way to the pyramids and to Luxor, the Indian tourist rushes from the Ballard Pier to the Victoria Station on the way to the Taj Mahal, Delhi and Benares. But in all other respects Bombay is the Paris of India. It is true it does not possess the beautiful, and, according to Lebrun, the honest, smiling river—

La *Seine* aux bords riants, nymphe tranquille et pure,
Ports son doux cristal, ennemi du parjure,
A l'immense Thetis:

but it has instead one of the most splendid harbours in the world, about which the old Portuguese Viceroy, Antonio de Mello e Castro, wrote to the King of Portugal, D. Affonso VI, in 1662: 'Moreover, I see the best port your Majesty possesses in India, with which that of Lisbon is not to be compared, treated as a little value of the Portuguese themselves.'

The history of the two cities has hitherto proved that they are both endowed with powers of recuperation to meet the effects of disaster. But while Paris possesses the vitality of a virile constitution, seasoned and braced up by the lapse of some centuries, to guarantee its future, Bombay is yet too young to justify any dogmatic prognostications of continued prosperity. History, like drama, delights in contrasts and coincidences. But if the historical parallels of the past were logical arguments in relation to the changed conditions of today, the tragic fate of nearly all the cities in western India, whose existence could hardly be counted by the cycle of three centuries, would lead us, indeed, to gloomy forebodings. Ahmedabad, with its houses of brick and mortar and tiled roofs, the broad streets, the chief of them with room enough for ten ox-carriages to drive abreast, and 1000 stone mosques among its public buildings, each with two large minarets and many wonderful inscriptions, rich in painters, carvers, weavers, and embroiderers; Bijapur, with its Ark-Killah, the Sat Mazli, the mehels, mosques, tombs and palaces, its goldsmiths and jewellers; the emporium of Surat, 'a city of a very great trade', as Barbosa describes it in the beginning of the sixteenth century, 'in all classes of merchandise'; Goa, the Rome of the East, built on seven hills, with its magnificent cathedral, its churches and convents, three fine hospitals, the dungeons of the Inquisition as famous as those of the ducal palace at St. Mark's Square in Venice, rich in mansions and in the produce of every part of the globe, a grand arsenal, a naval depot conveniently located, the sheltered stronghold of the Portuguese squadrons, where they returned to refit and rest in absolute security until some renewed need of action called again for their services—all these can now write upon their portals 'the glory is departed', while many others, such as Bassein, Chaul, Golconda, Ahmednagar, Gulburga, etc., are now little more than mere heaps of ruins.

I will not claim to possess the prophetic instinct to foresee what is in store for Bombay. But as it has adopted the happy motto of *Urbs prima in Indis*, it may be hoped that this will prove of good augury, and that among other privileges Bombay will own that of priority among the Indian cities for longevity in undecaying prosperity.

Since these notes were written, many new works, both official and unofficial, on Bombay, relating especially to the early British period, have been published. Still, there is a good deal to be learnt. One may, indeed, say of Bombay, in the words of La Fontaine: 'That is a field which cannot be so harvested that there will not be something left of the latest comer to glean.'

Impressions of Bombay

Khushwant Singh

Bombay, you will be told, is the only city India has, in the sense that the word city is understood in the West. Other Indian metropolises like Calcutta, Madras and Delhi are like oversized villages. It is true that Bombay has many more high-rise buildings than any other Indian city: when you approach it by sea it looks like a miniature New York. It has other things to justify its city status: it is congested, it has traffic jams at all hours of the day, it is highly polluted and many parts of it stink. Arthur Koestler compared his arrival at Santa Cruz airport to having a baby's soiled diaper flung in his face. Bombay discharges the sewage of its ten million or more inhabitants into the sea so close to the shore that a good bit of it is carried back to the land with incoming tides: used condoms can be picked up in the shallows. The stench of human shit prevails over some parts of the seafront. Since it has very few public conveniences, its bazaars smell of stale urine. Twice a year, early in spring and autumn, fish along the coast die in their millions and the acrid smell of rotting fish is overpowering. Bombay has no parks or gardens worth speaking of: only a few small parklets where people go round and round narrow paths like animals in cages. Usually the only place where one can take a walk of sorts is Marine Drive, running from the Chowpatty sands to Nariman Point. This has a dual highway crowded with speeding cars and buses on one side, and massive cement-concrete tripods along the sea walk to prevent it from making further inroads. The tripods are placed at convenient angles which make it easy for the citizens to rest their feet, let down their trousers or pull up their dhotis to defecate. Nevertheless, Bombaywalas throng to Marine Drive in their thousands every morning and evening to jostle their way through masses of humanity. Old people sit on

---

From *Truth, Love & a Little Malice* (2002).

benches placed en route to take in the sea air and gossip. Marine Drive is Bombay's pride and its joy. After sunset, as the street lights are switched on, they gape at it in amazement and call it a queen's diamond necklace.

However, there are some points in favour of Bombay. It has a heterogeneous mix of races, religions and linguistic groups. They mind their own business and do not bother with their neighbours, nor are they unduly concerned if they are happily married, divorced, having affairs or living in sin. People of diverse ethnic and religious backgrounds get on reasonably well. Till 1982 Bombay did not have many communal riots, but it would be wrong to conclude that the different communities have affection for each other. Every community thinks it is better than the others and behind their backs uses derogatory expressions to describe them. Parsis regard themselves as a cut above everyone else. They are indeed the most prosperous, and have given to Bombay more than other communities. They are conscious of their superiority and look down on the rest as 'ghatees'—coastal trash. Others regard Parsis as effete, senile Bawajis, most of whom are highly eccentric and on the verge of lunacy. Since they are very voluble, they are also known as 'kagha khaus'—crow eaters. Then we have the Gujaratis, largely in trade, commerce and industry. Their language, Gujarati, is more widely spoken than Marathi, the language of the more numerous Maharashtrians. The Gujaratis are generally peace-loving, law-abiding and vegetarian. Behind their backs they are referred to as Gujjus. Bombay has a variety of Muslims who, though they have little to do with each other, get together when there is anti-Muslim violence. Besides the major divisions into Sunni and Shia, there are Ismailis (of two kinds), Bohras (of two kinds), and Memons (Cutchee and Halai). They are lumped together as Mian Bhais. There is also a sizeable community of Christians, both Catholic and Protestant, known to the rest as 'Makapaos'—bread eaters (from pao, Portuguese for bread). The latest arrivals are Sindhis and Punjabis. Slowly but surely they have captured a sizeable chunk of the city's business and real estate and are consequently eyed with suspicion as grabbers. But Bombay's outsiders outnumber the self-styled insiders who call themselves Sons of the Soil and insist on calling Bombay by its original name Mumbai, after its patron goddess Maha Amba. No educated Indian calls it anything other than Bombay.

Bombay is much the richest city of India. More than half of India's income-tax comes from this one city. Bombay is also India's most corrupt city: more than half of the black money in circulation is generated in Bombay. It has more millionaires than the other three metropolitan cities put together. It attracts an endless stream of outsiders who hope to make their fortunes here. It also probably has more prostitutes and call girls than any other city in the world. Bombay's rich live very well: in large air-cooled apartments facing the sea, with rooftop gardens and bathing pools. A Sindhi multi-millionaire has a glass-bottomed pool above his bar-cum-sitting room. Whenever he has parties he hires young girls to bathe in the nude so that his guests can watch them from below while they sip their Scotch.

*

Churchgate, being an upper-middle class locality, did not have many street walkers. If there were any I was slow in recognizing them. One evening while returning home after dinner, a lady standing under a street lamp asked me for the time. The Rajabai Tower clock stared us in the face but I consulted my watch and told her the precise hour. She thanked me in polished Urdu: 'Bahut shukriya, Sardar Sahib!' It was only when going up in the lift that it occurred to me that the lady meant to proposition me. Another girl who attracted my attention lived on a pavement near a gas station which also had a couple of paanwalas and a bhelpuri seller on the drive-way leading to the pumps. She was a beggar in her mid twenties and on friendly terms with the bhelpuriwala who gave her his leftovers. I never saw her solicit anyone, nor as much as look up at strangers. She was mentally unbalanced and had apparently been thrown out by her husband. Much as I tried to draw her in during conversations with the paanwala or the bhelpuri seller, she ignored my presence. I got to see what she looked like after the monsoons broke over Bombay in the second week of June. The outbreak of the monsoon is an experience not to be missed. Weeks before its advent the pavements around Churchgate have people selling umbrellas and gum-boots. It finally comes in cascades, flooding the roads with knee-deep water. I was curious to know how the beggar woman coped with the inclement weather. On such days the bhelpuriwala couldn't have had many buyers, and I thought that perhaps I could buy the evening meal for the girl. When I went to fetch my paan there was no bhelpuriwala. The girl lay huddled on the steps of a shop barely an inch above the swirling rain water. She obviously had no worldly goods and not even a change of clothes. She haunted my mind through the night.

When I woke the next morning, the Rajabai Tower clock showed 5 a.m. It had poured all night and flooded the maidan, making it look like a lake. The rain had now come down to a drizzle, but the sky was overcast. In the greying light of dawn I saw the figure of a woman draped in a dirty white dhoti in the middle of the maidan. She was sitting on her haunches splashing water between her thighs with a tin can. She was evidently cleaning herself after having defecated somewhere behind the bushes. I got out my field glasses and focused them on her. Having done with her ablutions, she looked around to assure herself that she was not being watched. Then she took off her dhoti and poured muddy rainwater over herself, paying special attention to her breasts and middle. It was the beggar woman. I watched her till she put on the same dirty dhoti round her wet body and sloshed her way back to her pad near Churchgate Station. How was it that no one had spotted this beggar maid in this vice-ridden city? I found the answer a few days later. I had been passing by her pavement lodging every night but not seen her there. Had her husband taken her back? I could not contain my curiosity and, while buying bhel, which I had no intention of eating, asked the vendor as casually as I could what had happened to the woman. His voice choked as he replied: 'Kuchh na poochho Sardarji'—don't ask me anything Sardarji, 'bharoohey phusla kay lay gaye'—pimps inveigled her away. The poor thing probably ended up in some brothel in Kamatipura.

★

The monsoon brought other experiences. Often I had to take a spare shirt to the office and carry my chappals in my hands when wading through the muddy water. When it poured, the umbrella barely protected my turban from being drenched. There were other unexpected hazards. One morning, as I approached Flora Fountain I saw a large sewer rat coming towards me pursued by kites and crows dive-bombing on it. I thought it safer to cross to the other side. So did the sewer rat. I was in the middle of the road when it scampered after me and, finding no other shelter from its persecutors, sought refuge between my legs. It tried to claw its way up my trousers. I jumped about in a frenzy trying to shake off the rodent from my leg and waved my umbrella to ward off the kites and crows now hovering over my head. A crowd collected on the pavement to watch the spectacle. I managed to knock off the sewer rat and ran across to safety. Far from eliciting the sympathy of the spectators, this led one man to taunt me: 'Arré, Sardarji choohe say dar gaya!'—Look at this big Sikh getting scared of a mouse! I tried to protest that it was not a chooha but a big sewer-rat. But of course there is no word in Hindi to distinguish a rat from a mouse . . .

Long after I had left the city, scenes of Bombay kept haunting me: oddly enough it was not the people but the monsoon, the sound of dancers' bells practising for Gudi Padwa along Marine Drive, the sheets of rain coming down like a gossamer curtain, and the dogs who wagged their tails as I passed them on my way to office.

Three Uneasy Pieces

Adil Jussawalla

I

Another Normal Day

The palms on the road divider are difficult to maintain. Set in neat white rectangles, almost squares, they go down half the length of Cuffe Parade, varying in size from a few fronds just a foot off the ground to trees about twenty feet tall. It's a hot day.

Lines of cars stream north, the sun bouncing off their chrome and metal, fewer cars stream south. Rising above tin-plate, din and fume, the taller palms try to hold their own.

A strange pair of men is trying to help them. Palm trees normally look pathetic at this time of the year, their fronds covered in dust, drooping listless; there just isn't enough water for them to drawn on. This time someone has thought of feeding them on a regular basis, or perhaps I never noticed it being done in previous years. The watering device is a peculiar contraption. It consists of the two men I mentioned, a handcart, a water-barrel strapped onto the handcraft, and a large rectangular tin. The watering process goes thus:

Push handcart-with-barrel next to required tree. Dip large tin into water-barrel and empty whatever amount of water it catches onto base of tree. Do this three times, whether tree is small or tall. Move on to the next tree.

I watch from the balcony, fascinated. I notice smoke to my right. Since I can't see where the smoke's coming from, I think one of the

Versions of 'Another Normal Day', '18th Floor Blues' and 'A Destination of the Heart' first appeared in the *Daily*, *Gentleman* and the *Times of India*, respectively.

rooms of the Hotel President is on fire. The smoke billows, pale-grey and wispy. I hear a fire engine and watch it yodel its way past our intrepid gardeners. Life in the street is normal as far as the eye can see. No one looks up at the smoke.

Traffic signals change colour. It's the time of day when even cyclists have to respect them. The men gathered around the cigarette-and-newspaper corner chat and smoke as they always do.

I telephone a writer to give her a London address. We talk for a while. A ball of black smoke rolls into the grey. I hear more fire engines.

'The President's on fire,' I tell the writer.

'What!' she exclaims.

'I don't think it's serious,' I say.

Back on the balcony I notice nothing has changed, except that the smoke is blacker. The water-contraptionwalas have finished one side of the street. Then I notice a group of people staring at the smoke. The direction of their gaze indicates that the fire is not in The President, but beyond it. Which high-rise building could it be now? I wonder.

On the street, walking towards the fire, it strikes me: It's not a high-rise, it's past the World Trade Centre, it's the slum again. Yet I'm puzzled by the normalcy of things. A chauffeur twirls his master's car keys indifferently. A security guard yawns at his post; children, not rich, gambol in a dusty space.

It's when I approach the road stalls that supply bhajias and Pepsis and the dhobis who hang the clothes they've washed on long clothesline in the streets, that I see them: lines of people facing the fire, some quiet, some talking normally. A girl with a worried look on her face scans the smoke and tries to cross the road but is firmly pushed back by a rough-looking man. If she wants to find someone or something in the fire, she'd better not try, his attitude suggests. 'Ja!' he barks. Go wait.

Another man, rougher looking and totally drunk, tries to smash one of the windows of a passing car.

It's when I notice the objects piled around the people that I realize how stereotyped my ideas of poverty and slum-life are. Here is a yellow mixer, the name Sumeet written in black, here is a steel-blue desk, there a chocolate-brown table fan. The men wear colourful bush-shirts, splodged with large prints, the women wear printed dresses. The clothes that peek out of bundles, large and small are made of printed fabrics. A young man wears pin-stripped trousers, another blue jeans.

This could be a middle-class neighbourhood, I think, this woman could be a nurse, that one a secretary, that boy a college student. I try to tell by the clothes. Except for one thing. The cost of living in a slum is grime. Colour tries to struggle through it but fails to.

It's not the soot from the fire. I've seen it before but I've forgotten. A young man haunts me (let's call him Subodh). He's not a persistent beggar but the grime on him, from his head to his bare feet has begun to look like thick oil. Yesterday he asked me if I could give him a pair of old trousers. Since I had a pair I was going to get rid of, I told him to meet me at the corner in an hour. He didn't show up.

Smoke comes our way. My eyes begin to smart, I go deeper into the smoke. A BEST double-decker breaks out of its depot and floats towards me, a tearaway iceberg in the mist, I begin to choke.

So this is how we die, I think, on smoke-filled ships, struggle to get on deck, in discotheques, in hotel rooms. Smoke finishes what the fire couldn't. I breathe in sandpaper. I start gasping. I turn back. Others, disappearing into the smoke, seem unaffected.

There's a place I know close by. Going towards it, I hear a familiar voice behind me, it's always behind me.

'Sir.' It's Subodh.

'You didn't turn up,' I say.

'I did. I waited. Ask the chaiwala.'

'You didn't,' I say.

He holds a tin box about a foot deep. 'Only the other day I got a small corner for myself—to protect me from the rains. Now it's gone. They did it on purpose.'

'Anyone killed?'

'Many children,' he says. I enter the place.

The man who lunged at the car, trying to break one of its window, is there, with friends, trying to provoke them. He staggers about the bar. I fear he'll turn on me. One of his friends talks about children. He saved so many, how they were crying.

'Hang the children,' shouts the rough one. 'You should have saved the furniture!'

'Everyone has tension, Uncle,' someone says to me. 'Not only the poor. Isn't that so, Uncle?'

He doesn't hear what I say and turns to his companion. 'If he didn't have tension, why would he come here?' he asks, gesturing towards me. 'True or not, Uncle?'

I say I'm hard of hearing and haven't caught a word.

II

18th Floor Blues

A contributor to the *Asian Age* tells me that I live in an ugly concrete block. He also says that the block I live in, and others like it, have spelt the death of conversation as he knew it. He tells me that he, Ambedkar and Mulk Raj Anand used to sit and talk on a bench facing the sea before the sea was destroyed and ugly concrete blocks came up in its place. I know the bench he's talking about.

It used to sit directly opposite the building in which Mulk has his rooms. Since that building, itself in danger of being done away with, faces the block I live in, I used to be able to see the bench from my position of privilege, eighteen floors high. I was able to look down on the bench. The day I moved into the flat I realized I'd be held accountable for that position of privilege for as long as I lived in the flat.

Almost twenty-nine years after moving in, the demand to be accountable, the accusations, the envies, the rip-offs, the trade-offs, the harsh truths and the filthy lies haven't stopped. In fact, they've increased, sometimes finding their way into the flat from a long way off through the insinuating coils of a phone.

I feel odd, as though I'm getting the 'flu. But it's not the 'flu. It's the eighteenth floor blues. This is how they feel, or something like how they feel—

How do you do
Up there

Just as low as you
Down there
As low as a canoe
Up there
Got the 18th floor blues.

The lows began with Mulk
Down there
They said I'd blocked his light
Up there
That started off a fight
Somewhere
And my 18th floor blues.

The men who carried loads
Up there
Building my abode
Up there
Got hit by trucks on roads
Down there
Got their 18th floor blues.

Got down before one died
Down there
Couldn't help him if I tried
Up there
Help moves in horizontals
Like a chair
And I was
Verti-
cally
Blue.

Khushwant, Shobha stayed
Right there
On lower floors

No flat keeps open doors
Up there
They sang of sex and shoes
Down there
I got a dose of blues.

Pearl had heart and voice
Down there
When guests asked
'What's that noise?'
Out there
'Pearl is casting swine'
I'd say
And put on Ella's blues.

A giant touching sky
Up there
My feet on History's
Bench
Down there
What dwarfs old giants make
As I stare
They make me sing the blues.

They think I think I'm god
Down there
I am. A
Verti-
cally
Challenged
god
Up there
They must have got the news
Out there
They're setting up the rack
Down there

They're getting at my life
Up there
Got the 18th floor blues.

III

A Destination of the Heart

Like Salman Rushdie, I was delivered to Bombay by Dr Shirodkar. I can't say I've appreciated that fact. All the same, being born seven years before Salman had one clear advantage. For those seven years, he couldn't tread on my turf. After those years, we went to the same school, lived on the same street and finally he wrote my novel, *Midnight's Children*. Everyone born in the forties wanted to write *Midnight's Children*. Only he went and did it.

I was a sick child in a sick city. Pneumonia dogged me from year one. For me, the predominant Bombay colours during the years before Independence were pale blue, pale yellow and the whites of my father's doctor's suit and nurses' uniforms. I lived in his clinic not because of my ill health, but because we had no other place. That had its advantages too. In the clinic I saw Congress leaders come and go. A broken Yusuf Meherally was handed over to my father after the allopaths had done their bit. My father couldn't save him. I remember his body being carried through the clinic's corridors, the nurses' heads bowed.

For a while, because of the presence of Congress leaders in the clinic—they had a fondness for enemas—the place was under police surveillance. Can I possibly remember the violence that followed the Quit India call at Gowalia Tank (now August Kranti Maidan)? I think I can. The clinic was on Cumballa Hill (now August Kranti Marg). Unknown to Dr Shirodkar, whose clinic was quite close to my father's, he had not only delivered me to Bombay but to a momentous bit of its history.

I really wish he hadn't. Or couldn't I have waited till that fateful stroke of midnight when everything was over? As it happens, I was delivered to a violent time. I remember photographs of suburban trains set on fire, my father having to visit us before curfew (my parents lived separately for a while), talk of war, and one day soon after I'd turned four, the sound of three tremendous explosions. The Fort Stikine, exploding at Ballard Pier, sent shockwaves to Cumballa Hill. Curtain rods fell from their sockets, a door-latch got twisted. A tall tree of smoke rose behind Malabar Hill. The grown-ups said Japan had attacked.

These images are part of my poem, 'A Letter for Bombay', and similar images occur in a sequence of poems, 'Missing Persons'. When people point out the violence of some of my images, perhaps it's because they spring from a violent time.

Still, we had our American films (even if they reached Bombay two years after their Hollywood release), American chewing gum and thanks to Mr Phirozeshah Taraporevala's New Book Co. (he was my best friend's father), an endless supply of American and British comics. There were morning shows of Batman, Superman, Captain Marvel and Flash Gordon at the Capitol Cinema, there was Superman, the Saint and Dan Dare on the air.

All that changed in the fifties when Morarji Desai became chief minister. He launched programmes of fearful and numbing austerity, and the import of foreign 'culture', in the form of comics and even books, were banned. From a violent and occasionally happy city, Bombay became a dull city, for me the dullest in the world. I disliked school (not the school's fault, perhaps), Bombay's institutes of higher learning looked like dumps and were spoken about as if they really were. There was little to do in the evenings, nothing to read. I had to go.

I spent about eleven years abroad. People ask me why I came back. Why? When even in 1970, more and more people were beginning to realize the old only survive in Bombay. Not live in it. And why do I stay? When all its old problems have got magnified and when its poverty clings to you, drags you down, immobilizes you as only this country's poverty can. Perhaps there's an answer in 'A Letter for Bombay'.

In the poem, I speak of wandering like a medieval apothecary abroad and in a 'pouch wriggling against my ribs, carry a quintessence of you

(Bombay) not wholly without potency.' The pouch wriggling against my ribs is my cockeyed way of referring to my heart.

And another poem, this time by R.S. Thomas, called 'Here'. Why is he where he is, why does he stay there, he wonders in the poem, and ends:

> It is too late to start
> For destinations not of the heart.
> I must stay here with my hurt.

> Bombay, for me, is or has become a destination of the heart.
> I must stay here with my hurt.

The One Billion Rupee Home

Paromita Vohra

No Man's Land

There were seven of us on the floor, all women—me, Ramona, Shirley, Bitti, Priya, Naina and Rukhsar. There was someone in the corner room but she kept changing, so I won't count her.

But that was later. First, in the monsoon of 1992, there is only me, the two girls in the corner flat, who are never home because of bosses or boyfriends or something, and the family across from me—Shivaleela and her many children. I never quite figure out how many children. They seem interchangeable to me, all their heads shaped like grapes, or perhaps there are twins who create this optical illusion. Despite their small heads, they cry ferociously. Each Sunday morning, I wake groaning to the sounds of their favourite TV show, the Hindi version of *The Jungle Book*, the theme song of which is lustily belted out by a child: 'Jungle jungle baat chali hai, pata chala hai, chaddi pahan ke phool khila hai, phool khila hai.' ('There's a rumble in the jungle, a new flower is born and it's wearing undies!') I hear the kids voices echo the last phrase in delight—chaddi pahan ke phool khila hai, phool khila hai! Undies are something of a theme with Shivaleela's family. Her husband, for instance, wears brown VIP Y-fronts. I know this because he displays them of his own accord every evening when I come home from work. Holding a steel tumbler of rum, he leans against the doorframe, regarding me with slow bewilderment and generic affection as I sidle past in the narrow corridor, and furtively open my lock. Each night is a contest—will I get in before he gets me? Just as I think I have almost made it he catches the tail end of my quickly thrown half-nod half-smile and says, just as he has the previous night—'Kya bhabi, aaj bahut dinon baad?' (So sis-in-law, long time no see?)

Leave and Licence

Living on my own is not turning out to be what I had imagined. My fantasies of myself as a single woman in a Bombay flat perhaps had a greater resemblance to life in Manhattan, but then, I hadn't really seen any women living alone except in American movies, had I? Bombay had been a sort of home, where I came to stay with my grandmother every school vacation. My grandmother lived in Bandra and for me, the city began at Carter Road with the sea, the sunset and bhelpuriwala, and ended at Linking Road where I accompanied my mother as she bought slippers, bits of fabric and sunglasses, and if I didn't harass her too much, green kulfi in a cone from the stall near Lucky's.

Afternoons in Bandra were sleepy in the shade of bougainvillea bushes, spent playing with my miniature tea sets or reading Richie Rich comics in the cool, dark cocoon of the old Cadillac parked in the back compound. Sometimes, when an uncle visited from abroad and stayed at the Taj Mahal hotel, there would be the long drive from home to downtown, carried forward in the city's glamorous dark, with lights that whizzed and buildings and billboards that loomed and exciting traffic. When you saw the red-and-white striped concrete awnings you knew it was almost Pedder Road and in a bit you would be debouched into the air-conditioned smell of a five-star hotel. While grown-ups drank and talked in a distorted buzz behind, you could sit at the window and watch the overstuffed tourist boats and the small figures of people at the Gateway of India.

My idea of living alone in Bombay was Bandra by day and Manhattan by night. I could picture myself at the large window of my flat, in loungy pyjamas, a glass of wine in my hand, looking out at the twinkling lights of the city. But soon enough, like in the movies, fantasy collides with reality to the screech of tyres.

Reality is a special Bombay thing called Leave and Licence.

This is not a term that celebrates the liberated life. It is, cruelly, the very opposite. It is a living arrangement under which you are not a tenant with rights under the Rent Act but merely a passer through— someone who has been given leave to live (and license for nothing) in a flat for one day under eleven months. (Living in the premises beyond eleven months would give you tenant's rights and make it very difficult for the landlord to expel you.) At the end of eleven months you could revise your agreement—and the landlord usually does, by raising the rent and refusing to fix the leaking ceilings. However, nothing can stop the landlord from terminating this arrangement with a month's notice should you show unruly habits or a little too much cheek and nowadays, perhaps the wrong politics.

Refugees and PAPs

As a lowly assistant in documentary films at the absolute margins of Bombay's film industry, I was getting to be a veteran leave and licencee. I had a brief stay in a flat on Yari Road, which did indeed face the sea. If I ignored the intense smell of drying fish from the fishing colony across, the disapproving looks of the neighbours whenever I opened the door and they saw that I owned nothing but a mattress and a cardboard box, or that I had to stand all my vegetables in a plate of water so the ants wouldn't get to them—well, it was almost there, lapping at the hem of my fantasy. Another year and I could afford the glass of wine. But then I was thrown out so I moved further out to a flat near a sort of hill—well, actually a mound—which I fancied was a view. The charms of the view were a bit obscured by the glare of the fluorescent yellow walls and the fact that the water came for only ten minutes in the day and the rent was more than half my salary and that at the end of the month, either my electricity got cut off for non-payment or I had to figure out which friend I could discreetly hit on for dinner.

I was a refugee from Leave and Licence. If something did not come along, I feared that I might lose my nerve and go home. So that's how I came here to PMGP.

A friend who works for a big Bollywood director tells me film assistants (at least those in the know, unlike me) are all talking about this place called PMGP. It has one room with a little kitchennette and an attached bathroom and the rent is only 700 rupees. So we get into an auto rickshaw and venture into the inner reaches of Andheri (East).

The further we go, the more I will the rickshaw to stop at every passing block of flats we pass—let this be it, it looks nice. But it is a while before we turn into a wide but broken road, lined on either side by tiny grey buildings with a valiant trim of red. In one step, I go from my fantasy to my father's worst fear—that, rejecting every decent middle-class option he has struggled to provide, I would move to Bombay, join the movies and live in a chawl.

Technically, PMGP is not a chawl—that Bombay phenomenon of one-room tenements with common bathrooms and a communitarian balcony corridor. PMGP is blocks of very low-cost housing for people who had earlier lived in a slum near a factory they call Aeltee. I later realize they mean L&T—Larsen and Toubro. The slum has been uprooted by the construction of a new road and they had been relocated to this neighbourhood—a working-class enclave in the middle of an upper-middle-class area. My neighbours are people who development experts called Project Affected Persons or PAPs.

But no one actually asked the PAPs what kind of house they wanted to live in. When the Congress Party was celebrating the centenary of its founding, Rajiv Gandhi—the party's head and Prime Minister at the time—announced a billion-rupee grant for slum redevelopment, improvement and urban renewal in Bombay. Of this bounty was our colony built and so christened PMGP—the Prime Minister's Grant Project. Clearly the housing was designed more for middle-class people—yes, it was only one room, but it did have an attached bathroom and a marked-off privacy from the neighbours. To my middle-class heart, this made it different from a chawl. But to working-class people, this was no good. They could not afford the monthly charges for water and electricity and maintenance. They didn't like living this way, all separated off and hemmed into a ten-foot by twelve-foot room. If they sold coconuts or utensils, it was pretty hard to carry their stuff up and down the stairs. Besides, it wasn't close to where they worked. So it was that they found another slum or chawl on the other side of Aeltee, rented out their rooms and in a strange twist of development, became the more powerful party of a Leave and Licence Agreement, while middle-class folks like me, supplicant and resentful, moved our mattresses and cardboard boxes in, all the better to live the Bohemian Life.

Off, Off Mahakali Road

To find a place in PMGP is not difficult, but you have to go there first. The road does not quite have a name. You have to turn off Mahakali Caves Road and then turn into a road off that and then you ask someone on the street for a Mr Kante. Mr Kante is a short man with his hair combed back and a perpetual look of childish distaste. Cheating you does not upset Mr Kante. He did it with a sense of duty, with a mournful look. It was he who had brought the Leave and License to PMGP. He once worked as a mechanic but was quick to pick up on the possibilities of the situation and, like a good Bombayite, turn it into commerce and become a property broker—unregistered, of course. Word travels quickly in urban villages, so he was doing pretty well by word of mouth. If he got you a place and it needed some fixing up—an extra plug point, a little whitewash—he would have it done. Broker, contractor, what's the difference?

The colony has one wide central road with a slope towards the end. Each building has two wings, five floors. Each floor has seven flats, (with red doors and windows, a sort of cuteness for the masses). That makes seventy families per building. No lift, of course. As I walk up, I can look inside the houses because hardly anyone closes their doors. On the first floor, the owner has already asserted his personality and painted the red door brown and the white wall pink. He has a large framed photograph of Bal Thackeray right in front of the door. In the corner room of the second floor lives the onion-seller from the corner. His walls are painted an aqueous green and they glow at the end of the dim corridor. In front of the door is an iron bed, on which he sometimes sleeps if it is his wife's turn to mind the shop; under the bed, high piles of deep pink onions. On the third floor there is a Keralite family with two kids, their noses round and eyes densely black and I have to step over their toys to get to the next flight of stairs. The mother, slim, long-haired and very pregnant, cooks some fragrant coconutty thing over a kerosene stove and glances at me with her long shy eyes.

Finally, I come to my floor, the top floor, where I sidle past Shivaleela's husband and let myself into the room with the uneven floors, which I am trying to make home.

My Maternal Uncles

The day I move in, I deposit several cardboard cartons and my two cane racks in the house and stand looking out at what really is a view. Small green hillocks house the Mahakali Caves for which our road is named. There is a mist of monsoon drizzle and standing in the balcony, I think, well, everyone has to start somewhere. I will start next week. So I go off to stay at a friend's for a few days.

When I return I see the cardboard cartons still tied and taped but torn off at the top. Someone has gouged out a hole in each of them. I stand there in shock, my heart trembling. How had they got in? The door was locked. Could it have been the windows? What could they possibly want from my modest possessions? When I open the cartons I see that a hole has been tunnelled into the boxes from top to bottom, as if an electric saw has gone through it, cutting up everything in its way—clothes, books, candles, plastic mugs. Why has this happened? Is it just anger against a middle-class person moving here, or malicious harassment of a woman living alone? My mind searches wildly for an explanation and I sit down and weep.

A few days later, coming home late with my friend I stop to fix my shoe and she calls out—'Look out!' I see a dog running full speed at me and can't move past in time. It hits my leg with all its weight and as its long tail slithers over my foot I realize the dog is actually a rat. A big, bad Bombay bandicoot. This is the kind of creature that has tunnelled through my boxes.

In Bombay people do not say the word 'rat'. They say Maama which means maternal uncle in Hindi. 'Don't leave the door open, Maama will get in.' They fear invoking the name will cause it to materialize. I wish I had learnt this earlier because I say 'rats' all the time and obligingly, they infest my house. I keep a broom by the side of the door. I unlock the door, enter, lift the broom, and as two or three rats scramble on hearing me enter, I desperately chase them out. But they are bold and resourceful. They make homes inside the pile of old newspapers, behind the kitchen utensils, in the bathroom loft. They scrabble and shit and make my house smell. They eat up my clothes and books routinely. They are huge beasts with the demonic ability to squeeze under doors and through cracks in the window if you don't shut it tight. I stuff the bottom of the balcony door with magazines to stop them from coming in. But I'm a bundle of nerves, kept up all night by the sound of them gnawing to get in. In the morning, drained as a survivor from *Jurassic Park*, I open the door to see half the magazines eaten up, dangerously close to the door's edge.

Late one night there are sounds outside my door. I ignore them but they get louder and I open the door. Six men who I've often noticed sitting in a group at the front of the building stand there. Scarred by my serial evictions, my heart sinks. They say they are the building maintenance society and they want the monthly payment. All the time their eyes keep trying to look over my head into my room. Annoyed, I say—'Well, this is no time to ask for it.'

'What do you want us to do?' one man asks roughly. 'We work all day and after that we get the time to do the building stuff.'

'Well would you like it if six men came to your house at 11 when your daughter was alone?' I shoot back, pleased by my balance of aggression and appeal to their paternal instincts. 'What!' shouts another man, 'We are old enough to be your uncles. Are you casting aspersions on our character?' Tricky territory. We stand there staring at each other. I backtrack a little. 'Anyway I don't have it now. I'll give it to you later.'

'When?'

'I'm going out of town for a day or two—so after I return.' They mutter a little and leave. Before I can get back into bed, there is a knock again. A young man from the posse stands there.

'Yes?'

'Er . . . I was wondering, are you an air hostess?' he asks hopefully. I stare in outrage, knowing that air hostess is boy shorthand for available and loose. 'NO,' I bark. He backs away from my glare, 'No, it's just that you said you were going out of town for a day or two and . . . ok, goodnight, sorry.'

Kya Cheez Hai (Quite Something)!

There are a handful of people like me here, all working in the movies, living alone, keeping odd hours, wanting to buy strange things from the grocers. I go in and ask, 'Cheese hai?' (Do you have cheese?) The shopkeeper looks perplexed—'Kaun si cheez?' (What thing?) No working-class person would blow forty rupees on a tin of cheese. Or corn flakes. Or Maggi noodles, that staple food of those who live alone. For these luxuries we must walk down to Takshila market in front of where the white-collar folks live.

The PMGP locals regard us with a mixture of curiosity and hostility. We regard them gingerly, with a class uncertainty—not knowing how to live next door to the people whose houses we had never previously been inside. Sometimes, at Andheri station I get onto an auto rickshaw and the driver says, 'PMGP, right? I've seen you around, I live in No. 8.' My friend's household help lives on the ground floor of her building. On the surface, like a socialist ideal, we all live in the same type of house, but the interiors belie our different worlds. They have aluminium utensil racks, Godrej cupboards, laminated shelves, maybe a box bed. We have handloom cushion covers, chatais, a Van Gogh print taped to the wall or a kitsch Hindi movie poster, handmade coffee cups and books and tapes. One man looks long and assessingly at my rack full of music cassettes and finally asks—'Do you have a music shop?'

But slowly our numbers grow. More people working in film and TV begin to move in. Some even have the money to buy their apartments, liberating themselves from the eleven-month cycle of you-know-what. Renovations and improvements, each designed to build an illusion of space, become the centrepiece of conversation. 'Did you hear R has broken down an entire wall and made French windows?' 'I heard V has a full-length mirror in his bathroom. I pretended I had to go so I could see it with my own eyes!' 'You should check out H's new sliding windows—powder-coated a fabulous yellow.'

Strolling down the street I get used to someone calling out from their window—'Hey, I'm making fish, want to come have dinner?' Or, going out of the house to look for an electrician, being waylaid by someone who says—'Coming for a movie at Pinky cinema?' I begin to lose that don't-look-at-me-I'm-not really-here walk. I am no longer careful. I stand at the crossing and chat with a friend till 3 a.m. in the cold night air. This is a parallel universe, the Left Bank of Andheri (E). I live in PMGP, but in my head it's somewhere else. I still need to meet my neighbours but they are from a distant place of maintenance money and quick staircase smiles.

Slowly PMGP is changing. More of us enter, more of the original inhabitants leave. Slowly my hostile neighbours are becoming a little, could it be, obsequious? Like Mr Kante, the property agent, they are getting in the brokering game, asking me on the stairs—'Madam, aapka koi dost hai, room ke liye?' (Madam, do you have any friends looking to rent a place?) 'Tell me, I will arrange it, two months rent as fees. But for you, a discount.'

A chai shop opens and quickly expands to marble fronting and laminated benches. It is owned by two Shetty friends. They serve tea and eggs and bread, samosas—food to dawdle over. We gather here routinely—'So that guy who used to assist P is finally directing his own serial for HTV. Me? I'm putting in a few proposals, they say BiTV is commissioning interesting stuff with decent budgets . . .' The film assistants are being joined by theatre actors from the Delhi stage, coming to try their hand at TV. Thin girls who always wear make-up, smile sweetly, though their eyes hold a hint of strain—they want to be attractive casting propositions but after all they don't want to make themselves cheap. Romances blossom but never quite bloom, the hard urban ground not fertile with trust. Best friends come to find the gold together, stay up long nights with tea and rum, writing the perfect script on pages of foolscap and when nothing comes through, become disenchanted with each other because one seems to have lost his purity and the other seems to be living in the reality of Allahabad or Benaras or Jhansi. They're all on their way to something better; there is a desperate optimism in the street.

Nothing Happened

One winter morning in 1993, I wake to the sound of thudding feet on the roof. A short while later, a banging on my door. In the building across, people are standing on the roof, pointing to something in the far distance. I go up—there is a fire somewhere in Jogeshwari. It is 6

January and the city, just calming from terrible communal riots, flares up again.

There is chaos on the street, boys running past, chains in hand. A friend who sees me says, 'If you have somewhere to go, just go there now and don't come back for a few days.' The boys with chains have been chasing a Muslim woman across the quadrangle inside the colony and my friend's brother runs to stop them. They hit him on the head and while he bleeds, no rickshaw stops to take him to the hospital and no one helps him. This is not the worst thing that I hear and see over the next few days as the riots eat through the city like the rats ate through my cardboard boxes.

Two weeks later, I venture back and stop to pick up my clothes from the dhobi. 'Oh, we slept in fear these last days,' he says, in his UP accent. 'Boys running up and down in the night. But nothing happened, they were just calling out obscenities, nothing happened.'

Message in a Dosa

All things come to she who waits. And two things come to PMGP—Shetty's Dosa Cart and Prakashbhai's telephone shop.

The first offers a new delicacy—spring dosas, i.e., dosas stuffed with crisp slices of capsicum and tomato and crunchy onions, cut up like a Chinese spring roll. The second offers a message service. Prakash bhai has not one, but three phones. For a small fee, that phone could ring for you and Prakashbhai, chewing paan and speaking mostly in grunts, will take down a message. You may collect this message at any time but he will not come up to give it to you—unless it is a matter of death, says a big notice on the wall.

It is not long before the long-haired actors and the unemployed strugglers are ensconced in the steel chairs, waiting for the phone to ring. This is not something Prakash bhai has bargained for. After a few abuses and loud complaints, he puts up pieces of paper that say—'No loitering' and 'Sitting in the shop without work is strictly prohibited and will be presecuted.'

Prakash bhai knows exactly what's going on in our lives. You may be discreet and studiedly casual when you pass by for the eighth time asking, 'Any calls for me?' He looks at you intently and says—'No, he didn't call' and you scurry off blushing. Or if you happened to be walking past on the main road he calls out loudly—'You got a call, about a job.' You run anxiously to the shop and he allows you to break the line of people waiting to make STD calls—'Let her call, it's about a job.'

But it's not enough for Prakashbhai to be privy to every detail of your life. He also feels he must tell others about it—'Did you hear that M was called for an audition for some role by B.R. Chopra? Arré, but his luck is bad, and actually he hasn't got that special something, you know? I have been in Bombay for many years, I can take one look and I can tell you he is not going to be a star.'

So of course when M does not get the role, we all look away guiltily.

Prakashbhai often loses his temper and will throw people out, abusing loudly, if he doesn't like your attitude. I am treated fairly well. This is partly because my racy status as a single woman in the colony has been usurped by the ever-growing numbers of aspiring actresses, all curvaceous and enticingly dressed. Not only are they walking on the central road in shorts, but they are also on TV and this somehow makes them public property. In the light of their morally ambiguous position, I become a venerable elder, a respectable prior inhabitant, with greater right to deference and claim to space than the new immigrants.

*

Sometimes, between serving spring dosas, Shetty coyly slips the women a card for Saumya Beauty Parlour, which is located in the building behind where the cart stands. 'My wife,' he says, shyly and goes back to loudly distressing the dosa batter. The wife operates the salon with a very thin and timid helper, while her daughter, three-year-old Saumya, walks in and out with the certitude of someone who knows the place is named after her. She usually chooses to do this as you sit with your legs apart and your skirt hitched up, having your legs waxed. The wife never shuts the door, so the women next door—as they cut vegetables or make bidis or bindis—are given one more gaping view of your foreign behaviour. Complaints bring only a shy little laugh from the proprietor. Somehow you feel this husband and wife team will go far on the strength of that laugh.

★

Behind PMGP, a whole new MHADA colony is coming up and the central road winds upwards between its pink and mauve buildings, as yet unoccupied. Some nights, my friend and I walk up this empty road. The neon lights shining off the perfect unused road and the full moon make us feel like we are on a film set. Any moment now the rain will come down and we will sing a song of love under a black umbrella.

East-West

I go away for six months and when I return PMGP looks different. More shops of course—a medical store, a jeweller! Old shops are getting shiny counters and gleaming jars. The sugar isn't wrapped in paper any more but poured into a plastic bag. When I argue that it's not a good thing, the owner laughs. 'You're very strange, madam. The others will start fighting with us if we don't give them a plastic bag. Everyone wants to go forward and you want to go backward.'

The two girls who moved in at the same time as I are gone. The benches outside the chai shop are vacant. Shetty's dosa cart is missing. On the ground floor of my building is a shop with inscrutable tinted glass windows. The sign says 'Detective Agency'.

Prakashbhai tells me many people have moved. Suddenly there are so many new TV channels and so much work, their upward mobility has accelerated. They are all gone—the cameraman and his girlfriend who lived in the corner flat, the editor and scriptwriter who lived in No. 16, the assistant director and the actor couple from No. 13—moved on up to Poonam Nagar or Gokuldham and Saibaba complex in Goregaon (East). The ones who really did well have moved to Lokhandwala Complex or Yari Road in Andheri (W) where they can live next door to Amrita Singh or Akshay Kumar.

A few days later I do run into one of my older friends on the road. He's house hunting. 'Moving back here?' I ask. 'Oh, no. I can't do that. I mean once you've moved to the West, you can't move back to the East. People will look at your number and when they see it begins with 8 instead of 6, you could lose work.'

But what about the dosa cart Shetty? 'Oh, he has bought a shop in Takshila market.' Indeed it's there, the first Udipi on Off Mahakali Caves Road—Shreekrishna Udipi. He smiles shyly when I enter. Nestling by the side of the Udipi restaurant is the better half of the enterprise—Saumya Beauty Parlour. As I am leaving, little Saumya flounces out in a pink frock, leaving the door ajar. A woman, her face covered white with bleach, is revealed to the street for a few moments.

Home Alone

Gentrification: the process by which higher-income households displace lower-income residents of a neighbourhood, changing the essential character and flavour of that neighbourhood.

Analyses of the changes in a neighbourhood like PMGP would use that word when the film assistants replace the coconut sellers. What's the word when the film assistants leave to be replaced by another category of people who come from a no-man's land of shifting class?

I am a bit adrift. My playmates are gone to their true homes—the two BHK (two Bedroom-Hall-Kitchen) kind of homes. They are in Vijay Sales, buying red refrigerators and new TVs.

In pursuit of their dreams, they do not mind moving to Kandivili because Bombay for them lies where the film and TV offices and studios are and the commute takes them maybe as far as Bandra. They are at large in a different city from mine.

When I moved here, just the thought that saving so much money on the rent meant I could have a life I enjoyed and which only this city offered me—going to Town, sitting on Marine Drive, eating a Frankie while I lovingly surveyed my purchases from New and Secondhand Bookstore or the scratchy 45 rpm wrapped in protective plastic bought from Furtado and Sons.

Now, after three years, there is a big question in my mind. To commit or not to commit?

I buy the room right next to mine because even though the

neighbours are unfamiliar, the fourth floor of building 17 A seems like home. At least moving will be pretty easy.

On my floor there are two new families. On my left is Shirley, a glistening dark-skinned Catholic girl, her flamboyant sister Ramona and Ramona's daughter Bitti, an earnest and quiet eight-year-old with a katori cut. On their door they put up a little plaque with the Infant Jesus that says Bless this House. On their walls they put up mounted photographs of Bitti standing next to the movie star Kajol, inexplicably with a towel around her waist. They also have a Karaoke machine and several enthusiastic friends who come in to drink and sing loudly each night. On my right is Rukhsar, a ravishing woman with long dark hair, flawless skin, a big innocent smile, languid eyes, a womanly walk and a son, Shoyu, as cute as his mother is beautiful.

The long-eyed woman on the third floor has doubled her family and the floor outside her door is lined with shoes in various miniature sizes. The onion seller still sleeps on the iron bed with the onion treasure underneath. But the fourth floor is a different matter. Women keep their doors open and there is constant traffic between houses— 'Rukhsar, you have any coriander?' 'Shirley, is Shoyu in your house? My god, this boy will just kill me one day, he keeps crawling off and disappearing.' If they see me at the door they hesitate, drop their voices and carry on. Sometimes Rukhsar says—'Sorry, madam.' I suppose I should be relieved she doesn't add a 'ji' to it.

I really feel that I am alone, at home.

★

I come up the stairs carrying too many things. The women are standing on the landing chattering loudly. The women watch my balancing act as I try to unlock the door with half a hand. I drop a bag of milk, which bursts in a big white bruise over the floor. Before I can control it, the word slips out—'Fuck!' The silence spreads as thickly as the milk. Then they help me mop it up. This is the first time I am actually talking to them.

A little later, Shirley comes to my house holding a cup of milk. 'It's morning, no, so I am sure you went to get it for your coffee. I thought you might be needing some.' I am nonplussed by her kindness. I say, 'Oh, no no, it's ok, I'll get some more later.' 'Take no, men,' she says. 'We are all neighbours only. And you know what I say, you and me we are both the same no, single. These people here won't understand. Us single girls must stick together.' I smile inanely. Before going she says, 'I know you only drink coffee, I never see tea leaves in your garbage, no.'

Shirley and I find much to unite us after this event, other than our singleness and the fact that we both speak English. For instance, we both tend to burn the rice because we start doing something else after putting it on the fire. We both like to work and to spend time alone. Both our sisters are beautiful and more sociable. In fact Ramona is not only sociable but positively bountiful. She is often to be seen surrounded by red chillies soaking in a bowl, fish or meat lying heaped on a thali and ivory slices of garlic as she scrapes coconut for its milk. Ramona loves to make cauldrons of green curry crab, red fish curry, sausage pulao and pepper chicken and feed it to others. She looks at my pale soups and pert salads and says, 'We can't eat your food, men, what all ghas phus.' In fact, she clearly thinks I shouldn't eat my food either because each mealtime my doorbell rings and Bitti is sent with the message, 'Coming for dinner?' Once in four times I agree, which makes that pretty much every other day. I take along the ghas phus anyway as my contribution because it alarms me that they never cook any vegetables ever. To these meals, Rukhsar brings her bit—usually a chicken stew made Madhya Pradesh-style, thin, intoxicating with coriander smells and super spicy. Rukhsar understands no English, and Ramona and Shirley both frequently say things about her to me in English, while she looks on sweetly. When I suggest this may be rude, Ramona looks perplexed—'Why? What is there? We are not saying anything bad. If your heart is good who cares, men?'

Of course I am curious about these robust women. But I am too genteel to ask the questions. How can you afford this food when you don't seem to do any regular work? Where are Shoyu's and Bitti's fathers? I am also scared to ask questions, because despite the outward conviviality, I don't really want to share my feelings. These I keep for my other friends, the ones who don't live here anymore.

Eventually intimacy comes by the most trite route—alcohol.

While we eat Ramona's food, she drinks a half bottle of whisky, and Rukhsar accompanies her. They get drunker and louder and both their stories are always about how much money they had, how they *showed* the people who treated them badly. 'You won't believe it, you know, I was dripping with diamonds,' Ramona says. 'But I was stupid, I used to give things to anyone who asked, and in my time of need, there was no one.' Rukhsar counters, 'Arré, I used to wear gold bangles all the way up to my elbows. And my hair, you know now it has become half, but it was so thick the plait was as thick as my wrist. But the same—people come and ask, then how can you say no? Isn't it, madam? I would just take off a bangle and give.'

One day, a little under the influence myself, I ask—'So how did you earn all that money?'

Ramona looks a little sheepish and says, 'Well actually you know my mother was a smuggler.' 'Right,' I say politely, trying to look as if this is a regular occupation. 'I used to also do, lot of back and forth, Hong Kong, Bangkok, Dubai. Ask them, I used to bring suitcases full of things.' 'And now?' I persist. 'Now why I need to work. My husband is there, no.' 'Oh, Bitti's father,' I say. 'Arré, not him, what he will do? He used to beat me you know, every time I was landing up in hospital, sometimes hand is broken, sometimes face is broken. It took me years to walk out. Just trapped me with sweet words. You won't believe, he used to speak such good English. Then I got divorced. Not him—my second husband.'

She is referring to a surly, burly man who comes a couple of days a week and sits in brown shorts and gold crucifix, watching TV and eating fried chicken. I say nothing about it because in my body and in Ramona's too-wide smile and that gaze that seems direct but is a little off centre, I see the truth.

Rukhsar is quiet through this because the conversation happens in English.

★

Shirley gets married but her husband works in the Gulf. So, though she now wears a couple of gold chains more, our female conferences continue as before. She confesses—'I don't mind we are married, but I am happy living like this only with you all.' Bitti, now a teenager, joins a hobby class in the summer holidays to learn how to do mehendi. She practices long hours on my feet, making peacocks which look like ducks. Shoyu starts to walk, his hair tied in a fan-shaped ponytail on top of his head, making him look like Little Lord Krishna.

Shirley's husband comes home for Christmas. He gives me a box of Quality Street chocolates. Shirley gets pregnant. The Detective Agency board on the ground floor is replaced by a board saying Supreme Car Service, but the windows are the same forbidding tinted glass and I'm darned if I've ever seen a car being serviced downstairs.

We get two more neighbours—Priya and Naina. They too have one or two children but don't seem to work.

The Ballad of Raj and Shoyu

'Raja, why are you crying?'

It confuses me, the way Rukhsar always calls her son Raj or Raja. Surely one pet name per child is enough, Shoyu being short for Shoaib. Breaking my rule of silence yet again, I ask Rukhsar—'What is his name really?'

'I call him Shoyu, but his father calls him Raj.' I am mystified because I have never seen his father.

But of course I am naive. Shoyu can after all have a father without Rukhsar having a husband. Shoyu's father is Hindu while Rukhsar is Muslim. How did they meet? Well, Rukhsar came from Madhya Pradesh as a young girl, very beautiful and from a poor family. She got a job as a dancer in a bar. Of course she was popular, she was graceful and heart-stoppingly beautiful, with the childlike blankness which makes it so easy to turn her into your fantasy. Raj's father was the manager of the bar. She fell in love and he said he would take her away from it all, so he did. She got pregnant, he rented her a place in PMGP. Occasionally he visits, which is when he calls Shoyu Raj. He gives her 25,000 rupees a month, she claims, and why should I contradict her? Marriage? Isn't that a bourgeois kind of question. Anyway, he's

Hindu and she's Muslim and his mother is a heart patient and that's entertainment.

So, More Lonely Nights

Everyone is gathered on the landing and they are giggling. I open the door to check out the scene and see Shoyu, walking in a zigzag line. He looks at me with unhinged eyes, smiles a woozy smile and sits down with a hiccup. If he weren't two and a half years old, I'd say he was drunker than a drunk in a movie. The women all laugh.

Actually, he is drunk. 'What to do madam, he fights with me. He doesn't keep quiet if I don't give him a little.'

The nights are painful. Rukhsar cries with love and desperation. Sometimes she befriends an autorickshaw driver and asks him up. Some nights she drinks with the other neighbours. Some nights she drinks alone and who wants to do that, so she shares a drink with her one and only son. Everyone thinks it's cute, how a little kid acts like a grown up. 'Do you know madam, yesterday, I was cursing his father, and holding my head and he came up to me with the bottle of RC and plonked it in front of me and said, 'Tension mat le. Le, drink le.' (Stop stressing out. Here, have a drink).

It's not long before we have to take him to the doctor who shakes his head and says there's something up with the liver. Shoyu squirms and calls the doctor 'behenchuth' in his baby accent. The doctor asks, 'What did he say?' 'Oh, nothing,' Rukhsar hastily says, 'he asked for his father.' In spite of everything, we have to giggle.

Some nights are more painful than others. Some nights it is Ramona who cries, because her husband is not her husband and actually someone else's. Because he brings her money from his illegal construction business but actually he borrowed all her money some years earlier to start this business and that's why she sold her legally constructed house and so he's got her, hasn't he, with love and money? Shirley, not prone to sentiment, gets a hard anger in her eyes and says, 'Curse our mother. You know, she threw us out because our stepfather didn't want us. You know we had to stay in an orphanage and the nuns gave us one pao and some curry water—that's all, to eat in the day.

That's why I say, never say no to anyone for food. And I won't cry when my mother dies, it won't be a day too soon.'

By morning, everyone appears spent and calmed from their nights of release and cleaning and cooking go on as before.

*

For reasons of ignorance or obtuseness, I am often oblivious to the meaning of people's days. For instance, Priya and Naina in the room across wake late and spend each day scurrying after their babies or standing and gossiping in nighties and petticoats. They seem like quiet, North Indian girls who watch *Kkusum* and wear mangalsutras. In the evenings they bathe, and I hear the tinkling of pooja bells. Later I see them go off, dressed in salwar kameezes with little knapsacks on their backs. They keep to themselves and I never really wonder about when they come back home and where their husbands are.

A family with seven children of all ages move into the room next door. Their mother, whom everyone calls Bhaiyin, is a gigantic woman with a sweet face. Their one room is lined wall to wall with mattresses; their balcony stacked with utensils and clothes and about thirteen pairs of shoes straggle down the corridor up to my door. Her two older daughters follow the same routine as Priya and Naina. The evenings become a religious contest. Bhaiyin's daughters believe in electronic prayer and play bhajans on their stereo in the evening. Priya begins to do the same. The volume of each stereo ratchets up each day as they compete for piety. Then they all come out in their salwar kameezes and knapsacks and go off to work chatting down the stairs.

All the girls work in bars in and around Andheri, as dancers. If you are that young and pretty, you get to be a dancer. When you get older you would have to be a waitress. Rukhsar is relieved she no longer has to do it. So what if she's had to have five abortions. She is happy to have folks like her to hang out with, unlike those who help her in many ways, but will persist in speaking English over her head and try to make her send Shoyu to school.

Bhaiyin also has two younger daughters, aged six and eight. Radhika and Anmol wear little velveteen and chiffon ensembles studded with crystals. They dance in the corridor singing *Bhumro, bhumro, shyam rang bhumro*, their eyes darting from one side to the other archly.

Ramona says, 'Yeah, these people start early. After all it's in their family line.' Apparently the two families belong to a caste of performers who have come to this city to work in its beer bars.

Feeling bolder for having community around, Priya and Naina have been transformed. They now keep their door open, the radio running loudly. They send their babies to play loudly in the corridor and if I complain they take them in for a minute and let them out as soon as my door is closed. They throw old chapattis outside their doors, so the rat population once again begins to climb. Bhaiyin sweeps outside her door every day and neatly deposits the dirt outside my door. When I ask who has done it she looks so innocent you could cry. When I catch her at it, she looks even more innocent and says, 'Oh it isn't me, it's just this once.'

Ramona doesn't like this takeover of the floor or losing the supremacy she has so far enjoyed. I want to keep out of it but she won't let me and her daily tirades get stronger. 'Really these building people, they don't think who they rent to, they take anybody. Must our children play with these sorts of people now.'

I try to ask, 'Come on, what do you mean "these sorts of people". You were friendly with them too earlier.'

'Not me!' she says vehemently. As I gape at her rather convenient memory she says, 'Never, you can ask anyone, I only keep respectable friends. Really something should be done.'

Doorbells

Winter mornings in my room are my favourite time. The doorbell rings. It's just dawn and it's the paper and the paowala. The sun comes up slowly, and the entire room is aglow in long slants of deep red. Sitting on my table, watching the glass bottles on my window sill glow like jewels in the red-gold light, I drink a cup of coffee, listen to the sound of my modem connecting to the Internet, smell the parathas that the third-floor lady makes for the kids' tiffin and watch the butter melt on a fresh *brun pao*.

At 3 p.m. the doorbell rings. Two men outside—one in a garland, the other without one. The one with the garland stands smiling, hands folded and looking strangely familiar. The one without tells me, 'This is our esteemed local Samajwadi Party candidate. Please vote for him.' I listen in a resigned fashion to his many good qualities and plans for the neighbourhood. He smiles a little more and says, 'Recognize, no?' Recognize yes! It's the dosa cart Shetty. After serving us idlis for eight years he wishes to serve us in other ways. He loses, but that's only if you're being literal.

H, who moved out of PMGP and moved back again, reports excitedly that she saw Sunil Dutt outside the ration shop giving a speech. 'But there were only a few people around him. And anyway he was talking complete rubbish.' Better to take Shetty's route and remain silent while someone else does the talking. That way he can't be blamed for losing at least.

Another day, another doorbell. It's 8 p.m. Two ladies who look like the Chemistry and Sanskrit teachers from my school stand there. Turns out they are teachers by day and census takers by evening. They spread out the fascinating sheets, long and lined. They think I am being a smart ass when I say I don't know my caste. They give me that look that says: straighten out or it's 100 lines of imposition for you. I would wither if I was being a smart ass but I really don't know my caste so I withstand the gaze bravely.

'Mother tongue?' they ask.

'Well, don't know—I guess Punjabi or Bengali—or English I guess. Can I have two mother tongues?'

'Madam, you can only have one mother tongue.'

They don't seem to like the fact that I was born in Pune, that I came to Bombay from Delhi and there is much discussion about what to put in the columns. Exasperated, they ask, 'How many people living in the house?'

'One.'

'One?'

'One.'

'Marital status?'

'Single.'

'Age is thirty-two, no? Single?'

'Yes.'

'Hmm.'

They shuffle off next door. I wonder how they will fare at Bhaiyin's and Rukhsar's and at Ramona and Shirley where the three people in the house have three different surnames.

★

Rukhsar's crying. Shoyu's father is getting married. He's told Rukhsar—'This is it, no more money for you.' She asks him how she is going to manage with Shoyu and he says—'You can work, can't you?' So she has to go back to work in the bar but now she's been downgraded to a waitress. She is always tired and rarely smiles. No one wants to look after Shoyu because he is naughty and abuses and looks at people in a mean way.

The corner room has a high turnover of tenants who seem to operate on leave and licenses of about two months. A family moves in with two grown sons who don't seem to work or study, and one Pomeranian that always lies with its head disconsolate across the threshold. It's not long before Rukhsar is smiling at the younger son as he walks around bare chested, and plays with Shoyu. 'My god,' Ramona says, 'she has no shame, she won't even leave that young boy.'

When they leave, they are replaced by a Bengali woman who someone insists is a prostitute. 'Er, you aren't supposed to say that, you should say sex-worker,' I demur. Everyone laughs. 'Yeah, yeah,' they say, 'This is just like when something happens you say we should call the police and turn to the law instead of giving that person one tight slap. What world are you living in, Paro?'

★

I am shooting a workers' protest in Matulya mills in Parel. There is an impasse between workers and management and I sit outside the whole day, waiting to shoot whatever happens. Me and the policemen. The cops are concerned that I won't go eat anything in case I miss the action, so they send for some vada pao for me. As it gets later they are worried about how I will go home.

'Where do you live?' one cop asks.

'Andheri (E).'

'Oh, that's far,' someone says.

'Not really,' he counters, 'I live there too.'

'Where?' I ask.

'PMGP.'

'Really! So do I.'

He looks at me suspiciously. But then I ask, 'Is your building also having a water problem because of that new pipe which the health club is making?' and he relaxes. I feel as if I have met someone from the home country.

The MHADA colony behind PMGP is also fully occupied now. A music recording studio opens on the ground floor of my building. Although there are a couple of newer shiny shops, there are also many more vendors on the street than before, selling plastic flowers, lurid calendars, hair baubles for five rupees, cheap steel vessels. A clearing has been made in one of the quadrangles for cricket so kids don't play in the central street as much. There are cars outside all the buildings. Prakashbhai is thinking of shutting shop because everyone has phones at home and also STD rates are going down. 'What about a cybercafe?' I suggest. I don't really want him to move since he is one of the few remaining people from the old days. 'Oh cybercafe is a bad idea. Everyone is making a loss.' He nods towards the colony's cybercafes, which sit side by side. One charges twenty rupees an hour, the other nineteen. 'Let me see for a bit and then decide' he says.

Shetty's chai shop has shut and been turned into a driving school. Greta from downstairs, who makes dabbas and delivers them on her two-wheeler, also passes my friend a card which says Driving Lessons for Ladies only. 'Times aren't what they used to be,' Prakashbhai says.

A crazy man lives on the ground floor. His eyes are crossed and angry. He abuses anyone who walks past and the children either make fun of him or are scared of him. I'm a little nervous myself. I wonder how he is always so neatly dressed though, how he lives. One day I come down the stairs and see he has a roommate, a man who is tenderly combing his hair. As I turn the corner, he gently touches his friend's cheek.

Another day I go down and see the door of the house has been pulled out. The door lies diagonally across the doorframe, the edges jagged as if it had been torn out. The crazy man sits on his bed glowering and muttering. Greta tells me he tore it out himself the previous night in a fit of rage. Why is this man so angry?

We May Be Poor, But We Have Our Respect

Our building still hasn't registered itself as a cooperative. But it doesn't mean we can't act like one. A big board downstairs lists some rules. 'Resell or matters releting to renovations without prior permission is strictly prohibited.' Eventually the landlords are given a talking to. Bhaiyin's family has bought a place in No. 16 but are not being allowed to shift into it because the building people don't want dirty families with dubious professions. Why must our building not have high moral standards? We may be poor, but we have our respect.

Rukhsar has found herself a new lover who she says is her brother. Around the time her landlord tells her he won't renew her lease she marries him and moves to Vashi in New Bombay. She forgets to take her two katoris in which she'd given me that super spicy stew. Priya and Naina are also asked to leave. When I suggest to Ramona that this isn't fair, what if people ask us to leave because we are single, she says, 'Don't be silly, we are respectable and educated. And those people used to make such a mess and a nuisance, no? Always making a noise and creating garbage.' I am forced to agree. 'Well, that's why their lease was not renewed, not for any reason. After all this is a building not a slum, no.'

Over the years I too have lost my middle-class ways. Sometimes, when it gets stiflingly hot in summer, Bombay's intense humidity mixes with my genteel self-imposed poverty to stir up a big sweat and I have to open the door. I've even lost my middle-class decencies and sit in a tank top and shorts, revealing my shoulders for the world to see as I work at my computer. My friends are uncomfortable and always shut the door when they come in.

The building has its own soundtrack—the theme tune of *Kyunki Saas Bhi Kabhi Bahu Thi,* the pressure cookers, the clanging vessels, the kids crying, the unemployed grown ups yelling at them. After a while it all gets too much for me and I shut the door and turn up my jazz CD. Somewhere in a corner of my progressive heart, there is, perhaps, a place that is for ever two BHK. I am uncomfortable that I do this. I shut the door on that as well.

The Cult of the Golden Bull

Nina Martyris

With a bundle on a stick and trousers that didn't quite make it to the ankle, he was an unlikely symbol of greed. But Raj Kapoor in the 1955 classic *Shri 420* gave modern India its most enduring fable of avarice. In the grip of Nehruvian idealism, K.A. Abbas wrote a heart-rending delineation of Raj Kapoor's Chaplinesque innocence being corrupted by the lure of big money—and by Mumbai.

The plot unfolds to find Kapoor and the unscrupulous Seth Sonechand float a fraudulent company that promises homes to the poor at a hundred rupees (a swindle that perspicaciously predicted Shiv Sena chief Bal Thackeray's electoral promise forty years later to gift 40,00,000 slum dwellers free homes). Thousands pay up their hundred rupees. Beggars put together grimy stacks of ten paise coins to make up the amount. Along the way, Kapoor pawns his most prized possession—his honesty medal.

Such willingness to suspend disbelief has, over the 140 years, fuelled scam after Bombay scam. There was the cotton bubble of 1862, the reclamation con job of the early twentieth century and the stock-market fiddles of 1992 and 2001. As the city erupted from swamp to skyscraper, the yearning to believe in schemes that offer 36 per cent interest manifested itself with unfailing regularity. In *Shri 420*, Nadira is the svelte vamp who propels the young Raj along the slippery road of sleight with a song that exhorts him: *Mud mud ke na dekh*. This has become the theme song for a city that refuses to learn from its foolhardiness.

Wind back to 1862 the hands of the Rajabai clock tower (a structure built by Premchund Roychand, the stock broker largely responsible for the collapse of the Bank of Bombay in 1865, bringing thousands to destitution). The American Civil War spurred Bombay's eager trot into a wild gallop. Four years before the war, a southern American senator James Henry Hammond wrote confidently, 'Without the firing of a gun, without drawing a sword, we could bring the whole world to our feet. What would happen if no cotton was furnished for three years? England would topple headlong and carry the whole civilized world with her. No, you dare not make war on cotton! No power on earth dares make war upon it. Cotton is King.'

Little did Hammond or his red-necked plantation aristocracy realize that a snook would soon be cocked at them by the fierce enterprise of a small fishy island in the eastern hemisphere, populated by people whose skin was only a few shades lighter than that of the slaves whose sweat watered their cotton fields. That island was Bombay, and when Britain turned to India for cotton, Bombay thrust all its energies into feeding Lancashire's mills.

Overnight, the price of cotton rocketed and a white mania was unleashed, presaging the digital bubble that would envelop dotcomrades in the late twentieth century. Bombay's tidal wave of prosperity carried on its crest the banker, the farmer and the port hand. The windfall was so huge that peasants in the hinterland began to embellish their cartwheels with their surplus silver. The only commodity in short supply was good sense.

From 1862 to 1865, whipped on by the manipulative genius of the leading sharebrokers, Bombay seemed to go crazy. At that time, the export to China of one-kilo opium balls—known as cannon-balls of the mind—was a hugely profitable business. The three Js—Parsi barons Jamshetji Tata, Jamsetjee Jeejeebhoy and Cowasji Jehangir—were among those who built their fortunes on opium's addictive power. As thousands poured in from the countryside to share Bombay's prosperity, land itself became the most valued commodity. This spawned a rash of reclamation schemes and at least eight land companies, the most notorious being the Back Bay Reclamation project. At peak, Back Bay Reclamation shares touched the unbelievable sum of Rs 55,000—a figure that has not been matched by any Indian company even a century later. Writes historian Teresa Alburquerque, 'Each share was prized as a gold mine, fetching a profit of 2500 pounds before a load of gravel had been emptied into the bay.'

Everyone wanted a piece of the action. People even tore open old mattresses to sell the cotton stuffing, displaying the sort of derring-do that propels Mumbai's present-day residents to enclose their large-sized balconies and lease them to a paying guest. Bombay's leading baker, Salvador Patricio, was among those who started an informal bank and he speculated headily with the money of the Goan seamen who had entrusted him with their savings. But the end of the Civil War pooped the party. The end came one overcast monsoon morning in 1865. Baker, broker, mover and shaker all went belly-up, taking with them thousands of investors. The enormous volume of notional paper transactions that had been made during the period had the value of confetti.

The Bombay Chamber of Commerce, which had watched the city pile up its teetering castle of cards, set about attempting to ensure that future commerce in Bombay would not be built on the quicksand of speculation. It didn't get very far. The methods employed in the great cotton crash of 1865 would be used again to engineer the securities scams of 1992 and 2001: Prices were inflated steadily by a handful of key brokers; the people heading the banking and financial institutions were persuaded to turn a blind eye—and, in some cases, participated in insider deals; thousands of investors lost their minds and then their money.

That's what happened when, in the early nineties, a poor boy from small-town Raipur turned the stock market into a whirlpool. The darling of the stock-market until his great fall, Harshad Mehta masterminded a six-billion-rupee securities scam with an evil genius that even his detractors grudgingly admired. Single-handedly, Mehta unleashed a nation's greed, catapulting shares of specific companies to fantastic heights and triggering wild bull runs. As matadors, the banks and regulating authorities proved worthless. Then, in the summer of 1992, came the familiar crash. Mehta's ignominious death in a jail cell, wrote business journalist Sucheta Dalal, who broke the story of the securities scam, 'was the unceremonious end to the man who was the first broker to become a mega-star of the Indian capital markets and fire the greed and imagination of every middle-class Indian in the early 1990s'.

Less than a decade later, the market was sent into a similar frenzy by

Ketan Parekh, a modest businessman who soared to fraternize with the country's leading politicians and film stars. On a particularly ebullient day in June 1999, when the stocks of Ranbaxy rose from Rs 550 to Rs 1264, the liftmen at the stock exchange and the paan sellers around it made a killing. But the global meltdown of technology stocks put an end to the fun and games. The police came for Ketan Parekh on 30 March 2001.

Ever blind to the lessons of history, Mumbai threw its heart and its money into dotcom firms only a few years later. Anyone with a half-baked idea and fistful of capital thought they could set up an empire. Bankers dropped out of well-paying jobs to start up matrimonial websites. Housewives who had turned their beauty parlours into art galleries when the art market had boomed in the eighties now turned the art galleries into cyber cafes. Cartoonist Hemant Morparia captured the insanity with his sketch of two beggars, one with an empty begging bowl labelled 'money', the other's full of coins saying 'money.com'. If the dotcom boom had a signature line it was provided by that mysterious portal called Home Trade. 'Life means more', its advertisements said, endorsed by the country's three biggest pop icons: cricketer Sachin Tendulkar and matinee idols, Shah Rukh Khan and Hrithik Roshan. Home Trade fleeced several cooperative banks of Rs 250 crore before the police caught up with its young promoter, Sanjay Agarwal.

Perhaps it's hard not to dream of a millions-before-midnight lifestyle when one lives and works in India's biggest money mart. After all, Mumbai plays host to more than 90 per cent of India's merchant banking transactions. It has two stock exchange towers; 80 per cent of India's mutual funds are registered there, and it is home to the country's debt markets, money markets and forex markets. India's central bank, the country's three largest retail banks and two largest commercial lenders are based in Mumbai's business districts. The city pays more corporate tax and personal income tax than any other Indian city. Its ports handle 40 per cent of the country's maritime trade. Still, amidst the wealth of opportunity for legitimate speculation, the city's bylanes hide establishments devoted to taking the shirt off your back with games of chance: there's money to be made on the horses and cricket and *satta* and the *matka* numbers game. Seeking absolution in the city's gambling streak during the economic downturn of 2002, some small Mumbai firms that found themselves unable to pay out annual Diwali bonuses gave their employees lottery tickets instead.

Of course the scams won't dry up. The City of Gold loves the Midas trope—cotton is white gold, opium black gold and real-estate brown gold—and it's restless for the next gold rush, the next bull run. Mumbai has the best skill pool in India, it pays the best salaries, but sometimes the best is not good enough. It is not good enough because we believe that in Mumbai straw can turn to gold and that Rumpelstilskin isn't a fairy-tale figure but Dhirubhai Ambani himself, who turned himself from a petrol-pump attendant into a petrochemical magnate. Everyone wants to get there, yesterday.

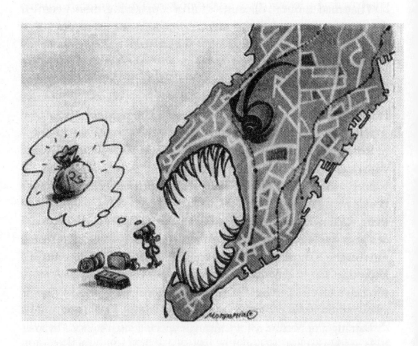

Bajrang—The Great Indian Bustard

Vilas Sarang

Bajrang arrived at the beach with Shalini. Winter in Bombay is seldom very severe, but it happened to be rather cold this year. A chill wind blew in from the Arabian Sea. Bajrang and Shalini walked along the beach, lifting heavy legs in the sand. Since it wasn't a Sunday the beach wasn't crowded. The sun had just set, and the sky was still bright.

They made a round of the small strip of beach. On this beach near Shivaji Park there is a huge gutter pipe which pours out the filth of Bombay into the sea. The gutter's giant mouth has a small dome-shaped structure of concrete to let out gases. Bajrang told Shalini how a man, obviously a visitor from some small town, had once approached him and asked solemnly: 'To which god was this temple built?' Shalini laughed, and Bajrang put his arm around her shoulder.

Bajrang started looking about for a place to sit near the walls by the beach. It wasn't dark yet, but later the walls would become crowded with couples and it would not be easy to find a secluded spot. Bajrang wanted to settle down in a good place while there was still time. Few people chose to sit beside the cemetery wall, so Bajrang selected a spot there. Bajrang liked to sit by this wall partly because it reminded him of a passage by Albert Camus, in which he spoke of Algerian boys and girls having assignations under the cemetery walls. It was thrilling to know that Bombay, together with a distant city like Algiers, contributed towards love's triumph over death. Bajrang saw a vision of cemeteries all over the world besieged by passionate youth.

Bajrang and Shalini sat against the wall. Bajrang had to listen to

From *Fair Tree of the Void* (1990).

Shalini's chatter until it was quite dark. Playing with the fingers of her left hand, Bajrang gazed out at the horizon. The sea was darkening. The tide was low, and the water was far away from the wall. Near the water's edge, little waves rose and fell in tiresome sequence. Since it was turning very dark, slum-dwellers were beginning to come onto the beach to defecate. They crouched at a modest distance from one another near the water, their silhouettes outlined clearly in the evening glow.

One man who looked rather old got up after his bowel movement, and went towards the water to wash himself off. Standing where the waves were breaking upon the shore, he lowered his buttocks. He didn't want to go into the water and wet himself any more than necessary. His idea was to clean himself against the wave just as it was about to break on the sands. He lowered his buttocks when he saw a wave coming in, but panicked thinking that the wave was high and would soak him to the waist. As he raised his body hastily, the wave passed beneath him without so much as touching him. He lowered his buttocks once more and waited for the next wave. Again he misjudged the height of the wave and it passed under him. This happened four or five times. It amused Bajrang to watch the old man alternately lowering and raising his buttocks as if he were engaged in a physical exercise, or practising the motions of a dance, or as though he were a puppet moved by invisible strings. Then the man seemed to have made up his mind, and remained still as the next wave came against him, soaked him to his chest. It was dark now, and the man was far away, so Bajrang couldn't see the expression on his face, but he thought he could imagine it. Life's like that, Bajrang said to himself, and idly wondered if he should send his anecdote to *Readers' Digest*.

As darkness fell, the breeze turned colder. Shalini snuggled closer to Bajrang for warmth. Bajrang felt cramped after sitting for so long against the wall. He decided to get up and stretch before they began necking seriously. Gently pushing away from Shalini, he stood up and brushed off the sand. Stretching himself, he glanced around. Couples were sitting along the wall on both sides of him. Bajrang noticed that the distance between each pair was about the same as that between the slum-dwellers on the beach earlier. Turning around

Bajrang looked over the wall. A corpse appeared to have been brought to the cemetery. As they waited for the crematorium attendants to build a pyre, men sat around the *tirdi* like ants around a dead beetle.

Bajrang was about to sit down again when someone stood up unexpectedly on the other side of the wall. Bajrang wouldn't have paid much attention, but something struck him. He looked across at the man. Good God, it was Kanchan Kothare, he thought. What the hell was he doing out here?

Kanchan had also recognized Bajrang. 'Hey, Bajrang,' he shouted. 'What brings you here?' Kanchan was one of Bajrang's close friends at college. He was somewhat hare-brained, and you could never be sure what he would say or do.

'I came to piss against the wall, and I hadn't the least idea you'd be on the other side.'

'It's a long time since I've seen you.'

'But how come . . .'

'Oh Bajrang, my mother died, you know,' Kanchan's voice changed suddenly. Tears came into his eyes. 'I've come here for Mother's cremation. Bajrang . . .' for a moment Kanchan seemed unable to speak further. Bajrang knew that Kanchan was extremely fond of his mother. 'Bajrang, you'll never know how wonderful my mother was.'

Bajrang didn't know what to say. Shalini, sitting beside him in the dark, looked at him with raised eyebrows. Kanchan was an old friend, but he had no business bothering Bajrang at this time, and in this place. Bajrang was about to say goodbye to Kanchan brusquely, when Kanchan cried, 'Bajrang . . .' Kanchan's body was shaking, and Bajrang thought he might collapse at any moment. Kanchan came forward a little and leaned against the wall. Bajrang felt Kanchan's breath upon his neck.

'Bajrang, how can I tell you my feelings,' Kanchan said. 'And I hate all these people.' He waved his arm towards the men in the distance. 'As for my father, he sighed with relief when mother died. She was in bed for two years, you know. Then all these people who call themselves relatives came out of nowhere. Like vultures flapping down to the ground. I'd never seen any of them in my life. But you can count on relatives to turn up at funerals. And at weddings. They'll come from the most god-forsaken village in the country. Always willing to lend a hand. This one, he's an expert in tying the tirdi—he takes the lead. And so it went. They tied her up in no time. As tight as they could.'

Kanchan's cheeks were wet. 'Bajrang,' he said. 'Could you come over the wall for a while, just to keep me company. I'm frightened of these people, you know. You'll come, Bajrang, won't you?' Kanchan rested his hand upon Bajrang's shoulder. Bajrang looked into his eyes. Then he bent down and whispered into Shalini's ear, 'Shalini, darling, look, I'll be back in just a few minutes. Will you wait here . . . please. Please darling.' Shalini shook her head. Bajrang wasn't sure if she meant yes or no, but without waiting to find out he jumped over the wall. He put an arm around Kanchan and walked with him towards the tirdi.

The pyre was built, and Kanchan's mother was placed on it. Arms folded, Bajrang stood by the pyre as the last rites were performed. It was quite cold now.

Flames leapt up when the pyre was lit. The faces of the men standing around the pyre looked red, like painted masks. The warmth of the fire made Bajrang feel better. He watched the varying shades of red on the faces of the motionless men.

Kanchan dragged me away from the warmth of Shalini's body, but his mother's body is warming me anyway, Bajrang thought. And what about Shalini? She's beyond the wall, alone in the cold. Bajrang's heart was suddenly filled with tenderness for her.

The warmth of the fire had taken the edge of the cold. Bajrang felt invigorated. Then, looking at the silent men ringed around the pyre, it occurred to him that they might have killed this woman so that they could warm themselves on a cold day. He could see their faces gratified by the warmth of the fire.

Where would a person find this warmth during a cold winter in Bombay? They had certainly made a first-class bonfire.

Kanchan's the only one here who isn't in on the secret, Bajrang thought. He looked at Kanchan, who was staring vacantly into the distance. He seemed to have completely forgotten that he had specially asked Bajrang to come.

As the flames leapt higher, the heat became intense. Yet, Bajrang's hands and back hadn't received their share of the warmth. Stretching out both hands, Bajrang spread his fingers in front of the fire. He turned them around a few times, until both sides were properly warmed. Then he turned his back to the fire.

When his back had absorbed enough warmth and his front was beginning to cool off, Bajrang turned his face again towards the pyre. Then he noticed that the people around him were whispering among themselves, casting frequent glances towards him. Perhaps it's because they don't know who I am, Bajrang thought. He decided that this wasn't an appropriate time to introduce himself. He spread out his fingers again before the fire.

Soon he saw two men advancing in his direction. He thought one of them was Kanchan's father. 'The monster, has he come to attend a funeral, or to enjoy himself beside a bonfire?' Bajrang recognized the voice of Kanchan's father. Before he knew what was happening, the men fell upon him.

Bajrang extricated himself from the grappling arms, and dashed to the other side of the pyre. He crouched there for a few seconds planning his next move. Kanchan seemed to have caught on to the situation by now. 'Bajrang, Bajrang...' he cried out, and, pushing people out of his way, ran to Bajrang's rescue.

Bajrang made up his mind quickly. He couldn't escape towards the wall by the sea, where Shalini was sitting. He would have to run for the wall in the other direction. Once more, he made a quick dash around the pyre.

Looking back he saw that he had hit the pyre as he was running around it, and that the logs on one side were tumbling down. A glance over his shoulder revealed that Kanchan, who had started to move towards him, had tripped over the logs he had dislodged. Sprawled on the ground, Kanchan thrust his arms and legs into the air as charred pieces of wood fell upon him.

Bajrang reached the wall, climbed up and, before jumping down on the other side, had a last look behind him. Kanchan had disappeared under a pile of wood, and his mother's half-burnt body had slid down towards him. Kanchan, who had been shouting Bajrang's name, now started crying out, 'Mother, mother . . .' and violently hugged her body. Some of the men had seemed bent on following Bajrang, but when they saw what had happened to Kanchan, they faltered. Most of them abandoned the pursuit to pull Kanchan out of the mess. One or two men continued half-heartedly after Bajrang. Bajrang looked upon this scene for a few moments and then leaped down from the wall. He kept on running.

One of Bajrang's beliefs was that he was a Great Indian Bustard, a species of birds now on its way to extinction. Bajrang alone knew the secret of the apparent contradiction in the name bustard: the bustard is a large swift-moving bird, but its name 'bustard' derives from the Latin *avis tarda*, slow bird. You think you can catch me easily. Bajrang said to himself as he ran, but I'm a Great Indian Bustard. 'He's a slow bird,' you say to yourselves. 'We'll have him in no time.' But I'm gone before you've uttered those words. Try as you might, you can't lay hands on me. If you got me, though, it would be a sad day. The Great Indian Bustard is on the verge of extinction, and you might really wipe us out. As one of the few survivors of a vanishing species, Bajrang knew that it was his duty to protect his own life. Pride welled up in his heart, and a kind of wistful love.

Bajrang reached a street that looked deserted, and stopped for breath. He glanced in the direction of the cemetery, but didn't see anyone coming after him. He relaxed.

The area was in darkness, but there were a few lights here and there, as there always seem to be, wherever you go. Bajrang stood in the street undecidedly. Then he started walking, perhaps in the direction of home. He suddenly remembered the time he had been at the beach at midday. Everyone goes to the beach in the evening, so Bajrang once went at midday, just to see what it was like there then. There was no one on the beach except for few dhobis, who had brought large bundles of freshly dyed saris, and were spreading them out. Under the blazing sun, Bajrang had stood that day watching long stretches of colourful saris drying on the sand.

Urban Fabric

Naresh Fernandes

Narayan Surve keeps the myth alive. The myth that you can make it anywhere if you can make it in Bombay.

It's also that he can't think of living anywhere else. 'I have a *relationship* with Bombay,' explains the man who is among Maharashtra's most respected poets.

As Surve runs his fingers through his greying hair, the deep furrows of six decades of life in the raw cut across his face. He takes a deep drag of his cigarette, exhales thoughtfully and searches for the right words. 'I couldn't possibly reside anywhere else,' he says. 'But sometimes I can't recognize this as the city of my birth.'

Though he isn't sure exactly when he was born, Surve does know that he was abandoned in a dustbin by his natural mother. He was found and adopted by a man employed in one of the city's cotton mills. Surve worked his way through middle school and went on to find employment in the Bombay Municipal Corporation, first as a peon and later as a primary school teacher. He now runs the Pragat Pratisthan, an institution that encourages progressive Marathi literature.

Surve's poetry resonates with the thunder of the local train to Victoria Terminus, with the shouts of the head loaders in the city's docks, with the chaos of the streets. And it echoes the clatter of the looms in central Mumbai's textile mills, in which Surve worked for three years from the age of thirteen.

He's come a long way since, but his office—tastefully decorated with the works of young painters—isn't far from where he spent his childhood. It's on the edge of Parel, a neighbourhood whose residents often refer to it as Girangaon, the Village of Mills. It's at the vortex of

---

A version of this piece first appeared in *India Magazine*, July 1996.

Mumbai's whirlpool of change. As the city's real-estate prices soar even higher and encourage mill owners to the realization that cotton textiles are no longer profitable, glass-and-chrome towers are springing up where factory sheds once stood. Wooden-beamed chawls—a residential arrangement for mill workers unique to Mumbai—are being replaced by new office blocks. Senapati Bapat Marg, dotted with sooty chimneys, is being transformed into the city's Madison Avenue. Yuppies in floral ties now pore over television-viewership ratings in cavernous halls in which, till recently, white cotton fibre hung low.

For social scientists, this is a fascinating study of how economics impinges upon all else. For those in the eye of the storm, it's simply traumatic. Says Surve, 'Parel is changing. But worse, our mental landscapes are being altered too.'

To begin with, levels of unemployment have risen dramatically. Two generations ago, spinners and weavers took it for granted that their sons would find work alongside them in the mills. Not many cotton textile labourers today cling to the hope that their children will be employed here. Or anywhere else. At its peak, Bombay's cotton manufacturing industry employed 2,32,326 people. In 1976, 27 per cent of Bombay's unionized labourers found work in the mills. This year, 12.5 per cent of the organized workforce—80,000 people—will take home salaries from the city's fifty-four cotton mills.

The transition from a manufacturing to a service-sector economy is being hailed as a sign that Mumbai is maturing along the pattern observed in cities around the globe. But mill labourers and the rest of the working class are bewildered. The service sector demands skills that they simply don't possess. Few of the new jobs created in Parel have gone to mill workers or their children. 'Do you think these people want to become advertising copywriters?' asks Meena Menon, an organizer of the Girni Kamgar Sangarsh Samiti (Committee for the Struggle of Mill Workers).

The deindustrialization of Mumbai has created a pool of frustration from which fundamentalist organizations—most notably the Shiv Sena—have drawn deep. They've profited from the agony of displacement that the left-wing Surve expressed in his poem 'Mumbai' (as translated by Mangesh Kulkarni, Jatin Wagle and Abhay Sardesai):

My father withered away toiling
so will I, and will my little ones?
Perhaps; they too face such sad nights
wrapped in coils of darkness.
My heart wells up,
seeks an outlet;
for it was my father who sculpted
your epics in stone.

*

The dimly lit office of the Bombay Mill Owners Association is crowded with portraits of its chairmen wearing a fascinating variety of Indian and British headgear, charting sartorial and political evolution over the organization's twelve-decade history. In his speech at the hundred and twentieth annual general meeting last year, the current chairman, Hrishikesh Mafatlal, made his demands clear. Bombay's mills are dying, he claimed. Mill owners should be allowed to roll down the shutters and sell the land on which their factories stand.

He didn't say anything about the stakes: 2.3 square kilometres of the sixty-eight square kilometre island city. The mill owners could take home upward of Rs 60,000 for each square foot.

With so much money involved, it isn't surprising that everyone wants a piece of the action. The bullets that killed Sunit Khatau, owner of Khatau Mills, laid bare the previously fuzzy links between the mill owners, Mumbai's vicious underworld and the official trade union that purports to represent all the city's textile labourers. Khatau was gunned down in May 1994 as his car waited for a traffic light to turn green. His company was attempting to shift its operations to Borivili, on the outskirts of the city, and had allegedly paid off gangsters to help convince reluctant workers that the move was in their best interests. But the deal seemed to have gone awry and the gangsters turned on their patron. Textile-industry analysts think it may be more than a mere coincidence that Sachin Ahire, general secretary of the official Rashtriya Mill Mazdoor Sangh (National Mill Workers Association), is the first cousin of notorious gang leader Arun Gawli.

But mill owners deny all links with the underworld. And they insist that they haven't turned into real-estate speculators. V.Y. Tamhane, secretary general of the Mill Owners Association, says that Mumbai's textile manufacturing shops have no option but to sell out. He insists that the city's mills simply aren't viable. He says his members pay higher wages and have higher infrastructure costs than the small-scale and unorganized powerloom textile factories. He also has another consideration. 'We are causing massive congestion in the heart of the city,' he pleads.

It isn't easy to gauge the health of the industry from a casual reading of reports by such trade organizations as the Mill Owners Association or the Indian Cotton Manufacturers Federation. These publications are a study in paradox. Their data juxtapose high sales volumes with low profits; increasing production with shrinking employment; record growth rates with rampant sickness. The textile industry is India's biggest employer after agriculture. Last year, it earned 8.3 billion dollars, accounting for nearly 30 per cent of the country's export earnings. Five of the top ten industrial houses on the *Economic Times* 500 list made their fortunes in textiles. The Tatas have sold off their mills, but the Birlas, Ambanis, Singhanias and Mafatlals retain their interests.

The textile industry also has more sick units than any other sector of India's economy.

Many workers maintain that it was the strike of 1982 that tipped Bombay's textile mills into the spiral of destruction. Called by firebrand leader Datta Samant to demand a wage increase, the agitation lasted eleven months and, technically, hasn't yet been called off. In the initial months, Samant and his Maharashtra Girni Kamgar Union (Maharashtra Mill Workers Union) inspired fanatical devotion. His demonstrations attracted hundreds of thousands of people, disgusted with their low salaries and working conditions. They were also demanding the repeal of the Bombay Industrial Relations Act, a piece of legislation from 1948 that ensures that Bombay's textile workers can only be represented by the Congress-controlled Rashtriya Mill Mazdoor Union.

But as the strike drew on, it became more difficult for the strikers to put meals on the family thalis. Mangalsutras and wedding bangles poured into the narrow shops of Girangaon's jewellers, who doubled up as pawn brokers. The agitation slackened when workers left Bombay to wait out the strike in their native villages, where they would be assured of food from their fields.

For the mill managements, the situation wasn't quite so tough. They used the strike as an opportunity to sell off their excess inventories, then sent yarn to be woven in the powerloom sweatshops of Bhiwandi and Malegaon. This, as it later turned out, was a fatal move. The powerloom sector has grown rapidly since then: it now produces 72 per cent of India's cloth, in contrast to the 6.4 per cent that the mill sector scrapes together.

When the strike finally petered out, the managements of ten mills chose not to reopen. Six of those resumed operations only two years ago, while four remain dormant. The Kotwal commission, appointed by the government to report on the effects of the strike, provided these statistics: production losses were estimated at Rs 985 crore; workers lost Rs 90 crore in wages; only 1,20,000 of the 2,32,326 strikers were rehired. The commission also said that 46,575 workers hadn't been paid their dues six years after the strike. And during the eleven-month agitation, at least 2600 workers had died.

Mill owners contend that the industry hasn't yet recovered fully from the events of 1982. Tamhane says that recovery hinges on the textile factories being allowed to sell the land on which they stand in order to buy modern machinery. This is a view to which the Rashtriya Mill Mazdoor Sangh firmly subscribes, says its president, Govindrao Adik. 'How else can the owners raise such massive resources?' he asks.

But Samant's MGKU has dug in its heels. 'The builders and the government have got together to sell our city. But we won't let them,' he told a crowd that gathered at a Girangaon playground in April to listen to his pitch for re-election to his Lok Sabha parliamentary seat.

Samant's rhetoric went down well, as evidenced by the cheers. But he nevertheless lost the election to Shiv Sena candidate Mohan Rawle. Rawle and his party's Girni Kamgar Sena (the Mill Workers Army) too have promised to stall all further sales of mill land. And Menon's Girni Kamgar Sangarsh Samiti has taken to blockading mills that owners are attempting to clear of machinery. Said activist Balkrishna Nar, as he and other agitators stopped trucks from carting carding machines out of Piramal Mills at the end of May, 'We don't want voluntary retirement packages. We want to keep our jobs.'

*

To many, Mumbai's hopes of regenerating itself lie in Parel. 'This is the opportunity for the city to avoid urban disaster,' says Rahul Mehrotra of the Urban Design Research Institute think-tank. He believes that cheap housing and parks can be built in Girangaon.

Seemingly with a view to fulfilling these very objectives, the Maharashtra government revised its Development Control Regulations in 1991 to allow mills to sell their land if the units were sick or wanted to modernize. Mill owners who sell land must surrender one-third of the area for parks and playgrounds, while another third will be reserved for public housing. There is, however, a loophole: These provisions don't apply if the mill decides to sell less than 15 per cent of its total area. That's allowed seventeen mills to begin construction projects so far without any land reverting to the city.

The state government, clearly, is of the opinion that Mumbai's mills are obsolete. For the officials, it's only a question of negotiating the best possible redundancy packages for the workers. Explains Neela Satyanarayanan, Maharashtra's textile secretary, 'History marches on. We have to consider whether this land is being used in the most economical manner.'

The mill lands play a vital role in the plan drawn up by Bombay First, a foundation funded by private industry, to develop the city into a global financial centre. The foundation believes that Mumbai's geographical location offers it the advantage of being able to do business with the world when Tokyo is asleep, but London and New York are abuzz with activity.

This would, of course, accelerate the growth of Mumbai's service sector. But even government planners warn that such a trend could be disastrous. The Bombay Metropolitan Regional Development Authority blueprint for the city over the next two decades says that continuing industrial stagnation could send its economy into a tailspin, resulting in serious social unrest. The BMRDA planners point out that the city of London had to introduce massive rejuvenation programmes after jobs in the manufacturing sector dropped by more than 50 per cent in two decades, to 5,80,000 in 1983 from 1.4 million in 1961. Ironically, Bombay First is modelled on a similar British organization called London First. Says Arvind Adarkar, an architect involved with the Nivara Hakk Samitia, a housing rights organization, 'It's so stupid. Why do we have to make the same mistakes that they made?'

★

The foundation of Mumbai's much-vaunted cosmopolitan culture was consolidated in Girangaon in the mid-nineteenth century. Many of the early textile workers were drawn from Maharashtra's lush Konkan coastal strip (so much so that many of those districts developed into money-order economies, dependent largely on remittances from relatives in the metropolis). But in a break with traditional caste-determined occupational patterns, Marathas and Kunbis worked alongside Bhaiyyas from Uttar Pradesh, Padmashali weavers from Andhra Pradesh and people from just about every part of the subcontinent. They expressed their desire to forget customary stratifications to forge a better future when, in 1881, they formed India's first trade union, the Bombay Mill Hands Association.

That idealism spilled out of the factories after they finished their shifts and went home to the same sprawl of chawls. Many of these now-crumbling extended-family dwelling units sprang up in the 1920s, when the Bombay Development Directorate took it upon itself to provide comprehensive industrial housing for 50,000 workers. In the end, the agency only managed to build 16,000 rooms because 'the people for whom they were being provided refused to occupy them until thousands of rupees had been spent modifying them into something remotely fit for human habitation,' wrote architect Claude Batley.

The improvements, such as they were, were rudimentary at best.

Consider this description of the average chawl dwelling from Kiran Nagarkar's novel, *Ravan and Eddie*: 'Each room was 12 feet wide and 24 feet deep with a wide wooden partition separating the drawing room-cum-study, library, playpen or whatever from the kitchen, which doubled as a dining room and bathroom (a tiny four-foot washing space with a tap was cordoned off on one side with a two-foot wall on which were stacked pots of water).'

In the seven decades since they were built, the claustrophobia of the chawls and the almost-total lack of privacy they afford have fostered institutions that emphasize community above all else. In Worli's BDD chawls, in Sewri and in Naigaon, the rhythms of life duplicate themselves. In dingy vyayamshalas, teenage boys pump iron under posters of Sunil Shetty, Shivaji and Schwarzenegger. Bhajan mandals are the perfect way for the enthusiastic and the unmelodic to seek the truth. Festivals are celebrated across community boundaries with the same vigour. In fact, when Lokmanya Tilak devised the Ganesh Chaturthi festival just over 100 years ago as a means to encourage a nationalistic spirit, he chose to hold the first celebrations in a Parel chawl. The Elephant God has since become Mumbai's patron deity.

Girangaon also saw the flowering of a subaltern poetry and *shair* tradition. 'Talented people like Daya Pawar, Shahir Sable, Annabhau Sathe and Shahir Amar Shaikh lived here and found inspiration here,' says Neera Adarkar, an activist of the Girangaon Bachao Andolan or Save Girangaon Movement. Her organization has put together poetry readings and music concerts attempting to show Mumbai how much less vibrant it will become with the physical destruction of Parel. Says Gajanan Khatu, another supporter of the organization, 'The kind of cultural activity here is unique. It's a blend of forms from across the country.'

But it's evident that the battle is quickly slipping from their grasp. Though Mumbai's population has grown over the decade, BMRDA statistics show that Girangaon actually has fewer residents. That's evident in Nare Park Municipal School, on the edge of the maidan that was the venue for massive rallies during the Samyukta Maharashtra movement in 1956 and during the 1982 textile strike. As in the case with several other lower schools across the island city, the authorities can't find enough students to fill the benches. So they've allowed a non-governmental organization to set up its offices on the top floor.

The unemployed are moving back to their villages, while others have dispersed to larger tenements in the suburbs. With the wave of migration, the poets have turned to writing televisions scripts and many theatre groups have been disbanded. When the bulldozers moved in on Lalbaugh's Hanuman Theatre in April, they seemed to destroy much more than only the last performance space in Mumbai for the robust song-and-dance tamasha form. Narayan Surve, the Parel poet, has observed the disintegration from up close. 'There's no cohesive culture anymore, just a few remaining strands of custom and tradition,' he sighs.

*

More than a century after the great cotton boom, few Mumbai residents remember that it was the White Gold that allowed the city's best-known stone epics to be built. And few are concious of how the fibre has woven itself into the names by which they know their neighbourhoods. The most obvious nomenclatural indicator of the time cotton was king is, of course, Cotton Green. The Green has long been built over with boxy warehouses in which fewer cotton bales are stacked with each passing year. A million Mumbai office workers stop at Cotton Green for thirty seconds every day as their trains travel on to the commercial district beyond Victoria Terminus, but few hear history's whisper.

Similarly, few of the worshippers on their way to pay homage to the vermilion-faced goddess from whom the city may derive its name are alive to the past when they ask the bus driver to let them off at the Cotton Exchange stop. Paint peeling off its stone facade, the building that once was the hub of Mumbai's economy is now simply a convenient landmark to help the disoriented find Mumbadevi temple.

And almost no one hears the hum of the spinning rotor as the chimes of the Rajabai clock tower float out over the Oval Maidan every half hour. The magnificient Porbunder-stone tower was built by Premchand Roychand in memory of his mother. Roychand made his pile during the cotton explosion of the 1860s, when the American Civil War forced Manchester to buy massive stocks from the subcontinent. Prices on the Bombay Green leapt from Rs 180 a kandy to Rs 700 and exports more than doubled from Rs 16 crore to Rs 40 crore in the five years that the bubble lasted. The city earned approximately eighty-one million pounds sterling during that period and Roychand displayed the sort of acumen that would come to be associated with Harshad Mehta more than a century later. Roychand wangled his way into becoming a major shareholder in the Bank of Bombay and worked out schemes to withdraw Rs 1.38 crore. He added to his fortune by obtaining London cotton prices a little in advance of his Bombay competitors, dispatching smaller country boats to waylay mail ships by the lighthouse off Bombay harbour.

When the crash came with the end of the Civil War, the Bank had to write off a full 40 per cent of his advances.

By then, Bombay's first cotton textile mill had already been coughing out black smoke for eleven years. The Bombay Spinning and Weaving Company had been started in 1854 by a Parsi merchant named Cowasjee Nanabhoy Davar for the avowed purpose of fighting Manchester 'with her own weapons'. When it became apparent that he had a good thing going with cheap labour, easily available raw material and a large local market, Davar opened the city's second mill, four years later. By 1865, Bombay's skyline was dotted with ten chimneys. The mills had 25,000 spindles and 3400 looms, processed 40,000 bales of cotton every year and employed 6000 people.

*

Poet Namdeo Dhasal says that even though he can't quite comprehend Girangaon's metamorphosis over the last three decades, he thinks the changes are vastly desirable. 'The old methods of production have become obsolete,' he says. 'That's the imperative of progress.'

In 1972, he was among the founders of the radical lower caste Dalit Panther movement. Now a greying forty-eight-year-old, he continues to be involved in politics, as a member of the fragmented and fractious Republican Party of India. Across from the rugby field of the exclusive

Bombay Gymkhana, Dhasal holds court most afternoons in an asbestos-roofed cramped shed that serves as the headquarters of the Gavai faction to which he is now aligned.

Last month, he took on Congress bigwig Suresh Kalmadi in parliamentary elections in Pune. He lost his deposit, but doesn't seem to be bothered. Speak of the changes that are sweeping Mumbai, however, and he becomes instantly animated. 'Mumbai is my oxygen, my blood. I can't live without it,' he declares, his steel-rimmed reading glasses riding low on his forehead. Dhasal says he's perturbed by the fact that the culture of the working classes is being replaced by 'imperialist culture, the worst possible exports from the west'.

But he seems to be riding out the turbulence rather gracefully. Like thousands of others, he's moved out to a more salubrious neighbourhood. He occasionally visits his old home, on the fringes of the city's red light district, in his white Toyota Cerrida with windows that roll down automatically. Mumbai, it would seem, is his oyster. Or perhaps, to use his own metaphor, his strumpet. That's what he says in 'Bombay, My Beloved Whore' (as translated by Mangesh Kulkarni and Abhay Sardesai):

You be faithful to us
You warm up our beds
Play the flute of Eternity
Play around with our dreams
Breathe fire into our sperms
O footloose hussy
O churlish slut
O Khandoba's concubine
O wanton coquette
O whore with the heart of gold
I won't go away from you like a ragged beggar
I'll strip you to the bone
Come, throw open the gates of heaven to the poor devils
Bombay, my beloved whore
I'll take you for a ride
I'll strike you dumb
And go.

The Great Water Wars

Kiran Nagarkar

Built by industrialists as housing for their workers, Bombay's chawls
form the backdrop for Ravan and Eddie, *a novel of great charm and*
quirky wit.

—Eds

They should have killed for water, the men and women of the CWD
chawls. People have been known to kill for less: religion; language;
the flag; the colour of a person's skin or his caste; breaking the queue
at a petrol pump. One of these days they may get around to it but so far
Ravan, Eddie, their mothers and the tenants at the CWD chawls
haven't committed murder in the name of water. Though God knows
there have been times when they were close to it. There have been
words, nasty, bitter, venomous, corrosive words; genealogies have been
traced, incestuous sexual acts involving mothers, brothers and sisters
invoked in swear-words; hostilities have been declared, words have
led to physical fights. Frictions have festered, attitudes hardened and
prejudices led to Pavlovian reflexes of bellicosity and at times it's been
touch and go.

The causes have almost always been the same: supply cannot meet
demand. Planning and execution have met the needs of the population
figures of a decade or two earlier. Rains are an act of God in India. And
God as we know is a law unto himself. He is not responsible, neither
is He accountable. That is the essence of God: he gives with two
hands and takes away with eight more. Why else would Indian gods
and goddesses have several pairs of hands?

The nature of the municipal water tap is feudal and bureaucratic. It
replicates and clones the Almighty's manners and moodiness but never

From *Ravan and Eddie* (1995).

his generosity since its power is entirely derivative. It is a middleman, its patronage disburses what does not belong to it. The only way it can experience and feel power is to exert it erratically and often. Hence it is not enough that it calls the shots, it must perforce leave you in the dark. You are at its mercy. You are grateful for its bounties and contrite for its seasons of drought.

The unstable tyrant of the family in the CWD chawls is the man of the manor. Drunk, sober, employed, jobless, taciturn or gibbering, his word is law. His wife sustains and not infrequently supports the family and is more than happy to give her husband all the credit if only he will allow her to carry on with her work. But despite the boss-man's pretensions and the wife's sacrifice and self-effacement, the prime mover of life is water. You snapped out of anaesthesia, interrupted coitus, stopped your prayers, postponed your son's engagement, developed incontinence, took casual leave to go down and stand at the common tap, cancelled going to church because water, present and absent, is more powerful than the almighty.

You left the tap open before you went to sleep. When the water sputtered and splattered at 3, 4 or 5 a.m. and sometimes not at all, was when your day began. You cursed and cribbed and filled up every vessel in sight and tried to zip through a bath and if there was still a trickle left, woke up the children and gave them a speed bath that was more an act of the imagination than an exercise in cleaning. If it wasn't already six, you stumbled back to a twilight sleep where nameless fears and forebodings, all of them waterlogged, crawled and rose in phantasmagoric shapes from the floor of your subconscious and left you tepid and perspiring.

There's a water tap in the bathroom of every house in the CWD chawls, in the four toilets at the end of the left and right wing of each floor and the two common wash-areas opposite.

If the tanks on the terrace run out of water—two or three days at a time is not unusual—you are forced to troop down to the public tap. There's one for every two chawls. There's no law on the subject but the idea is to share the water amongst the 480 families who live in the two adjoining buildings. There is no court of appeal but by and large almost everybody adheres to the unwritten protocol.

'Those people' as the people on the ground floor were called in the CWD chawls, the 300 or so families whose very shadows polluted the others, had a couple of separate taps just as six taps were reserved for all the Catholics. When the water was short or if the papers gave notice that there was going to be a water-cut the next day, the untouchables were shooed away from their taps and water filled from them after the first woman in the queue perfunctorily threw a few drops in the direction of the brass nozzle of the faucet to make it clean and usable.

The municipal tap is the original cornucopia. It is plugged into the mains and supplies water twenty-four hours of the day. Twenty-four hours, as you know, is a flexi-time concept in our country, and can stretch anywhere between three to four hours. That's on the good days. The timings are fixed. When the water comes, you know it's come.

On any given day, there were anywhere between 100 to 250 pots waiting in queue. What a sight it was. Two thousand years of brass and copper craftsmanship. Long, slender necks, wide bodies, broad butts, svelte torsos, short-chinned stodgy tankers, tightly corseted, narrow-bottomed, prissy mouthed, there was no end to their shapes and sizes. Despite the perpetual water shortage, they shone like flares from newly sunk oil wells. That was thirty years ago, the brass and the copper have been replaced by cheap, exuberant plastics which the sun denudes of all colour and turns grey and anaemic within three or four months.

The women came down, stood by their pots and buckets, chatted, compared notes on which ration shops had sugar and kerosene, went back to their homes to feed their babies and send their children to school, returned, untied their hair and knotted it tightly at the back with effortless and casual grace, adjusted their saris and waited.

Hours passed.

The lead pipe went into a spasm, recoiled and kicked and threw up epileptic tantrum as if it were made not of lead but rubber. It made threatening noises, coughed and cleared a thirty-metre long throat, vomited seventeen drops of brown tepid goo, withdrew, brooded, went dry. Wring the neck and length of the pipe all the way back to Tansa lake and it won't yield a drop of water for the next fifty years. It shuddered. A quake, 7.5 on the Richter scale, shook it. It lashed out, the jet of water a venomous fist of fury that sent the copper pot under it skittering for shelter.

The response to the sight of flowing water is desperation, a frenzy of pointless activity and loss of sanity.

There were fights every day over water, but that didn't make them any less interesting. A good scrap was liberating, especially when someone else was doing the fighting. It always made you feel mature, objective and wiser. How foolish people were. What utterly ridiculous and petty things they fought about. It took all your self-control sometimes not to egg them on and join them and see some blood spill. No question about it, it was a great spectator sport, so long as you weren't at the centre of it. And frankly, sometimes it felt great letting go, standing there arms akimbo, saying the most God-awful things and believing that you were alone against the world, after all, look how your adversary for whom you had done so much, put her up for the nights when her husband had pulverized her and she had nowhere else to go, was repaying you. Well here goes, you kicked her water-pot, it keeled over and all the water drained away, she would have to go and stand at the end of the queue all over again. Look out, she had pulled your head down and thrown you back till you were sitting on your butt, you were not going to take it lying down, besides for some reason best known to them, a few other women had joined the fracas, you didn't know who was on whose side but that didn't matter, hell, this was a free-for-all, if you didn't take the offence, you were dead.

One of these days, it may be tomorrow or twenty years from now, the municipal tap in the CWD chawls is going to run dry while the forty-seventh woman is still filling her pot. The remaining 219 women will complain as usual and go back with empty pots hoping that they can stretch the water in the drums in their kitchens till the next day. But on the day Mrs Rele, Mrs Pathare and Mrs Ghatge saw the knife-grinder walking into the CWD chawls compound with his unwieldy grinding wheel slung over his shoulder and brought their knives down to be sharpened. Did the sun shine in Mrs Ghatge's eyes or did a fly buzz too insistently around Mrs Rele's face or was it that Mrs Pathare didn't like the colour of Mrs Rele's eyes? All we know is that Mrs Pathare plunged her yet-to-be-sharpened knife between Mrs Ghatge's third and fourth ribs. Mrs Ghatge was thrown off balance but managed bring down her meat-cleaver on Prabha Salunke's head and open it up as if it were a coconut. It was Prabha's engagement tomorrow. More knives appeared, all you had to do was scamper up to your kitchen and rush down. That day blood flowed freely in the CWD chawls.

Water. Blood. Is there a difference?

The water wars had started. It had taken a long time but the CWD chawl women had finally begun to understand the value of water.

Clearing the Slums

Jeremy Seabrook

There have been periodic efforts to clear squatters and slum dwellers from Bombay. In 1981, the then Congress (I) administration of the city sought to clear people illegally occupying public space. The attempt was a clumsy and insensitive move—demolitions were undertaken at the very height of the monsoon and people were left exposed and stranded as the flood water carried away their few belongings. This lost the municipal authorities much of the sympathy they might have gained from those keen to see Bombay rid of its squatters. The clearances became the object of a court injunction and the final appeal was heard in the Supreme Court which gave its judgement in July 1985—four years after the initial evictions. The Supreme Court declared that local authorities had the right to remove people obstructing public footpaths or encroaching on public land. Anand Patwardhan made a film about the 1981 demolitions. It records them in all their brutality in images reminiscent of engravings of evictions of peasants during the Irish potato famine, or the breaking of the crofts during the Highland clearances. The film illustrates to what extent 'the hutments, whatever the quality of their construction and their space standards, represents a substantial and precious investment made over time by the poor in terms of their resources and labour'.

The familiar prejudices of the rich against the poor are nowhere more clearly articulated than in India's richest city; and even the less than impartial words of the Supreme Court judgement sound like the strictures of middle-class Victorian London voicing its fear of the dangerous classes. Of the street dwellers, the Supreme Court said, 'They cook and sleep where they please. Their daughters come of age, bathe under the nosy gaze of passers-by, unmindful of the feminine

From *Life and Labour in a Bombay Slum* (1987).

sense of bashfulness. The cooking and washing over, women pick lice from each other's hair. The boys beg. Menfolk without occupation snatch chains with the connivance of the defenders of law and order.' Such official verdicts permit the wealthy of Bombay to express in authoritative tones their familiarity with the lives of poor people they have never spoken to: they are, it is asserted, dirty, lazy and criminal. They have come to Bombay in search of an easy life. They pay no rent, they obstruct the pathways, they add to congestion, they live by stealing, drug dealing and begging.

Indira Jaising, the lawyer who argued the case of the slum dwellers evicted in 1981, actually got the Supreme Court to acknowledge that 'the eviction of a person from a pavement or slum will inevitably lead to the deprivation of his means of livelihood . . . and consequently to the deprivation of life'. The one concession to the pavement and unrecognized slum dwellers of Bombay was that if they could prove they were living in the city at the time of the 1976 census, they would have the right to be housed elsewhere. But since that census was notoriously haphazard and unreliable, and since the pavement dwellers were not counted anyway, this made little difference to those in the greatest need.

The resonance of this judgement goes far beyond India. By the year 2000, over half of the world's population will be concentrated in cities and towns, hundred of millions of them living in conditions like those in Bombay, with its inadequate services, corruption and inertia, as well as its crumbling buildings. Scarcely a month passes without the collapse of a tenement block somewhere in the old city, often with considerable loss of life. The policy of the city authorities to create a 'sunder Mumbai' (beautiful Bombay) by planting trees and displacing people only shows how profoundly ignorant they are of the social and economic pressures which lead to urbanization. They believe they can reverse the flow of people into the city by physical removals, as though their presence had nothing to do with developments in the villages and countryside which are dispossessing people of their traditional modes of subsistence and creating new reservoirs of landlessness and poverty. The attempts to clear people so far have been sporadic and discrete. For one thing, there is simply nowhere for people to go: the idea of 'sending them back' has about the same level of feasibility as the ideas of those in Britain who talk of 'repatriation'. Most of the children and young people living on the pavements of Bombay were born there; more than 50 per cent of pavement families have been in the city for more than two decades.

One recognized slum demolished early in 1986 was in one of the richest parts of Bombay, Colaba. The site of this slum, a relatively small enclave, housed about 2000 people, some 300 families. It had originally been formed as a camp of migrant workers and their families, specifically brought to Bombay by contractors to work on construction projects on Cuffe Parade on the narrow tongue of land reclaimed from the sea on Back Bay. The workers who formed the core of this settlement, called Sanjay Gandhi Nagar, worked on the building of commercial premises, luxury flats and hotels which, many people say proudly, makes Bombay look more like New York than a characteristic city of the South. That the slum dwellers are not idlers and vagrants is there for all to see. When asked to provide documentary proof of their presence in the city before 1980, they point to the buildings and say, 'How do you think they got there? They didn't grow overnight.' No more tangible proof could exist. A man who worked as a mason on the Oberoi Towers Hotel said bitterly, 'There is shelter for transients who can afford 1000 rupees a night, but the people who built it have nowhere to go.'

The slum was destroyed without warning on 12 March 1986. Police and municipal workers invaded the community and told the people to evacuate the area immediately. They were allowed to take the belongings they could carry and the clothes they were wearing. The slum had been in existence for about ten years. The structures were of wood, corrugated iron, the roofs covered with faded blankets, polythene and hessian, weighed down with stones to prevent them from blowing away in the strong sea wind. Because the site was small, the huts were close together, forming narrow alleys and rocky passages. All the materials, dismantled with hammers and crowbars, were taken away on lorries. The one building untouched was the Shaila Welfare Centre, a brick structure which served as a school. As a 'humanitarian' gesture, the people were told they would be permitted to remain on the pavement on the side of the road opposite Sanjay Gandhi Nagar for a further month. This meant they could stay until the end of the school term, until the children had finished their examinations. The compound—littered with rubble, broken pieces of wood, bricks that had been used for cooking stoves, shreds of polythene, splinters of glass, jagged metal and rusty nails, torn and faded fragments of cloth, torn pictures of gods and film stars—were surrounded by a barbed-wire fence. A metal gate, also covered with barbed wire, was opened at the beginning and end of each day, so that the children could come and go to their lessons.

The people were shocked and disbelieving. Since the construction project many had worked on had been concluded, all had found alternative employment. Indeed, all the surveys indicate that families squatting in such places have a higher proportion of economically active members than any other group. The people who come to the city tend to be among the most able and the most resourceful; they are nearly always young, and therefore at an age when they start building a family. Far from being a drain on the resources of the city, they offer crucial services and labour on which the lives of the rich depend. The people stigmatized for their lack of shelter are cobblers, painters, masons, sign painters, construction workers, watchmen, public transport workers; vendors, sellers of flowers and vegetables, of ice-cream, snacks, drinks; domestic servants, hotel, restaurant and catering workers. This particularly true of Colaba, where there are so many hotels servicing the tourists—for whom Bombay is a major port of entry into India—businessmen and the rich from the Gulf who come to Bombay for medical treatment. They are also reclaimers of waste, recyclers of rags, paper, metal and plastic—one woman in Patwardhan's film was making wigs from the hair of the dead. They work in factories, workshops, the docks; they are office cleaners and property guards.

The people displaced from Cuffe Parade built themselves fragile and temporary shelters facing the derelict site where they had lived and where many of their children had been born. These consisted of bamboo poles fixed into the wire fence behind them (itself enclosing another site awaiting a new skyscraper), tied to poles resting on the edge of the pavement and flimsily covered with bleached rags and blankets, pieces of hessian and rattan, palm leaves which can be peeled from the trees. Although these structures appear crude and improvised, the way in which the limited space is used by the sojourners on the pavement is a wonder of economy and care. It is the women who are the supreme conservers and arrangers of the living space; they are the uninstructed designers, planners and architects, who have the surest instinct for the best ways of minimizing labour and conserving energy. One day, along Cuffe Parade, one family said, 'Come into our kitchen and have a cup of tea,' beckoning us on the part of the pavement where there was a faded blanket set out beneath the threadbare sacking that provided some shade from the sun.

However poor, the people here keep their living place absolutely clean. When they emerge in the early morning for work, nothing about them tells of the humiliation of living in this exposed way on a public thoroughfare; no one will have seen them washing in an empty paint pot, with no more than two or three pints of water, or cleaning their clothes in the gutter and hanging them to dry overnight on the roof of their shelter. These people came here from the countryside, pliable, adaptable labour to augment the already saturated city markets. No one told them of the price they would pay, not only in terms of the separation from a familiar environment—they knew about that—but of the contempt of the rich and persecution by the authorities. To the people looking at Bombay from afar, only its lights and its wealth are visible; the other, negative things appear only in close-up. When asked what they found most striking when they first came to the city, many people say, 'The nights are never dark.'

The Cuffe Parade eviction followed several others elsewhere in Bombay. The Sanjay Gandhi Nagar community formed an association affiliated to the Nivara Hakh Surakhasha Samiti which leads the resistance to further demolitions. It is very difficult to organize city-wide struggle. For one thing, people cannot afford to travel and few can take time off work because their jobs last only as long as they present themselves for work each morning. The forfeit of a day's pay is unthinkable because it means the difference between eating and going hungry. But a group of slum-dwellers, supported by members of the radical Lawyers' Collective, Anand Patwardhan, journalists and teachers, met and decided to reoccupy the vacated land and symbolically to re-erect a single hut. It was to be a peaceful protest, a quiet and dignified statement to the city authorities. A young student living in Colaba, Suresh Kanojia, who is studying for his Commerce degree, was so angered by the evictions that he went on a spontaneous public hunger strike immediately after the demolitions. After some days he became ill and was removed to the hospital.

The meeting to organize the reoccupation is held one evening at 8.30. By that time, people have returned from work and finished the evening meal. All along the pavement fires are smouldering; women are cleaning the cooking utensils, scouring them with grit until they shine before washing them; others are finishing their meal of rice and chillies and vegetables. Here and there, children are sleeping, naked, on a piece of sacking on the edge of the busy road itself. They look extraordinarily vulnerable, in spite of the mothers who keep watch and give their babies the breast. Suddenly the whole scene is illuminated by the theatrical beam of the headlights of a passing car. Older children do homework by the orange light of smoky woodfires or the pallid blue glare of the street lamps; an occasional oil lamp sheds a muted glow through the thin sacking. It looks like a stage set; only the lives and privations that attend them are real enough.

Some of the people have painted placards and fixed them above their shelters, in Hindi, Marathi and English: 'No Jobs in Villages. No Shelter in Cities. Where Shall We Go?' They have constructed a high awning which serves as shelter for a meeting place. There, they have been painting posters—'No Demolitions'—and pictures of themselves being turned out of their homes. The men bring some benches and charpoys to sit under the awning. The women and children sit on the ground, even though it is the women who will play the greater part in the campaign. It is they who will court arrest, because the wages of the men, which are higher, must not be placed at risk. They also believe—perhaps mistakenly—the police and officials will deal less harshly with women, many of them nursing mothers.

By half-past eight here, are perhaps seventy or eighty people crammed into the meeting place. It is a hot airless night. A policeman, swinging his lathi, goes past. He looks with curiosity, but then moves on. This evening's meeting is primarily to keep up people's morale. Most have no choice but to remain where they are and see what happens. Their work is in the immediate vicinity of Sanjay Gandhi Nagar; even if they were given an alternative site to build their homes in another part of the city, they would not be able to continue their work.

There is discussion about the form of next week's direct action. They plan to take over the site, build a single rudimentary shelter. It is essential to make sure that TV cameras are there. Some celebrities have expressed their willingness to take part—film stars, writers, academics. If the slum dwellers alone demonstrate, the media will not be interested—it is too commonplace an event for that—and they may well be badly treated, beaten by the police; they risk being detained in jail and losing their jobs.

Gurbir Singh, who is a journalist, leads the people in a chant of 'Zindabad' ('Victory'), 'Hamara zamin le chalenge' ('We will take back our land'), 'Subramanian murdabad' ('Down with Subramanian'). He is the State Housing Minister. He lives in one of the big blocks of new flats on Cuffe Parade, overlooking the slum. Some of the people worked on its construction. They respond with passion. Even small children, six and seven, raise their fists. It is impossible to be a slum dweller of any age and remain unaware of the malevolence of the authorities, the ill-will of the well-to-do. There is something extremely touching about these poor children, some of them the only comfort of mothers on their own. It is in their solemn and sometimes frightened faces that the real 'sunder Mumbai' is to be seen, the neglected beauty of this appalling and splendid city. All along the sidewalk, there are saplings, protected by metal cages, and labelled with the name of the company that donated them: Balsara Garden Centre, Nascent Chemicals.

The action is fixed for the following Tuesday at nine in the morning. The people will gather, the police will be taken by surprise. Before they know what has happened, a single dwelling will have been erected. Let the municipality demolish it: it will only demonstrate more clearly the modest and peaceful demands of the people—to be allowed to live in freedom to pursue their livelihood, to be able to bring up their children in security.

It doesn't work out as planned. Someone had tipped off the police. Soon after the daybreak four dark-blue police wagons with barred windows are parked on the two sides of the compound that are flanked by roads. The people assemble as planned. Some of the young people have taken time from work: Arjun, thirteen, who has left his family in Uttar Pradesh and works on a dry-snack stall at Flora Fountain, doesn't want to miss the excitement. By nine o'clock, there are perhaps 200 people, among them Shabana Azmi, whose new film is currently showing at the Regal Cinema in Colaba. The police post themselves around the empty ground, standing in front of the parallel loops of barbed wire. All have lathis, some carry guns. The people are completely without any form of self-defence. The crowd contains mostly women and older men. There are many children. Some of the women carry babies in their arms. There are few young men—mostly those who do not have work.

The first group, carrying 'No Evictions, Stop Demolitions' banners, moves across the road. The others follow and come to a halt in front of the line of police in their khaki militaristic gear. The police tower over the women, who look frail in their dark sarees. The police swagger; many of the higher ranks have bellies that sag over their trousers. The people are forbidden to trespass on the enclosure. 'Our homes are here.' The land, it appears, is required for a new fire station. In any case, it is far too valuable to be given over as mere living space for the poor. It is the kind of argument heard all over the world; the land where the poor live suddenly becomes urgently required for more vital purposes: a new office-block, a motorway, a shopping centre, luxury apartments. They try to engage the police in conversation. 'Have you ever been evicted from where you live, have you ever seen your wife and children cast out on to the road?' No response. 'We are going to take back our land.' They are warned against any attempt to do so. They move forward. Some of the men lean against the stakes that support the barbed wire: the posts have not been driven very firmly into the dry ground and they yield. There is something quite incongruous in people trying to occupy this barren, sun-baked piece of ground: it looks more like a prison camp—the sort of place you might expect them to struggle to escape from.

The supporting stakes sway and fall backwards. Immediately, some of the women try to clamber over the barbed wire. The police is on them, leaving another part of the fence exposed. This goes down and another breach is made. Some of the women go to the corner where there is an aperture in the wire. Within a minute, everyone is inside a compound. A cheer goes up. The police bring up the van close to the gates of the site. The police now assemble inside the piece of ground, line up and wait. The crowd continue to uproot the posts and trample the wire. Then they sit down in the shade behind the school building. Inside, the lessons continue. A schoolteacher comes to the door, and looks out in surprise. She retreats. The deputy police commissioner for Bombay has been sent for. When he arrives, he strides vigorously into the crowd and recognizes some of those in the demonstration— the playwright Vijay Tendulkar is there, lawyers, scientists, film stars. To the policeman in charge of the operations he says, 'I am extremely angry with you. They should never have been allowed to get inside.' The people start singing, somebody produces drums and string instruments. There are speeches. The women ask the deputy commissioner, 'Where can we go? How shall we live?' With that characteristic legalism of police the world over he says, 'That has nothing to do with me.' He decides that all those who are now trespassing must be arrested. The police wield their lathis in anticipation. The first of the police vans backs into the gates. A few people withdraw from the crowd. One woman argues with her twelve-year-old daughter, ordering her to leave. She wants to say, but she is the only earner in the family. If she is locked up, what will happen to them? The girl stands her ground. The mother seizes her by the hair, drags her to the edge of the compound and forces her into the safety outside.

The people who have been sitting rise. The first of them file voluntarily into the van. The police are surprised: they had surged forward, expecting them to resist. When the van is full, it drives away, the heavy wheels setting up a cloud of dust. The people wave and shout to each other through the close-barred windows. The second van drives in, the third, the fourth. The demonstrators walk peacefully into them. A few of the women with very young babies protest and are allowed to hand their children to other women standing outside the wire. Neighbours bring bottles for those mothers who prefer to keep their children with them.

By now there are about fifty people left inside the enclosure. As I go to leave the compound, a policeman forces me back: 'You're part of it.' The deputy commissioner says angrily, 'Let him go.' He is in a state of some agitation—film stars, Western journalists—it is all very embarrassing.

The View from Chinchpokli

Dilip Chitre

A fouled Sun rises from behind the textile mills
As I crawl out of my nightmares and hobble
To the sink. Then I luxuriate in the toilet
While my unprivileged compatriots of Parel Road
  Cross Lane
Defecate along the stone wall of Byculla Goods Depot,
I shudder at the thought of going out of this lane
Towards the main road. Hundreds of workers are
  already returning
From the night-shift, crossing the railway lines.
The bus stop is already crowded. I begin to read
The morning's papers and cover my naked mind
With global events. The ceiling fan whirs, but I sweat.
I breathe in the sulphur dioxide emitted
By the Bombay Gas Company, blended with specks
  of cotton
And carbon particles discharged by the mills
That clothe millions of loins. Then I shave
  and shower,
Dismissing all untouchables from my mind, fearing
More palpable pollution. On my way out
I shall throw a used condom and a crumpled pack of
  Cigarettes
Into the garbage. And like a glorious Hindu hero,
Reluctantly riding his chariot to the centre of the
  battlefield,
I will take a cab to the Manhattan-like
Unreality of Nariman Point. There I will shape India's
  destiny

From *Travelling in a Cage* (1980).

Using my immaculate gift. I will ride in a taxi.
I will pass the Victoria Gardens Zoo without blinking.
Byculla bridge will give me the first line of a poem,
And the Christians, Jews and Muslims on my way
Will inspire a brilliant critique of contemporary
Indian culture. Of course, I will ignore
The junk-shops, the tea-houses, the restaurants, the
  markets
I zig-zag through. I shall smoothly go past
The Institute of Art, Anjuman-e-Islam, The Times
  of India,
The Bombay Municipal Corporation, and Victoria
  Terminus
If I glance at Flora Fountain or the Bombay
  High Court,
It will be an absent-minded observation.
And if I seem to look at the University of Bombay's
Clock-tower and buildings it will only be the sulking
State of a dirty-minded alma mater-fucker at the old
  hag herself.
But beyond all lies my daily sigh of relief
Because the gross millions are temporarily out of sight.
Some culture is possible in that half a square mile
Where the wall of India cracks open and the sea is
  visible.
At Chinchpokli, once I return in the evening,
I plot seductions and rapes, plan masterpieces
Of evasion. The loudspeakers blare at me.
Bedbugs bite me. Cockroaches hover about my soul.
Mice scurry around my metaphysics, mosquitoes sing
  among my lyrics.
Lizards crawl over my religion, spiders infest my politics.
I itch. I become horny. I booze. I want to get smashed.
And I do. It comes easy at Chinchpokli,
Where, like a minor Hindu god, I am stoned
By the misery of my worshippers and by my own
Triumphant impotence.

Hoops, Hunger, and the City

Nikhil Rao

'There are eight million stories in the naked city.' The memorable
first sentence of the voiceover in Jules Dassin's seminal noir flick, *The
Naked City*, is probably as applicable to Mumbai as to any other
megalopolis. For the last several months I've been engaged in tracking
down some of these stories as a doctoral student struggling to collect
enough material to write his dissertation. Yet, as a sports fan, one story
has intrigued me for a while. Perhaps precisely because of its ephemeral
and tangential role in the sporting life of Mumbai, I have often
wondered about the place of basketball in the social fabric of the city.

I should explain that I am a hoops fan. As is probably the case with
fans of other sports, describing myself as 'a fan' is simply code, to be
deployed in polite company, for describing myself as pathologically
obsessed with basketball. For a long time now, playing in my regular
pickup game at the Central YMCA in Colaba, I'd heard stories of
legendary players. These sessions of reminiscing were themselves
memorable for our five younger players standing around sweating
after the game, swatting away moths in the near darkness, while one
animated older player favoured enough to have seen some legend in
action described the poetry of so-and-so's jump shot, or the strength
and aggression of such-and-such's rebounding ability.

When I finally set about trying to find out about Mumbai basketball
more systematically, what emerged is as much a story of basketball as
it is a story of the city. It is not simply a desi version of the story of
Harlem, or the Bronx or Watts—of dirt-poor ghetto kids achieving
fame and fabulous fortunes through sport. Rather, it is a story of
Mumbai, its neighbourhoods and its very own particular history.

The Sabina Chandrashekhar Manoranjan Maidan in Colaba is

From *Man's World*, October 2000.

where I usually play. It is a cozy space ringed by trees and completely enclosed by buildings. By day it serves as sports ground for the three schools and the Central YMCA that circle it. But in the evening, for two hours, it is the venue for the hottest pickup basketball game in south Mumbai. The squeak of rubber is accompanied by the usual courtside melange of sounds—people trash-talking and supplying intimate genealogies of the aberrant sexual lives of each other's forebears, always in an argot that combines basketball terminology with choice swear words in a few languages. On the post supporting the backboard, some local hoops-crazed artist has rendered a version of the leaning, dribbling player that is the logo of the American National Basketball Association. Someone else has emblazoned basketball jargon onto the post—'dunk,' 'alleyoop', 'finger roll'—and I recognize a kindred spirit. When one is obsessed with basketball, when one falls asleep visualizing a perfect head fake followed by a flawless crossover dribble, one feels the need to embody it somehow, it is as if somehow articulating the action through words or a figure could freeze the beauty of that moment for posterity.

Yet this court is merely the scene of lively pickup games. Even though the Central YMCA had produced respectable teams in the past, it becomes clear after asking around that this is not the epicentre of the Mumbai basketball scene. For this I have to go to Nagpada. Here, right next to each other, sit two legendary institutions—the Nagpada Neighbourhood House and the Mastan YMCA—consistently producing the city's greatest basketball players.

II

On a recent Saturday evening I head over to Nagpada to catch the finals of the Mastan YMCA Monsoon League. The club is in Mastan Talao, a former tank that was deemed a health hazard and was filled over during the Bombay Improvement Trust's great redevelopment of Nagpada in the early twentieth century. This is not some desolate urban ghetto—it is a vibrant working and lower-middle class neighbourhood. The YMCA ground is ringed by low, ramshackle buildings. Small enterprises of various sorts thrive—garages, workshops, small manufacturing units, many undertaking outsourced job work from more prosperous parts of the city. The minarets of two mosques are visible on the periphery. As I walk in I step past three goats nestling snugly against one another.

I arrive in time for the Men's Final. Several boys and young men sit around the court, watching the action. A podium has been erected for the guest of honour, a minister with local connections. The nets on the rims are red, white and blue. One of the floodlights is temperamental and chooses to turn itself off and back on. There are also elements of the unreal. The interlude between the Juniors and the Seniors, we are treated, bizarrely, to an array of 'lilting melodies'— (announcer's words)—by the Sea Scout Marching Band. Replete in white uniforms, white gloves and batons, with a full complement of bagpipes, the Band launches into a series of off-key marching tunes, leaving my friend and I marvelling at the incongruity of the whole scenario and yet thinking to ourselves, 'It could only be this way.'

It is clear that this event has deep significance in the community. 'Basketball is the main sport in Nagpada and Nagpada is the main breeding ground for Mumbai's players,' Iqbal Qureshi tells me a few days later, when I meet him in the early evening at the Mastan Y, to the sound of the muezzin calling the neighbourhood to prayer. Iqbalbhai, as his students call him, is the Head Coach of the Mastan YMCA team. We talk a little about the history of basketball in Nagpada and the role it plays in the community today. Why basketball? Why here?

Basketball was introduced to Mumbai by the YMCAs. In the mid-1940s, an American missionary group set up an institution called the Nagpada Neighbourhood House, designed to promote various kinds of services to young men. The sports coach was one Mr Longfellow, a basketball fan who saw the possibilities in marrying his favourite sport with the cramped space and limited resources of Nagpada community. The needs were minimal—one relatively small patch of earth, two posts with boards and buckets, one ball. Add adrenalin, testosterone and muscle. Stand back. With the arrival of the legendary Bachoo Khan in the 1950s, basketball in Nagpada really took off. There are numerous stories about him. 'Bachoo Khan was a real bhai. Even the local *dadas* were respectful of him,' Shahid Quereshi, a recent star of Nagpada tells me. By the sheer force of his personality Bachoobhai would will the most athletic kids of the neighbourhood onto the court and make them train hard.

This made Bachoo Khan a force, not just on the courts, but in the entire locality. In a relatively poor neighbourhood like Nagpada, the sporting facilities offered by clubs like the Mastan YMCA and the NNH were rare and seized upon. People realized that keeping their children on the courts meant that they would be off the street and less susceptible to the various malevolent temptations on offer. 'Why do you think we have the Monsoon League?' Iqbalbhai asks me. 'If we allow these kids to run around for these three months, who knows what new friends they may fall in with.'

Iqbal Qureshi moved from Nagpada Neighbourhood House to Mastan YMCA in 1978. He is now something of a neighbourhood figure, the way Bachoobhai was. 'Everything I am I owe to Iqbalbhai,' Ibrahim Lakdawala, a Mastan star, tells me. Most of the kids who come straggling in to the practice that evening are from the neighbourhood, from within a few minutes walking distance. As I sit by the court talking to Iqbalbhai, I notice that every kid who walks in makes it a point to come up to where we are sitting and shake each of our hands. The first few times this happens I perceive it as an annoyance. After several kids have come up to us to shake our hands, I see what is happening. This is yet another practice that Iqbalbhai has instilled into the kids, a habit that, through sheer repetition, is meant to encourage civility. I am moved by the simplicity and beauty of the gesture, by what it reveals of the concern Iqbalbhai and the other coaches have for these children. 'We often know and care more about the whereabouts of these kids than their parents,' Iqbalbhai remarks, as though he was reading my thoughts.

Because the club draws heavily from the neighbourhood and because the neighbourhood is predominantly Muslim, the vast majority of players in the two Nagpada clubs are Muslim. At Central YMCA in Colaba, most players tend to be Christian. I ask Iqbalbhai if this ever results in any kind of communal tensions during games. 'Absolutely not,' he tells me. 'When we go to play in Indian Gymkhana (in Matunga, where most players tend to be South Indian Hindus), we get maximum support and when they come here, they get all the cheering.'

Why basketball? I ask Tom Alter, the well-known actor and mediaperson, to speculate on reasons for the popularity of the sport in this area. Mr Alter has been involved with the basketball scene in the Mumbai Central area for more than fifteen years. 'I think it has to do with the symmetry and order of the sport,' he says. In the context of poverty and disorder, he suggests, young boys in areas like Nagpada are drawn to a pastime where the rules are clearly drawn and where winning and losing depend entirely on one's own abilities and efforts. Add to that the gritty, urban nature of the game and the opportunities for grandstanding it provides to young bucks from the neighbourhood and it's easy to see why this sport appeals.

All this apart, the game thrives in Nagpada simply because it's there. Everyone I speak to tells me that they started playing basketball because they live across the street from the court and used to watch people play there, or because their brother used to play, or because Bachoobhai or Iqbalbhai caught them one day and made them get on the court. The courts in Nagpada are inextricably embedded in the neighbourhood—if you live there and have energy to burn, then some channel or other will lead you to the point where you're dreaming about the perfect arc on your jump shot.

III

In a place like Nagpada, kids are drawn to basketball because there are no other sporting opportunities, and because excelling might lead to a job and upward mobility. However, in other neighbourhoods, playing basketball is more of a choice.

To find a counterpoint to the Nagpada scene, I go to Indian Gymkhana in Matunga, another ground that has produced great players in the past. It is set in a wooded middle-class neighbourhood that is quite different from Nagpada. Low, comfortably picturesque buildings circle the Gymkhana; their paint is peeling, but they have a shabby gentility. An immense tree casts its shadow over the tennis courts. The first thing that strikes me is the plenitude of space compared with the cramped quarters in Nagpada. In addition to the two tennis courts and two basketball courts, there is also a ground that is used for cricket and football. But when I show up one evening, the basketball court is empty. I speak to Mukund Dhus, an Indian Gym veteran and General Secretary of the Maharashtra State Basketball Association, 'Right now the kids are too busy to come and play,' he tells me.

We chat a little bit about the game in Matunga versus the game in Nagpada. He suggests that the Nagpada boys play a more physically aggressive game whereas Indian Gym plays a technique-oriented game. I pose the same question I did to Iqbalbhai, as to whether the communally specific nature of the major club teams ever leads to tension. He vociferously concurs with Iqbalbhai that there is never any friction of that sort. In fact, he says, the great thing about sport is that it transcends these communal differences.

The sociology of Matunga is utterly different from that of Nagpada, and thus basketball occupies a different place in the life of the community. The kids in Matunga have different sporting options. They can play tennis, badminton, cricket or football. Moreover, their middle-class background means that basketball can only ever be a hobby. Their first priority is studies: getting good marks in the phalanx of exams and getting into the right colleges. In recent years, with the proliferation of various coaching classes and other extramural academic programmes that appear to be mandatory, kids have no time or energy to play sports on a sustained basis. Hence, while good players may be bred here, the chances of their becoming great players are slimmer because they simply won't have time. While there have been illustrious players to come out of Indian Gymkhana—the names of C.N. Sharma, S. Kishnanand, and P.V. Prabhu stand out—they don't need to make basketball their life. They will become doctors and engineers and bank managers—all solidly middle-class occupations. They are not hungry the way boys from Nagpada are, they don't live for basketball in the same way. They don't have to. The Nagpada boys are more hungry because they are less privileged, because doing well in school is not presented to them as a way to move up in life.

Another reason for the decline of basketball in Matunga in recent years may have to do with the changing real-estate market and the resulting transformation in the demography of the neighbourhood. I notice that the Gymkhana is a less vibrant place than it used to be in the eighties, when I used to play tennis tournaments here. Until the late eighties, the Gymkhana used to host the famous Ramu Memorial Basketball Tournament, the biggest and most popular hoops festival in the city. Teams from all over the country would participate and fans would flock to the Gymkhana to see legends in action.

Now the formerly lush maidan is brown, rutted and uneven. The tennis courts appear to be in disrepair. I ask Vishwanathan Menon, the manager of the canteen, about the general feeling of malaise that seems to pervade the Gymkhana.

'The whole locality has changed,' he tells me. Following the escalation in real estate prices in the last two decades or so, the original predominantly South Indian base (which was also the core basketball constituency, both in terms of supplying players as well as fans) of Matunga has eroded considerably. Significant numbers have moved to places like Chembur, Mulund and Vashi. Mr Menon maintains that the new entrants don't place so much emphasis on sports for their kids. Several flats in Matunga are also currently vacant, he informs me, because the owners, people who've most recently moved to Thane or Vashi, are waiting for the market to pick up again before selling.

A comparison between the current state of the two main clubs in Matunga is illuminating. Indian Gymkhana is a classic middle-class club. It is somewhat ramshackle, but has a genteel, mellow charm. Matunga Gymkhana, which used to be a similar place, has now gone in for a thorough makeover. The whole place is rubble right now, but in its place is to be erected a posh club, with expensive membership fees and all sorts of luxury services. This contrast embodies the transformation in the neighbourhood. The old middle class has had to make way for new entrants with money to spend.

IV

If basketball in Nagpada is a story of the neighbourhood, it is also a story of getting out of the neighbourhood, at least metaphorically. For many boys from not-so-affluent backgrounds, basketball offers an entrée into a white-collar life. As with other sports in the Indian system, large companies and government agencies hire athletes on generous terms where the 'job' is essentially a sinecure, allowing players to practice and participate in competitions. On the basketball front, the Indian Railways—the world's largest employer with a staggering 1.4 million employees—alone fields about thirteen basketball teams. Other major employers include Income Tax, Central Excise, TISCO, and various nationalized banks. To learn about this, I set off to find Abbas Muntasir, Mumbai's Mr Basketball and Arjuna Award recipient. In the days before I finally met him, he acquired a mythic quality. When I told people I was writing about basketball, almost invariably the response, delivered in a hushed tone, would be, 'Well, have you spoken to Abbasi yet?' or, even more maddeningly, 'Have you seen Abbasi play?'

In person, Mr Muntasir is very real. He comes from a family of Kashmiri carpet merchants. He is not particularly tall for a basketball player—he stands about 5'11" or so—but, even at fifty-eight, he is powerfully built and radiates intensity. He is one of those people who leans into you as they speak, as though compelled to do so by the sheer force and conviction of what they are saying. As I appraise this legend of whom I have already heard so much, I recall what Tom Alter had said to me. 'He's not particularly tall and he's not a great shooter, but once Abbasi decides that he wants to steal the ball from you or that he's going to drive past you to the basket, then nothing is going to stop him.'

We sit watching the Railway team practice at the NNH. As a Sports Officer with Central Railway, he has personally recruited many of the young men we see playing. Across the street, overlooking the court and about forty metres from where we're sitting, is the building where Mr Muntasir was born and where he still lives. The space of the court somehow inscribes a certain form of sociability into the space of the neighbourhood. Despite the differences between neighbourhoods, what we're doing—sitting around watching a game, with passers-by on the street pausing to check out the action—could happen anywhere. Every now and then he heaps abuse upon the players for a slack pass, or a meek attempt at a rebound.

'The problem with players nowadays is that they don't hate to lose,' he says, succinctly offering his analysis of the decline in India's basketball fortunes. The scene now is a far cry from the days of Ramu Memorial at Indian Gym, when there would be a brisk black market trade in tickets to see stars like Abbasi play.

Mr Muntasir does not like to lose. In fact, he doesn't even like other people thinking he's going to lose. He tells me of an episode in Bangkok, during the Asian Basketball Championships in 1975, when he bet all his money on India coming out on top simply because a local resident had disparaged the Indian team's chances. Goaded perhaps by the wager, India ended up coming in fourth, an unprecedented high finish.

There are also structural reasons offered for the decline in stature of Indian basketball. I speak to another Nagpada legend, Abdul Hamid Khan, also known as 'Babu', who works at Central Railway. Of a generation younger than Mr Muntasir (he is about forty-two now), Babu and his older brother Ghulam Rasul Khan (aka Papa) grew up in the building next to Abbasi, the sons of a coal merchant.

'The structure of incentives isn't there to encourage young players,' Babu tells me. Despite the fact that he has attained almost every honour there is—he represented India on numerous occasions and received the Chhatrapati Shivaji Award when he was only fifteen—Babu appears embittered with the way the Indian sporting establishment treats basketball players. He's upset that he and his fellow players don't get enough respect for having represented India in international competitions.

Yet he too feels that many players today are simply not that hungry. It's as if the nature of the existing incentive structure dulls the urge to excel. Unlike marquee sports like cricket or football, the best they can hope for is a secure job with Railways or Income Tax. Knowing that their job is guaranteed if they deliver a certain minimum performance, they have no itch to transcend themselves. He tells me that when he and his brothers were young and playing in the Nationals, they would play both in the Juniors' as well as in the Men's divisions. Since quite often a team would have to play two matches a day, those playing in Juniors' and Men's would have to play four matches a day. On such days, Babu informed me with a dreamy look in his eyes, he would sometimes end up scoring over 100 points a day. They would simply keep changing vests and step out onto the court, hungry for action. I try and see if younger players are more enthusiastic about their prospects. I'm sitting with Shahid Qureshi in his family's business premises—the Super Taxicab Meter Manufacturing and Repairing Co. in Nagpada—watching him take care of business. Shahid is twenty-eight and is a recent international player from Nagpada.

At a bulky 6'2" or so, Shahid is an imposing figure, as much for his size as for his aggression and intensity. When he played professionally in Sweden, his team mates and opponents called him 'Djor', which is Swedish for 'The Bull'.

Shahid now has a job with TISCO. But he too is not enthusiastic about the support that players get. The money is not enough, there is not enough respect, there is too much politics. 'I now play because I love the game, not because of what I can get out of it,' he tells me. He has suffered a brutal knee injury and plans to go to the United States for a complicated surgical procedure.

However, people are still obsessed with playing the game. Abbasi doesn't play anymore, but shows up regularly at the court to watch and criticize and encourage. Babu still works out thrice a week with the Railways team. Shahid's knee has healed somewhat, and he now plays regularly, although with only a fraction of his previous intensity. He tells me of one recent Nationals where he would be carried off the court after every game, such was the pain in his knee. But he would get back the next day, ready to bang some bodies.

V

In posh areas like Colaba and Cuff Parade, basketball currently enjoys a certain surging popularity among wealthier youth as a result of their having travelled to the States or because NBA games are now broadcast on Indian TV. But the old basketball scene appears to be declining in popularity as well as in institutional support. Tom Alter traces the beginnings of the decline to roughly the mid-eighties. In neighbourhoods like Nagpada, he suggests, poor young men now have other avenues to upward mobility. Meanwhile, in neighbourhoods like Matunga, demographic changes and other pressures have contributed to the downward trajectory of the sport. Some say that the future lies in newer suburban clubs such as the Andheri and Ghatkopar YMCAs. But so far nothing like the Nagpada or Indian Gymkhana tradition has emerged.

Back in Colaba, I've just been humiliated on the court by Donald and Rajni, the two current kings of Central YMCA. They are probably not going to pursue basketball seriously although Rajni, especially, has long been bitten by the bug. He is now about nineteen, but he used to show up at the court as a kid of eleven wearing chappals. The older boys (I was one of them) wouldn't let him play. But he would hang around the periphery and, every time the ball went out of bounds, would run after it and grab it. Before we could get it from him, he would run into the court and launch one shot at the hoop. This is how he spent his evenings—waiting for that stray chance to launch the ball. So, perhaps there is cause for hope, despite the problems of Indian basketball. As long as the court, the basket and the ball are around, there will always be someone or the other, waiting, hoping to watch the arc of his jumpshots culminate in the sublime swish of the net.

Dekho, Dekho, Art Deco

Salman Rushdie

For many Bombayites, for us most definitely, Salman Rushdie is the storyteller of Bombay. The voice he adopts here is that of the narrator Rai, denizen of Villa Thracia, who tells us almost as much about Bombay as he does about the love affair between Vina Apsara and Ormus Cama, both singers, both fabulous confections with trace elements of many old Bombay stories and rumours.

—Eds

When you grow up, as I did, in a great city, during what just happens to be its golden age, you think of it as eternal. Always was there, always will be. The grandeur of the metropolis creates the illusion of permanence. The peninsular Bombay into which I was born certainly seemed perennial to me. Colaba Causeway was my Via Appia. Malabar and Cumballa Hills were our Capitol and Palatine, the Brabourne Stadium was our Colosseum, and as for the glittering Art Deco sweep of Marine Drive, well, that was something not even Rome could boast. I actually grew up believing Art Deco to be the 'Bombay style,' a local invention, its name derived, in all probability, from the imperative of the verb 'to see'. Art dekho. Lo and behold art. (When I began to be familiar with images of New York, I at first felt a sort of anger. The Americans had so much; did they have to possess our 'style' as well? But in another, more secret part of my art, the Art Deco of Manhattan, built on a scale so much grander than our own, only increased America's allure, made it both familiar and awe-inspiring, our little Bombay writ large.)

In reality that Bombay was almost brand-new when I knew it;

From *The Ground Beneath Her Feet* (1996).

what's more, my parents' construction firm of Merchant & Merchant had been prominent in its making. In the ten years between the birth of Ormus Cama and my own coming into the world, the city had been a gigantic building site; as if it were in a hurry to become, as if it knew it had to provide itself in finished condition by the time I was able to start paying attention to it. No, no, I don't really think along such solipsistic lines. I'm not over-attached to history, or Bombay. Me, I'm the under-attached type.

I return to my muttons. It is true, though it's got nothing to do with me, that the building boom that created the Bombay of my childhood went into overdrive in the years before my birth and then slowed down for about twenty years; and that time of relative stability tricked me into believing in the city's timeless qualities. After that, of course, it turned into a monster, and I fled. Ran for my wretched life.

Me? I was a Bombay *chokra* through and through. But let me confess that, even as a child, I was insanely jealous of the city in which I was raised, because it was my parents' other love, the daughter they never had. They loved each other (good), they loved me (very good), and they loved her (not so good). Bombay was my rival. It was on account of their romance with the city that they drew up that weekly rota of shared parental responsibilities. When my mother wasn't with me—when I was riding on my father's shoulders, or staring, with him, at the fish in the Taraporewala Aquarium—she was out there with *her*, with Bombay; out there bringing her into being. (For of course construction work never stops completely, and supervising such work was Ameer's particular genius. My mother the master builder. Like her dead father before her.) And when my father handed me over to her—when we sang our hideous ditties and ate our curdled ice-cream—he went off, wearing his local-history hat and a khaki jacket full of pockets, to dig in the foundations of building sites for the secrets of the city's past, or else sat hatless and coatless at a designing board and dreamed his lo-and-behold dreams.

V.V. Merchant's first love would always be the city's pre-history; it was as if he were more interested in the infant's conception than in her actuality. Give him his head and he would prattle happily for hours of the Chalukya settlements on Elephanta and Salsette islands two and a half thousand years ago, or Raja Bhimdev's legendary capital at Mahim in the eleventh or twelfth century. He could recite the clauses of the Treaty of Bassein under which the Mughal emperor Bahadur Shah ceded the Seven Isles to the Portuguese, and was fond of pointing out that Queen Catherine of Braganza, wife of Charles II, was the secret link between the cities of Bombay and New York. Bombay came to England in her dowry; but she was also the Queen in the NY borough of Queens.

Maps of the early town afforded him great joy, and his collection of old photographs of the edifices and *objets* of the vanished city was second to none. In these faded images were resurrected the demolished Fort, the slummy 'breakfast bazaar' market outside the Teen Darwaza of Bazargate, and the humble mutton shops and umbrella hospitals of the poor, as well as the fallen palaces of the great. The early city's relics filled his imagination as well as his photo albums. Hats were of particular interest. 'Time was, you could tell a man's community at once by the thing he wore on his head,' he lamented. Sir Darius Xerxes Cama with his chimney-pot fez was a last relic of those days when Parsis were called Topazes on account of their headgear. And banias had round hats and the chow-chow Bohras crying their unlistably various wares in the streets seemed to be carrying balls upon their heads . . . It was from my father that I learned of Bombay's first great photographer, Raja Deen Dayal and A.R. Haseler, whose portraits of the city became my first artistic influences, if only by showing me what I did not want to do. Dayal climbed the Rajabai tower to create his sweeping panoramas of the birth of the city; Haseler went one better and took to the air. Their images were awe-inspiring, unforgettable, but they also inspired in me a desperate need to get back down to ground level. From the heights you see only pinnacles. I yearned for the city streets, the knife grinders, the water carriers, the Chowpatty pickpockets, the pavement moneylenders, the peremptory soldiers, the whoring dancers, the horse-drawn carriages with their fodder-thieving drivers, the railway hordes, the chess players in the Irani restaurants, the snake-buckled schoolchildren, the beggars, the fishermen, the servants, the wild throng of Crawford Market shoppers, the oiled wrestlers, the movie makers, the dockers, the book sellers, the urchins, the cripples, the loom operators, the bully boys, the priests, the throat slitters, the frauds. I yearned for life.

When I said this to my father he showed me still lives of hats and storefronts and piers and told me I was too young to understand. 'Comprehension of historical appurtenances,' he assured me, 'reveals the human factor.' This required translation. 'See where people lived and worked and shopped,' he clarified, with a rare flash of irritation, 'and it becomes plain what they were like.' For all this digging, Vivvy Merchant was content with the surfaces of his world. I, his photographer son, set out to prove him wrong, to show that a camera can see beyond the surface, beyond the trappings of the actual, and penetrate to its bloody flesh and heart.

The family construction business had been developed by his late father-in-law, Ishak Merchant, a man so interminably choleric that at the age of forty-three his inner organs literally burst with anger and he died, bleeding copiously inside his skin. This was soon after his daughter's marriage. The daughter of an angry man, my mother had chosen a partner wholly lacking in anger, but couldn't handle even his gentle—and rare—reproofs; the mildest of cavils would unleash in her an astonishing storm of emotion that was more tearful than explosive, but otherwise, in respect of its extreme and damaging force, not at all unlike her dead father's rage. V.V. treated her gingerly, like the fragile thoroughbred she was. Which was necessary; but also spoke of trouble ahead, or would have, had either of the happy couple been listening. But they turned a deaf ear to all words of warning. They were deeply in love; which beats earplugs.

The happy newlyweds, Vivvy and Ameer, were plunged in at the deep end. Fortunately for them, the city needed every builder it could get. Two decades later, they could point out several of the art dekho mansion blocks along the west side of the Oval Maidan, and on Marine Drive too, and say with justifiable pride, 'We built that' or 'This one's ours.' Now they were busy further afield, in Worli and Pali Hill and so on. As we drove home from Juhu, we made a number of detours to take a look at this or that site, and not only those with Merchant & Merchant boards on wire perimeter fences. Building sites are, to a family of builders, what tourist sights are to the rest of the populace. I had grown accustomed to such behaviour and, in addition, was so excited about my encounter with my swimsuit goddess that I didn't even bother to complain. I did, however, ask questions.

'What's her name?'

'Arré, whose name? What do I know? Ask your father.'

'What's her name?'

'I'm not sure. Nissa or some such.'

'Nissa what? Nissa Doodhwala? Nissa Shetty? What?'

'I can't remember. She grew up far from here, in America.'

'America? Where in America? New York?'

But my father had run out of information; or else there were things he did not wish to reveal. Ameer, however, knew it all.

'New York State,' she said. 'Some stupid gaon in the backyard of beyond.'

'What gaon? Oh, Ammi, come on.'

'You think I know every village in the US? Some Chickaboom-type name.'

'That's not a name. Is it?'

She shrugged. 'Who knows what-all kind of crazy names they have there. Not just Hiawatha-Minnehaha but also Susquehanna, Shenandoah, Shehboygan, Okefenokee, Onondaga, Oshkosh, Chittenango, Chikasha. Canandaigua, Chuinouga, Tomoatosauga, Chickaboom.' They were her last words on the subject. Chickaboom, NY, it was.

'Anyway,' added my mother, 'you don't want anything to do with her. For one thing, that Piloo is her guardian now, and plus, she is well known to be nothing but trouble. One thousand and one per cent bad egg. She had a life of tragedy, that is so, my heart goes out to her, but just keep away from her. You heard how she talks. No discipline. She's too old, anyway; find friends your own age. And plus,' as if this clinched it, 'She's a vegetarian.'

'I liked her,' I said. My parents both ignored me.

'You know,' my mother changed the subject, 'those Red Indian names sound darn South Indian to me. Chattanooga, Ootacamund, Chitaldroog, Chickaboom. Maybe some of our Dravidian co-nationals sailed off to America yonks ago in a beautiful pea-green boat. Indians get everywhere, isn't it? Like sand.'

'Maybe they took some honey and plenty of money,' my father joined in. I saw that we had embarked on one of our traditional family kidabouts and there was no point trying to get things back on track.

'What's the point of wrapping honey in a five-pound note, anyway?' I said, giving in. 'And, p.s.,' I added, my thoughts turning back to my swimsuit girl, 'what self-respecting pussycat would marry a stupid owl?'

'Minnehaha, Laughing Water,' Ameer followed her own train of thought. 'So *haha* must be laughing, which means *Minne* is water. Then what's Mickey?'

'Mickey,' said my father sternly, 'is a mouse.'

The philosopher Aristotle was dismissive of mythology. Myths were just fanciful yarns, or so he opined, containing no valuable truths about our natures or our surroundings. Only by reason, he argued, will men understand themselves and master the world in which they live. For this view Aristotle had, in my childhood, some minority local support. 'The true miracle of reason,' Sir Darius Xerxes Cama once (or, actually, rather too often) said, 'is reason's victory over the miraculous.' Most other leading minds, I'm bound to report, disagreed; Lady Spenta Cama, for example, for whom the miraculous had long ago supplanted the quotidian as the norm, and who would have been utterly lost, without her angels and devils, in the tragic jungle of the everyday.

Also ranged against Aristotle and Sir Darius was Giovanni Battista Vico (1668-1744). In Vico, as for as many present-day theorists of childhood, the early years are the crucial ones. The themes and dramas of those first moments set the pattern for all that follows. For Vico, mythology is the family album or storehouse of a culture's childhood containing that society's future, codified as tales that are both poems and oracles. The private drama of the vanished Villa Thracia colours and prophesies our subsequent way of living in the world.

'Keep away from her,' said Ameer Merchant, but once the inexorable dynamic of the mythic has been set in motion, you might as well try and keep bees from honey, crooks from money, politicians from babies, philosophers from maybes. Vina had her hooks in me, and the consequence was the story of my life. 'Bad egg,' Ameer called her, and 'rotten apple' too. And then, dripping and bruised, she arrived at our door in the middle of the night, begging to be taken in.

Just seven days after our Juhu experiences, at six o'clock in the evening, it began to rain out of a clear sky, in hot, fat drops. Heavy rain, whose warmth did nothing to cool down the maximum-humidity heat wave. And as the rain increased in force, so too, in a freak of nature, the temperature also rose, so that the water, falling, evaporated before it hit the ground and turned to mist. Wet and white, rarest of all Bombay's meteorological phenomena, the mist rolled in across the Back Bay. The citizenry, strolling on the Parade for the customary 'eating of the air', fled in search of shelter. Mist obliterated the city; the world was a white sheet, waiting to be written upon. V.V., Ameer and I stayed indoors, clutching our poker hands, and in that bizarre whiteness our bidding became extreme, reckless, as if we intuited that the moment required extravagant gestures of us all. My father lost even more matchsticks than usual, and at higher speed. A white night fell.

We went to our beds, but none of us could sleep. When Ameer came to kiss me good night, I said, 'I keep waiting for something to happen.' Ameer nodded. 'I know.'

Later, after midnight, it was Ameer who first head the noises outside, the bumping and thumping, as if an animal were loose on the front veranda, and then an exhausted, tearful panting. She sat straight up in bed and said, 'Sounds like whatever Umeed was hoping for has turned up at last.'

By the time we reached the veranda the girl had passed out on the boards. She had a black eye and there were cuts on her forearms, some of them deep. Glistening serpents of hair lay across the wooden veranda floor. Medusa. It crossed my mind that we should look at her face only in a burnished shield, lest we be turned to stone. Her white T-shirt and jeans were sodden. I could not help looking at the outlines of her thick nipples. Her breathing was too fast, too heavy, and she was groaning as she breathed. 'It's her,' I said, stupidly.

'And we have no choice,' my mother said. 'And what will be will be.'

Dry, warm, bandaged, and eating hot porridge from a bowl, with a towel wound around her hair like a pharaoh's crown, the girl held court in my parents' bed, and we three Merchants stood before her like courtiers: like bears. 'He tried to kill me,' she said. 'Pillo the yellow-belly. He attacked me. So I ran away.' Her voice failed. 'Well, he threw me out,' she said. 'But I won't go back, anyway; whatever happens.' And Ameer, who had warned me off her, said fiercely, 'Go back? Out of the question. Nissa Doodhwala, you will kindly just stay put.' Which utterance was rewarded by a tentative, though still suspicious, smile.

'Don't call me by that bastard's name, okay?' the girl said. 'I left there with nothing. From now on I'll be whatever name I choose.'

And a few moments later: 'Vina Apsara. That's my name.'

My mother soothed her, reassured her—'Yes, Vina, okay, baby, whatever you want'—and then probed: what had provoked so violent an attack? Vina's face slammed shut, like a book. But the next morning the answer arrived on our doorstep, anxiously ringing the bell: Ormus Cama, beautiful and dangerous as the revenant sun, nineteen years old, with a 'reputation.' And in search of forbidden fruit.

It was the beginning of the end of my days of joy, spent with those Thracian deities, my parents, amidst legends of the city's past and visions of its future. After a childhood of being loved, of believing in the safety of our little world, things would begin to crumble for me, my parents would quarrel horribly and die before their time. Fleeing this frightful disintegration, I turned towards my own life, and there, too, I found love; but that existence also came to an untimely end. Then for a long time there was just me, and my painful remembering.

Now there is at last a new flowering of happiness in my life. (This, too, will be told at the proper time.) Perhaps, this is why I can face the horror of the past. It's tough to speak of the beauty of the world when one has lost one's sight, an anguish to sing music's praises when your ear trumpet has failed. So also it is hard to write about love, even harder to write lovingly, when one has a broken heart. Which is no excuse; happens to everyone. One must simply overcome, always overcome. Pain and loss are 'normal' too. Heartbreak is what there is.

Bhelpuri

Rahul Srivastava

It is a foolish exercise to try and trace a definitive history of anything. But nations and cuisines, in particular, are problem areas. Let's take nations first. How far back do you go in claiming a nation's history? Do you include the migrants from distant lands a thousand years ago? If so, then why not include 'foreigners' of four centuries ago? Why not consider the history of a neighbouring country as your own? Especially since your entire region may have had the same experiences for a millennium (if not more) and you became separate nations only fifty years ago?

The questions still puzzle historians and are fertile ground for fierce debates. But that does not compare to confusions generated by questions of origins about food and cuisine.

For example, it may now be a cliché to talk about the foreign origins of chillies to Indians. But it is still tempting to see the expression on their face when you say it again. A pang of pain and a look of disbelief inevitably greet such an assertion. 'Chillies are not Indian?' they say with utter disbelief even if they have heard this before. 'But then what did we eat before the Portuguese brought them here from Mexico in the sixteenth century?' The inability to imagine any food from the sub-continent without this spice can cause much anxiety to its inhabitants and even lead to deep anguish about their cultural identity. Consider the humble bhelpuri, which hides within itself analogies of great debates on history, questions of identity, definitions of cosmopolitanism and other such sociological concerns. In fact, trying to trace the origins of bhelpuri can actually help us look at the writing of history in a new way, with a newer, more productive emphasis on innovation, adaptability and enterprise.

This popular item is said to have originated in Mumbai (when it was still Bombay), and has multi-cultural influences of a most complex kind. Its main ingredient, kurmura, a kind of coarse puffed rice is commonly found in many north-and-west Indian temples as prasad. Most Sai Baba temples in the city, and even in Shirdi itself, serve it as their main prasad. It is cheap and easily available. Interestingly, the temple of Swami Samarth of Akkalkot in Maharashtra uses the bhelpuri itself (not just the kurmura) as naivedhyam, a daily ritual food offering.

Kurmura must have caught the eye of an enterprising working-class migrant either from Uttar Pradesh or Bihar. (This is pure conjecture. But consider the fact that most bhelpuriwalas come from these two states and it would not be so inaccurate to say that they had an important role to play in cooking up this concoction.) One imagines that memories of eating chaat in Delhi and eating farsaan (different fried savouries with high storage value) in Gujarati shops in the city all came together into one imaginative pot-pourri in the entrepreneur's mind and bhelpuri was born.

Basically, the kurmura is mixed with typical chaat sauces. One hot, made from chillies, coriander and mint, and one sweet, made from tamarind, jaggery, cumin powder and dried ginger powder. The sauces are mixed in various combinations according to the taste of the eater. (These sauces have traditionally been used in Indian snacks as chutneys to accompany savoury items. They can be found all over the sub-continent in different forms.)

Then you have the garnishes, tiny flecks of raw mango (especially in the summer, when the fruit is cheaply available), with coriander, raw onions, sev, a crushed hard puri, green chillies and a squeeze of lime. The sev is perhaps a derivative of the Gujarati farsaan. Bhelpuri is eaten with a hard small puri in place of a spoon. Now, this puri is quite different from the regular soft puris. It could very well be related to the pani-puri (or golgappa as it is known in the North), small puffed puris made from a mixture of semolina and flour. These are fried into small delicate table-tennis-size balls and filled with spiced water. When you fry them they must fluff up. If they don't then they are to be discarded or used in some other preparation. And our enterprising originator of bhelpuri must have decided to judiciously reuse them. Much of the pleasure of eating bhel comes from the crackling of crushed puris and the constant temptation to consume your edible puri-spoon.

When exactly the bhelpuri came out from the slums and the working-class enclaves of the city, is, to use a catch phrase from history text-books, 'shrouded in mystery'. But it would not be difficult to trace it by following the paths of hundreds of hawkers trying to earn a living in the city. A city that treats them as part of an illegal unofficial shadow-economy. And yet the bhelpuriwala is there on every street corner in spite of being part of this dark shadow-economy. He is there mainly because the people in the highrise buildings love his food and will ignore his illegal status. In the shadow-economy lies a shadow-market.

Today bhelpuri is also served in big food establishments with an air-conditioned ambience. The originator is dead and questions of patents are irrelevant to his family. However, the legacy lives on. That's all. That is the definitive history of bhelpuri.

Its subaltern origins and easy use as a metaphor for cultural diversity (all those mixed-up ingredients) have made it very popular with scholars of urban history and sociology talking about co-existence and cosmopolitanism. But it is perhaps equally important to see it from the point of view of enterprise, the main ingredient in the life of the migrants in the city. Migrants, who have contributed to its richness. Not just by being there but by innovating and adapting, a quality encoded in the cultural history of bhelpuri. If only historians rewrote nationalist histories from the vantage point of this humble food, much of the mindless debates about origins and authenticity could be discarded forever and a more dynamic history could shape our future.

A Brace of Bombay Ducks

Various

Bombay Duck is not a duck at all. In fact it should be spelt Bombay Dak. What it is, is dried fish (known in Bombay as Bombil) and when the British introduced the railway system to western India under their Raj, it started going in wagonloads to the interior from Bombay. The crates stank of dried fish, like stale penises. They were marked 'Bombay Dak', literally 'Bombay Mail'. At the time the railway was run by whiteys. The English may call a spade a spade, but they don't call 'stinking fish' by that name. They referred to it euphemistically as 'Bombay Dak', the Bombay Mail.

From Farrukh Dhondy's *Bombay Duck* (1990).

★

BUMMELO: A small fish abounding on all the coasts of India and the Archipelago; *Harpodon nehereus* of Buch. Hamilton; the specific name being taken from the Bengali name, *nehare*. The fish is a great delicacy when fresh caught and fried. When dried it becomes the famous Bombay Duck, which is now imported into England. The origin of either name is obscure. Molesworth gives the word as Mahratti with the spelling *bombil*, or *bombla*. Bummelo occurs in the Supp. (1727) to Bluteau's Dict. in the Portuguese form *bambulim*, as 'the name of a very savoury fish in India'. The same word *bambulim* is also explained to mean '*humas pregas na saya a moda*', 'a certain plaits in the fashionable ruff', but we know not if there is any connection between the two. The form Bombay Duck has an analogy to Digby Chicks which are sold in the London shops, also a kind of dried fish pilchards we believe, and the name may have originated in imitation of this or some similar English name. [The Digby Chick is said to be a small herring cured in a peculiar manner at Digby, in Lincolnshire, but the Americans derive them from Digby in Nova Scotia.]

In an old chart of Chittagong river (by B. Plaisted, 1764, published by A. Dalrymple 1785) we find a point called *Bumbello Point*.

1673—'Up the Bay a Mile lies Massigoung, a great Fishing-Town, peculiarly notable for a Fish called **Bumbelow**, the Sustenance of the Poorer sort.'—*Fryer*, 67.

1785—'My fried General Campbell, Governor of Madras, tells me that they make Speldings in the East Indies, particularly at Bombay, where they call them **Bumbaloes**.'—Note by *Boswell* in his *Tour of the Hebrides*, under 18 August 1773.

1810—'The **bumbelo** is like a large sand-eel; it is dried in the sun, and is usually eaten at breakfast with kedgeree.'—*Maria Graham*, 25.

1813—Forbes has **bumbalo**; *Or. Mem.*, i. 53; [2nd ed., i. 36]

1877—'**Bummalow** or *Bobil*, the dried fish still called "Bombay Duck".'—*Burton, Sind Revisited*, i. 68.

From *Hobson-Jobson: A Glossary of Colloquial Anglo-Indian Words and Phrases, and of Kindred Terms, Etymological, Historical, Geographical and Discursive*, by Col Henry Yule and A.C. Burnell.

★

BOMBAY DUCK: Small sea fish (the bummelo). Fresh, it is gelatinous with a delicate flavour, especially favoured by **Parsis**. But mostly it is sun-dried and spiced and used as a condiment. It has been said that the name is an Anglicism from the bazaar cry in Marathi, 'bomil tak'—here is bomil.

Bombay ducks: in British days and occasionally today, name used by Europeans in other parts of India for their compatriots living in Bombay.

From *Hanklyn-Janklin or a Stranger's Rumble-Tumble: Guide to Some Words, Customs and Quiddities Indian and Indo-British*, by Nigel B. Hankin.

★

Lalitha Luke's* hitherto top secret Bombay Duck recipe

Ingredients:

4 Bombay ducks (fresh)
¼ tsp turmeric powder
1 tsp red chilli powder
Salt to taste
10 ml tamarind pulp
Rawa (semolina) for coating
Oil for frying

Method:

Clean Bombay ducks, open them. The centre bones may be removed or left in as desired. Wash thoroughly.

Keep between flat plates and remove excess liquid. Dry on cloth. Grind together spices with tamarind pulp, vinegar and salt. Rub into the fish. Let it stand for one hour.

Heat oil in a frying pan to smoking point; lower the heat. Coat Bombay ducks with rawa and fry them.

---

* A woman of remarkable patience, Lalitha Luke suffered the capriciousness of the editors of this volume with grace and charm and typed out our 1,80,000-word manuscript with nary a complaint.

In the Gully

Sunil Gavaskar

It would seem improbable for any sport to flourish in a city as starved for open space as Bombay. But ever quick to turn adversity into opportunity, Bombay has used its makeshift concrete pitches to forge a uniquely disciplined batting style. As little boys get their first taste of the game, running between compound walls and parked cars, they learn to thump the tennis ball through the gaps with precision, so as to avoid broken window panes. The lessons of gully cricket, as Bombay's pick-up games have come to be called, served Sunil Gavaskar well as he slashed his way through the world's cricket stadiums. He became the first cricket player to score 10,000 runs in Test Matches.

—Eds

I may never have become a cricketer and this book would certainly not have been written, if an eagle-eyed relation, Mr Narayan Masurekar, had not come into my life the day I was born (10 July 1949). It seems that Nan-Kaka (as I called him), who had come to see me in hospital on my first day in this world, noticed a little hole near the top of my left ear lobe. The next day he came again and picked up the baby lying on the crib next to my mother. To his utter horror, he discovered that the baby did not have the hole on the left ear lobe. A frantic search of all the cribs in the hospital followed, and I was eventually located sleeping blissfully beside a fisherwoman, totally oblivious of the commotion I had caused! The mix-up, it appears, followed after the babies had been given their bath.

Providence had helped me to retain my true identity, and, in the process, charted the course of my life. I have often wondered what would have happened if nature had not 'marked' me out, and given

---

From *Sunny Days* (1976).

my 'guard' by giving me that small hole on my left ear lobe; and if Nan-kaka had not noticed this abnormality. Perhaps, I would have grown up to be an obscure fisherman, toiling somewhere along the west coast. And what about the baby who, for a spell, took my place? I do not know if he is interested in cricket, or whether he will ever read this book. I can only hope that, if he does, he will start taking a little more interest in Sunil Gavaskar.

My most vivid recollection of my childhood cricket-playing days is the time I almost broke my mother's nose. She used to bowl to me in the small gallery of our house where we played our 'daily match' with a tennis ball. Since the area was small she would kneel to bowl, or rather lob the ball to me. I hit one straight back and caught her bang on the nose which started bleeding. Although it was a tennis ball, the distance between the two of us was very short, which accounted for the force with which the ball hit her. I was frightened but she shrugged it off, washed her face and, as the bleeding stopped, we continued the game. But for the rest of the day it was only forward defence for me. I restrained myself and played no attacking shot.

Right from the beginning I wanted to become a batsman and I hated losing my wicket. This became such an obsession with me that if the rest of the boys ever got me out, I would fight and eventually walk home with the bat and ball. This would bring the game to an abrupt halt since nobody else had a ball or bat. The boys cursed and called me names, but the tension did not last long and we generally got along very well. Whenever I batted they would decide beforehand that they would appeal by a particular ball and whether I was out or not I had to go by the majority verdict. We often played matches against teams made up of boys living in the neighbouring building and there was tremendous interest in the 'trophies', as we called them. The trophies were small white-metal cups for which we all contributed and bought for as little as Rs 1.50.

In our neighbourhood were Sudhir Naik, Sharad Hajare and, of course, Milind Rege, who lived in the same building in which we had a flat. We often played against each other in those days. Years later, when all of us were in the Bombay Ranji Trophy team, it seemed as if Chickalwadi and Shivaji Park were representing Bombay!

Special Providence

Salim Ali

Until a few years ago the question of how my interest in birds originated never bothered me or anyone else. I grew up with it and the oddness was taken for granted—that was that. It was only much later, after the question was put to me by an inquisitive press reporter, that I began giving thought to the matter. I then realized that, considering my early background, his query was actually less irrelevant than it first appeared. Eighty-seven years is a long time to remember details, but I vividly recall our rambling family house in Khetwadi, a middle-class residential quarter of Bombay, in the now overcrowded area between Girgaum and Charni Road. Here I lived as the youngest of an orphaned family of five brothers and four sisters: my mother Zeenat-un-nissa had died when I was about three and my father Moizuddin two years earlier. We grew up under the loving care of a maternal uncle, Amiruddin Tyabji, and his childless wife, Hamida Begam, who were more to us all than any parents could be. They were guardians as well as to miscellaneous assortment of other orphans and children of absentee friends and relations of different ages, and very variable—sometimes even dubious—quality. There was no one in that very mixed ménage who, as far as I can remember, was at all interested in birds, except perhaps as ingredients of an occasional festive pulao.

'Nature conservation' was then a phrase only rarely heard. Partridges and quails were abundantly and freely sold in the mart, and six to eight birds per rupee of the former and sixteen to twenty of the latter made them cheap enough as a variant, on high days and holidays, of the eternal murghi, costing perhaps six to eight annas (thirty-five to fifty paise). The birds used to be brought alive to the Khetwadi house,

---

From *The Fall of a Sparrow* (1985).

crowded in round flat bamboo baskets with a burlap flap on top, and 'lawfully' halalled (had their throat slit). I well remember how, when about ten years old, Suleiman (a nephew two years my junior) and I used to rescue a few of these unfortunates on the sly and keep them as pets in a rough-and-ready open-air pen, made from wire mesh and old packing cases, with the help of Nannoo, the trusty old cook and factotum of the family and us children's unfailing friend, abettor and accomplice in all such enterprises. It is a wonder to all of us who knew him, and increasingly so in the context of current servant problems, how Nannoo ever found time to volunteer for all these 'extra-curricular' activities, and always with so much zest and cheerfulness. He ran the kitchen single-handed, cooking two full meals a day for seldom less than ten people, mostly children and teenagers with healthy appetites. This involved scraping and cleaning pots and pans (for he had no kitchen help), kneading the ata and baking a pile of chapattis which, in a sporting mood, he would challenge us to finish faster than he could produce while squatting on the ground at a smoky wood fire choola. The 'aviary' was run in partnership by Suleiman and myself and it gave us immense joy to sit beside the enclosure and watch the behaviour and action of the birds—among which our favourites were named—for hours together. On school holidays it was certainly a far pleasanter way of passing time than doing homework.

We made as frequent excursions as our pocket money of Rs 2 per month would permit to the bird section of Crawford Market to see if any new birds had arrived which could be added to our collection. In the early days our interests was confined chiefly to game birds, and our collection consisted of Grey and Painted Partridges, and Grey, Rain and Bush Quails. Occasionally when feeling particularly flush, as after a birthday celebration, we would acquire a pair or two of Grey Junglefowl or Red Spurfowl. But I never was nor have been successful in keeping captive birds and other animals or pets alive for long. After repeated disappointment and failure I finally gave up trying: and though I have from time to time in later years kept birds for various experimental purposes, I have always released them thereafter.

About this time, when I was about nine or ten, the father-uncle with whom we lived and whom we boys greatly hero-worshipped for his *shikar* exploits, presented me with an air gun. I well remember that it was a nickel-plated 500-shot repeater 'Daisy'—a popular make in those days, more toy than gun. Through a hole behind the front sight you had to drop up to 500 round lead pellets of BB size into a hollow cylinder round the barrel; after each shot you worked a hand lever to compress the spring which at the same time automatically slipped the next pellet into the breech. It was not much of a weapon as air guns go, extremely inaccurate and temperamental in its performance and needing a good deal of manipulation and allowances in aiming before you could hit a mark at thirty-feet range. However, a repeater air gun was an innovation and as such was the envy of my little companions, some of whom possessed equally innocuous single-shot affairs. To own such a 'sophisticated' piece of weaponry added greatly to my ego and I loved to show it off. In spite of its shortcomings, I soon acquired enough cunning with it to shoot house sparrows, of which a colony used to be in permanent residence in the stable. Spilt grain from the horses' nose-bags, sundry holes in the ceiling and walls for nests provided them with bountiful living. We boys, being correctly brought up as god-fearing Muslim children, knew that although the sparrow fell with the category of lawful meat it could only be eaten provided the birds had been halalled in the ordained manner. Under fear of dire consequences in the hereafter, and with timely warning from our elders, we were usually scrupulous in observing the ritual, but even at the risk of purgatory were sometimes tempted to cheat by cajoling Nannoo to cut their throats even after the birds were long dead and cold. Nannoo taught us how to deal with the sparrows after the correct obsequies had been performed, and some of us little boys became expert at transforming them, with masala, a blob of ghee and a frying-pan, into delicious morsels.

The very first bird note I ever made was during this era, at the age of nine or ten. It concerned an incident in the course of one of those sparrow hunts in that Khetwadi stable. Wooden pegs had been driven into the wall, on which harness was hung. One of these pegs had come off, leaving a hole in the wall which became a coveted nesting place for the sparrows. The observation made was on a female sparrow nesting in that hole. Crude and incomplete as it was when rediscovered nearly sixty years later, the gist of the note seemed relevant enough for publication in *Newsletter for Birdwatchers*, more or less in its original form, thus:

> 1906/7. The cock sparrow perched on the nail near the entrance to the hole while the female sat inside on the eggs. I ambushed them from behind a stable carriage and shot the male. In a very short while the female acquired another male who also sat 'on guard' on the nail outside. I shot this male also, and again in no time the female had yet another male in attendance. In the next 7 days I shot 8 male sparrows from this perch; each time the female seemed to have another male in waiting who immediately stepped into the gap of the deceased husband.

I am rather proud of this note because though intended as a record of my prowess as a hunter and made long before I was conscious of any possible relevance, it has proved more meaningful in the light of present-day behavioural studies.

Each year when school vacations began in summer the entire Khetwadi ménage migrated to Chembur—now a noisy part of metropolitan Bombay but in those days a delightfully quiet sylvan haven of secondary moist-deciduous jungle set among outlying hillocks of the Western Ghats. The highest of these, Trombay Hill, just over 300 metres and the venue of our youthful mountaineering exploits, now forms part of the Bhabha Atomic Research Centre's estate. It was thickly wooded in parts till uniformly denuded into a veritable Rock of Gibraltar by the relentless fuel-hunters from the janata colony which was established around its base after the Second World War. The Chembur of those days is memorable for its peaceful jungle flavour and the considerable wildlife it held despite its closeness to the city. The nearest railway station, Kurla, was three miles by foot or bullock cart. There were no industries, shopping facilities, schools or other social amenities in the neighbourhood. Motor cars and buses had not invaded the scene and practically no commuters resided in the locality. Such rare townsfolk as one occasionally met were, like ourselves, vacationing visitors or absentee landholders on weekend trips to their farms or mango orchards, of which there were a flourishing number around. The Chembur area has long enjoyed a well-deserved reputation for the excellence of its mangoes, especially alphonso and pairi. Unfortunately, such orchards as have not already succumbed to housing or industrial development are fast disappearing in the wake of rocketing land values with the growth and expansion of the city. The mango trees once so lovingly tended have vanished or stand gaunt and neglected spectres, overrun by the parasitic growth of *bandha* (loranthus) and awaiting the vandal's axe.

Most of the animal sounds, so evocative of our schoolboy vacations, have been long since silenced one by one with the inexorable encroachment of 'civilization'. The familiar howling of jackals at dusk and all through the night, inseparable from my Chembur memories, ceased years ago, and hyenas, scarce even then, have completely disappeared. The spirited song of the Magpie-Robin which regaled us at daybreak as we lay half awake, reluctant to leave our cosy beds, is one of the earliest and most cherished of my ornithological memories. They bring back those matchless, carefree school vacations in Chembur every time I listen to a Magpie-Robin's song, no matter where.

Like idle and thoughtless schoolboys everywhere, with no notion of the ethics of sports (whatever they be!) or conservation instilled into us either at home or in school—on the contrary with a certain Victorian aura attached to hunting and shooting as a manly sport— we roamed the countryside with our air guns, making a target of every little bird trusting enough to permit a close approach. I recall my juvenile elation if I managed to drop a honeysucker or similar small bird in this vandalistic sport. Happily, such occasions were rare. Part of a more regular hunting programme of us gangsters was to visit the tiny neighbouring hamlet of Deonar near sunset when large numbers of House Sparrows collected to roost among the stacks of rice-straw, piled up in trees to keep it out of reach of hungry cattle. The sparrows came just as it was getting dark and hurriedly tunnelled their way into the straw, and our strategy was to keep ready for their arrival and sportingly pot only the males before they disappeared within. The forays to Deonar often served a dual purpose since the family supply of eggs, vegetables and milk came from this village, and we were commissioned to bring back the hut-to-hut egg collection along with our own bag of 'game' (Eggs cost one *phadia* or four pies or one-forty-eighth of the old rupee!) As far as I can recall it was at this point, and as a fortuitous offshoot of one of these sparrow-hunting expeditions, that my first 'scientific' interest in birds was born.

While one of my victims was about to be halalled, I suspected something was wrong with the bird: it looked like any other female sparrow I sometimes got except that it had a yellow patch on the throat, like a curry-stain. My main concern at this moment was whether this sparrow was lawful meat for a God-fearing little Muslim or not. Unwilling to jeopardize my prospects in the hereafter, I prevented the halalling and instead carried the corpse back to the house to obtain an authentic pronouncement (fatwa) from Uncle Amiruddin, the shikari of the family. He examined the sparrow carefully and agreed that it was a different bird, apparently not having noticed one like it before. Uncle Amiruddin was one of the earliest Indian members of the Bombay Natural History Society (BNHS), having joined it soon after its founding in 1883, and became an active participant in its work. He gave me a letter of introduction to the then Honorary Secretary, Mr W. S. Millard, the head of Phipson & Co., Wine Merchants, asking his help in identifying the bird. My very first contact with the Society, then housed in the premises occupied by Phipsons, came about in this way. The visit was a thrilling experience and is still fresh in my memory.

Incidentally this building at the corner of Forges Street and Apollo Street was the former residence of the Chief Justice of the Bombay High Court. In those days there was practically no social contact between English people and Indians, much less so for boys of my age. The sahibs lived in the insulated little Englands they had created for themselves; their exclusive clubs were defiled by no black man's shadow, excepting, only the 'bearers' who poured out their chhota and bara pegs. They had built around themselves a mythical aura about their nobility and greatness and superior virtues, about carrying the black man's burden and all that. This myth took such firm root that even after forty years of independence it still survives. It was a rare occurrence for a middle-class Indian to meet and talk to an Englishman, official or otherwise, except purely on matters of business. A schoolboy's only contact with the English was perhaps when his classroom was visited annually by an educational inspector who, of course, always had to be a sahib.

I remember the feeling of nervousness—almost of fear and trembling—at the prospect of meeting a full-grown sahib face to face with which I entered the quaint old single-storeyed building through its magnificent solid teakwood portal. After due checking of my bona fides I was led up the shallow coir-carpeted steps by a supercilious khaki-liveried sepoy, the flanking walls covered with mounted heads of shikar trophies in terrifying profusion. Upstairs, in a corner of the wooden-floored room chock-a-block with desk showcases displaying seashells, butterflies, birds' eggs and miscellaneous natural history bric-à-brac, the walls were still more crowded with skulls and mounted heads of tigers and leopards staring glassily down at the intruder, or snarling with bared fangs more ferociously than they ever did in life. I was piloted to the sanctum sanctorum through this welter of animal remnants, stumbling over stuffed crocodiles and hoofs of sambar floor-rugs. In a corner of this congested junk shop, which was the Society's museum in those days, and partitioned off by swing doors, sat, leaning over his desk, the genial bald-headed Walter Samuel Millard, the Honorary Secretary.

This must have been somewhere in 1908, and my first contact with the BNHS was later to become such an important element in the shaping of my life and career. All my nervousness vanished completely in the face of the charming kindliness and consideration of Mr Millard. I then realized that perhaps *all* white men were not the ogres our youthful fancy had painted them from stories of unsavoury incidents on tea plantations and confrontations in railway carriages. As Mr Millard peered at me over his reading glasses I fumbled out my credentials and the little paper packet containing the mystery bird. He identified it at a glance as a Yellowthroated Sparrow (*Petronia xanthocollis*) and bid me to follow him to the reference cabinets, from one of which he produced several stuffed specimens for confirmation. There were numerous other species of sparrows in the collection, which he took great pains to show me, and explained the differences and points for identification. He patiently opened drawer after drawer for me to see the hundreds of different birds found in the Indian Empire, and I believe it was at this moment that my curiosity about birds really clicked. Mr Millard gave me a few bird books from the small library to read, and this is how I made my first acquaintance with Edward Hamilton Aitken's (EHA's) inimitable classics—*Common Birds of Bombay* and *A Naturalist on the Prowl*. They spurred my interest, and I have since read them again and again over the last sixty years or more with undiminished pleasure and admiration. At the request of the publishers, I had the rare privilege of annotating the first for a new edition brought out in 1946 under the altered title of *Common Birds of India*, which carries a short biographical sketch of the author by my friend Loke Wan Tho.

Mr Millard encouraged me to make a collection of birds as the best way of learning about them, and offered to have me trained at the Society in skinning and preserving specimens and keeping proper notes about them. He introduced me to a young Englishman in the next room who had lately been recruited as the first paid Curator of the Society. This was Norman Boyd Kinnear who, later, after World War I, joined the Bird Room of the British Museum (Natural History) and ended up as Sir Norman Kinnear, director of the Museum, in 1947-50. Kinnear, a dour Scotsman, appeared to me rather stand-offish and reserved, and therefore outwardly at least more like the pukka sahib of our youthful conception. Behind this façade of stand-offishness, however, he was rather shy, but kindly and helpful, and did much to encourage and foster my new-born enthusiasm, both during his curatorship of the Society and later from the Bird Room of the British Museum. He put me under the training of two young assistants, S.H. Prater and P.F. Gomes. They showed me over the entire bird collection and initiated me into the art of skinning, stuffing, preparing and labelling bird and mammal specimens for a study collection. Both these persons remained in the Society's employ to the end of their working lives. Prater, of whom I shall have more to say later, distinguished himself in several ways: as the Society's Curator in its most consolidative years, as a leader of the Anglo-Indian community in Western India, and as its elected representatives in the Constituent Assembly and Bombay Legislative Council till his retirement and emigration to England in 1948. P. F. Gomes, a rather stolid pachydermic Goan, was in charge of the Society's insect collection in his later years, a function which he discharged with phlegmatic efficiency. I remember chiefly for his neat handwriting, which can still be seen in the old accession registers of the Society, and on many of the labels in the reference collections. I remember Gomes also for invariably referring to tendons (while teaching me to skin) as 'nostrils', and that was with a soft Portuguese 't' which was puzzling at first but continued to amuse me the rest of the time.

The fortuitous incident of the Yellowthroated Sparrow opened up undreamt vistas for me. Thenceforth, my reading tended progressively towards books on general natural history, and particularly birds. Illustrated books on Indian birds were virtually non-existent in those days, and indeed for many years later, and there was little available to help a beginner in identifying and learning about the birds around him. The absence of illustrated books was in my opinion the most serious obstacle to the development of bird-watching as an outdoor hobby among Indians generally. Thus, most people who contributed to bird study in India in the early years were foreigners—mostly Englishmen—who had grown up in their home country in the time-honoured British natural history tradition and were already familiar with bird lore—if only as egg-collecting schoolboys—before they came out to India. Spurred by the wealth of bird life around them here, and perhaps by the opportunities as well as the social constraints in the lonely life of a district officer in the backwoods, some of them took to sport shooting and natural history as a serious pastime, or to collecting bird skins and eggs. Many blossomed in course of time into scholarly naturalists or highly competent ornithologists who helped to lay the foundation of scientific natural history in India. Jerdon's *Birds of India* (1864) and later the four-volume publication on Indian avifauna by Oates and Blanford (1898) were adequate for identification, provided you had an elementary familiarity with birds, the necessary ferreting zeal and a specimen in hand. The lack of illustrated field guides and good field glasses, however, seriously inhibited the cult of bird watching as we know it today. There is no doubt that I owe the beginning of my serious interests in birds to that enigmatic Yellowthroated Sparrow and the chain of events it brought in its train.

The Day It Rained Gold Bricks and a Horse Ran Headless

Jerry Pinto

'I was standing on the terrace of a building in the Fort, but the impact was tremendous. I was thrown off my feet. At first, I thought it was an earthquake. Then I thought the Japanese had attacked, because that was an ever-present fear in those days. When I got up again, I looked down and saw a horse careening madly down the street. Then a plate of glass flew from a building and sliced the horse's head off. It ran on, almost a few yards, blood spurting from its neck, before it fell to the ground.'

Augustine Pinto, then a young engineer and a recent emigrant to Bombay, would never forget that sight. When he told his children about it, they would never forget it either although they had not seen it. Their father standing on the terrace of a building, watching a horse being decapitated on the street, on the clear sunlit afternoon of 14 April 1944.

For on that afternoon, at 4.46 p.m., the SS *Fort Stikine* exploded, taking with it a large portion of Victoria Dock No. 1 in which it was lying at anchor. That moment still lives for many people as it did for my father.

Adelaide Pereira, now in her seventies, remembers the day vividly. Although Dhobi Talao, where she lived, was a fair distance from the docks, she says the impact blew her off her chair. 'Everyone was talking about the Japanese and so we were ready to believe that we had been bombed. A madman who lived in our building ran out on to the streets, shouting, 'They've bombed us. They've bombed us.' He forced some of the children into crouches, pushing them into stairwells and under handcarts, where he thought they would be protected. When I got home, my brother Daniel was missing. I went out to look for him and found him crouched under a car and crying.'

Journalist Shashikala Baliga's uncle, who was deaf, heard the blast, making it the only sound he ever heard in his life.

The *SS Fort Stikine* had arrived from Karachi more than twenty-four hours earlier carrying a highly inflammable cargo of cotton bales, resin, lubricating oil, torpedoes, detonators, one million pound sterling in gold ingots and 1200 tonnes of Category A explosive—the most sensitive kind.

What kind of captain would accept such a cargo? Every manual, every handbook warns against carrying cotton and explosives together. But Captain Naismith had little choice. England expected every man to do his duty and a captain's duty was to carry a full load in wartime.

In wartime. The words recur as the leitmotif of that afternoon. It was wartime and the ammunition was badly needed. It was wartime and so the *Stikine*, carrying explosives was allowed into Bombay's harbour. It was wartime and so the *Stikine* did not fly her red flag indicating an explosive cargo—this would make her a natural target for the Japanese bombers of Bombay's paranoid imagination. It was wartime and so the dock siren, which would have been sounded to clear the area, was not used since it was linked to the air-raid precaution siren. It was wartime and momentous things were happening all over the world and so Bombay was forgotten. This was also the wartime that left us with memories of Hiroshima, Nagasaki and an exultant America that wanted other Japanese cities to burn 'like autumn leaves'.

At 1 p.m. that afternoon, smoke was seen coming from the hold of the *Stikine* and a fire alarm was sounded—an ordinary one. Two fire engines arrived from Carnac Bunder and firefighting operations began but the firemen had no idea what they were dealing with since the *Stikine* was not flying a red flag. Seamen in the adjacent ships didn't know either; they watched for a while and then grew bored and went below, according to John Ennis in his book *Bombay Explosion* (Jaico, 1960). The firemen couldn't even see what they were dealing with since the cotton was being held down by scrap iron and smoke had filled the hold. Eight more arrived as the authorities began to guess that something was wrong. The Bombay Port Trust tug, *Doris*, and the water boat, *Panvel*, came to assist them but by then the fire was raging out of control. Everything was tried. The boat could not be scuttled because the valves were set not to let water in. A gas-cutter brought to the scene proved to be defective or else the fire might have been sighted and the water trained on to it.

And so eventually, 600 tonnes of explosive went off in the evening, blasting the ship into the sky, ripping through the docks, lifting the adjoining ship, the *Jalapadma* (6450 dead weight tonnage) clear out of the water and landing it on a dock nearby. The explosion set off a reaction in the city: partitions fell, and the evening sky was lit up as bales of burning cotton and oil drums set ablaze flew through the air.

The blast was felt in Simla where the seismograph registered a tremor. Closer to the 'epicentre', the lucky were temporarily deafened. Or hurt by flying glass. The unlucky were maimed or burnt alive. Panic grew. School principals, unused to such calamities, sent the children home even though transport was paralysed. The water mains burst. Electric stations caught fire. The bodies began to roll in. The St. George's hospital at Frere Road admitted 371 people in the first hour. The Sir J. J. Hospital opened a new wing, two months early, to cope with the influx of 264 patients. The city was dropping into chaos.

'I remember the pall of smoke,' says Adil Jussawalla, the poet, who was a boy then. 'It hung in the sky over the city, grey and ominous. The sunset was dark red, ochre, brown—those were the colours of the sky. By then, we had heard that something had happened at the docks and I remember wondering if the sky was reflecting something.'

Very likely. Brilliant sunsets are generally the result of refracting material—smoke, gases and the like. That was what was in the sky that evening.

Initially, the residents of the area simply fled, leaving the fires to rage untended. But by the night, the city was putting up a fight. Volunteer brigades began to be formed. The Akali Dal helped build firebreaks. The women of the American Red Cross set up a canteen to serve the firefighters. The Wrens in Bombay set up a first-aid post. Only, it wasn't much of a fight. There was no one to coordinate efforts, no one to ensure that the few resources left to the city were being put to the best use. As the *Free Press Journal* put it, 'Symbolic of the way the city met the disaster is the solitary figure playing his hose without knowing exactly how.'

'I remember we had been asked to write an essay on 'A House on Fire' in school that year,' Adelaide recalls. 'We always wrote about the sky turning red, about the brave firemen, about the crying people. Suddenly, it was all happening. But this wasn't just a fire in a house; it was the city. And it wasn't going out. The fire was spreading.'

Fire was now the enemy. It was raging in the docks, where 500 tonnes of coal in the *Jalapadma* had consumed the homes of the luckless who lived by the docks. Others had their homes razed to contain the fire. The city squatted by the sea, by millions of tonnes of water and it burned.

We know the numbers. We know that 200 soldiers saved 13,684 tyres and inner tubes from a godown. That sounds like a reasonable if slightly eccentric figure; it has the smell of a fact. We know that 231 people died and 146 were badly injured. We know that the government says that the outer number they were willing to put on the number of casualties was 1376. That figure doesn't make sense; it doesn't smell of a crowded dock with firemen, dockworkers, sailors; of a downtown area filled with civilians; it stinks of the bureaucracy.

If you look carefully, you see the figure of the bureaucrat, silhouetted against the flames. The Great Indian Clerk was hard at work, helping the fire. When the torpedoes were to be taken away, the railways protested that the rule book didn't allow transport of torpedoes in open trucks. When the firefighters asked why 211 pumps were not in use, they were told that those could only be commandeered by the government in case of an enemy attack. And since no one was bombing the city, since it was only a fire, these lay unused and the people formed a bucket brigade against the inexorable flames.

Eventually the fire was put out. An old man came forward to return some gold ingots which he had found driven into the wall of his balcony. It was no surprise that he was a Parsi. A memorial was built to the firemen who lost their lives. The two huge hundred-foot craters scooped out by the explosions have been filled in. The city has been rocked by other forces, chemical and communal.

But to those who lived through it, the images remain. The sky tinged with blood, a man sliced in two by incandescent steel, the sudden fear when the ambulances went by, the black market in grain, the debris floating in the bay, and for me, the image of a headless horse, still running, still spurting blood.

War Comes to Bombay

Khwaja Ahmad Abbas

The population of Bombay [during the Second World War] had grown
to more than a million and a half. Still the bus and tram and train fares
had not gone up, and there were empty flats to let . . . I had been aware
of the rate of Bombay's growth of population, from first-hand
experience of those who were forced by circumstances to sleep on
'beds of stones'!!

But the growth of population took a 'breather' when the war started
and there was danger of attacks from the sea by lurking German
submarines. The coastal area buildings suddenly were advertising
their flats 'TO LET', and through a friend who was living in a building
on the sea-front at Shivaji Park, I was able to shift to Shivaji Park,
which was then regarded a posh area next to Marine Drive (also called
the Queen's Necklace), the poshest area in the city.

I was already on the fringes of the Cinema business (generally and
wrongly called the film industry), being part-time publicity writer for
the Bombay Talkies Studios at Malad. I spent half a day there and by
3 p.m. I was back in the *Bombay Chronicle* office where I was being
asked to write film reviews, among my other activities. But I took it
more seriously than others, which involved editing 'MOTORING
AND AVIATION' and 'AGRICULTURE AND INDUSTRY' pages
which were mostly scissors and paste assignments but which brought
me a windfall when the 'AVIATION' editor received an invitation for
the inauguration of Delhi–Bombay postal flights, as the solitary
passenger of the four-seater plane which no less a pilot than Mr J.R.D.
Tata himself, was piloting. I did not know him when we took off from
Juhu airport in the darkness of the pre-dawn hour. So I committed a
faux pas by asking my pilot what salary he got, when he reluctantly

From *Bombay, My Bombay: The Love Story of the City* (1987).

replied, 'Three thousand per month.'

'Your pilots earn a lot,' I said, relative to the time before war, 'Your company looks after you very well.'

JRD brought me to a shattering climax when he answered, 'I am not exactly a pilot!'

I looked down at the fields under us, 5000 or 6000 feet, and asked nervously, 'You are not exactly a pilot? You are not an amateur pilot, I hope?'

He studied my nervousness and said, 'Don't worry, Mr Abbas, I am not an amateur. I have all the necessary licences. But I am not exactly a pilot. I am the Chairman of the Company.'

Then I knew that the youthful-looking pilot was the great JRD Tata himself.

But to come back to Bombay, at the beginning of the war, the Sethias were going back to Ahmedabad, Surat and Baroda, and large number of war-time job-seekers were coming to Bombay. These included the later famous Anand brothers—Chetan Anand who was an intellectual, a school teacher of English who stayed, to become a film director, and Dev Anand who was working in the war-time Censor office as a Sorting Clerk, before People's Theatre cast him in my play called '*Zubaida*'—and Prabhat of Poona took him over as a film hero. After that he never looked back—only looked ahead. It is difficult to imagine him in today's 'HUM NAUJAWAN'!

The population of Bombay was about two million during the war!

Many nationalities were represented amongst the Allied soldiers who were seen in Bombay during those days. One could meet them, mainly in the Fort of Bombay—British and (later) Americans, of course, but Canadian Americans, even French, Dutch, and Swedes and bedraggled Italian prisoners-of-war who passed through Bombay on the way to their P.O.W. camps in Maharashtrian countryside.

This influx brought with it a whole lot of magazines and papers of all languages which were sold at Lamington Road second-hand book shops of which I was an avid customer—they ranged from pornography to more serious magazines like *New Yorker* and *New York Times* magazine.

Seeing this (mostly) English-speaking potential clientele, local publishers started publishing a lot of cheap paper-backs—at a price of Rs1/8—mostly reprints of D.F. Karaka's books and novels, books on Yogas and Indian Spiritualism, even a little book of mine, *Indian Looks at America*, got published and sold well among American troops who wanted to know how an Indian writer looked at their country. There was a chapter about Negroes called 'The Darker Brothers' which brought quite a few appreciative letters from the coloured GIs and even from liberal-minded white troops—and a few abuse letters from soldiers from southern states who had the same mentality like our Brahmins and Thakur landlords who think nothing of burning Harijan villages.

Arriving in Bombay

Aldous Huxley

On the quay, awaiting the disembarkment of their relatives on board
our ship, stand four or five Parsi ladies—all ugly, as only members of
that exclusive inbred race can be ugly. They wear Indian saris, with
European blouses, stockings, and high-heeled canvas shoes. In one
hand they hold black umbrellas, in other garlands of flowers. The
black umbrellas are for using against the sun; the wreaths of tuberoses
and oleanders are to hang around the necks of their returning friends.
One of the ladies, we are confidentially informed, is an eminent woman
doctor.

A dozen coolies, thin-limbed like spider-monkeys, are drafted to
wheel up the gangway. They lay their hands on it, they simultaneously
utter a loud cry—in the hope, evidently, that the gangway will take
fright and move of its own accord. But their faith is insufficient; the
gangway does not stir. Sadly, with sighs, they make up their mind to
shove. A vulgar, commonplace, and tiring method of making things
move. But at least it works. The gangway rolls across the quay, is
hoisted into position. Passengers begin to leave the ship. The friends
and relations of the Parsi ladies at last come down the plank. They are
embraced, lassoed with flowers, and led off to the attendant Hupmobiles
and Overlands behind the Custom House. It is our first view of the
East.

The brown skins, the bare feet, the nose-rings, the humped
bullocks—all these thing were foreseeable, seemed obvious and
familiar from the moment of landing. The really odd, unexpected
thing about Bombay was its birds. There are more birds in the streets
of this million-peopled city than in an English woodland. Huge kites,
their wings spread and unmoving, go soaring along the thoroughfares,

From *Jesting Pilate: India and Burma* (1948).

effortlessly keeping pace with the traffic below. Innumerable grey-headed crows fly hither and thither, sit perched on every roof, every sill and wire. Their cawing is the fundamental bass to every other sound in Bombay. Kites and crows do useful scavenging works, and Bombay, which produces much garbage and few dustmen, keeps them well employed and copiously fed. Nobody, in this land where the killing of animals is all but murder, does them or their nests any harm. They increase and multiply, they are astonishingly unafraid. All over India we were to find the same abundance of bird life, the same trustful absence of fear. Coming from Italy, where, for nine months of the year while *lo sport* is in progress, the countryside is almost birdless, where armed men lie ambushed half a day for a hedge-sparrow, and migrant warblers are netted and eaten by the thousand—coming from Italy, I was particularly impressed by the number and variety of Indian birds.

Architecturally, Bombay is one of the most appalling cities of either hemisphere. It had the misfortune to develop during what was, perhaps, the darkest period of all architectural history. Most of its public buildings were designed and executed between 1860 and 1900. It is hardly necessary for me to expatiate or comment. All that need be said has been said perfectly in the guide-book: Secretariat, we are told, is in 'the Venetian Gothic style'. The University Hall (completed 1874), which is 'in the French Decorated style of the fifteenth century', rubs shoulders with the 'Early English' Law Courts (opened in 1879). The University Library, harking back to an earlier century than the Hall, is 'in the style of the fourteenth century Gothic'. The Old General Post Office 'was designed in the medieval style by Mr Trubshawe'. (Mr Trubshawe was cautiously unspecific.) The Telegraph Office (date not mentioned, but my knowledge of architectural fashions makes me inclined to a rather later epoch) is 'Romanesque'. The Victoria Station, of which the style is 'Italian Gothic with certain oriental modifications in the domes', confronts the Municipal Buildings, in which 'the oriental feeling introduced into the Gothic architecture has a pleasing effect'. More frankly oriental are the Gateway of India ('based on the work of the sixteenth century in Gujarat') and the Prince of Wales Museum ('based on the Indian work of the fifteenth and sixteenth centuries in the Presidency'). The architecture of the Hotel Majestic and the Taj Mahai Hotel is not described in the guide-book. It is a remissness; they deserve description. The Majestic is more wildly Mohammedan than anything that the most orthodox of Great Moguls ever dreamed of, and the gigantic Taj combines the style of the South Kensington Natural History Museum with that of an Indian pavilion at an International Exhibition. After an hour passed among these treasures of modern architecture, I took a cab, and in mere self-defence drove to the Town Hall, which is a quiet, late-Georgian affair, built in the thirties. Long and low, with its flight of steps, its central pediment, its Doric colonnade, it has an air of calm and quiet decency. Among so many architectural cads and pretentious bounders, it is almost the only gentleman. In Bombay, it seems as good as the Parthenon.

In the lounge of the hotel is a bookstall, stocked with periodicals and novels—my own, I was gratified to see, among them. One whole section of the bookstall is devoted to the sale of English and American technical journals—but technical journals of a single, rather special kind. Journals of gynaecology, of obstetrics, of sexual psychology, of venereal diseases. Rows of them, and dozens of copies of each. The hotel lounge is not specially frequented by doctors; it is the general public which buys these journals. Strange, strange phenomenon! Perhaps it is one of the effects of the climate.

From its island body, Bombay radiates long tentacles of suburban squalor into the land. Mills and huge grey tenements, low huts along the palm-trees flank the outgoing roads for miles, and the roads themselves are thronged with the coming and going of innumerable passengers. Driving out of Bombay along one of these populous highways, I felt (but more acutely) that amazement which often overwhelms me when I pass through the sordid fringes of some European city—amazement at my own safety and comfort, at the security of my privileges, at the unthinking and almost un-resentful acceptance by millions of my less fortunate fellow-beings of my claim to be educated, leisured, comparatively wealthy. That I and my privileged fellows should be tolerated by our own people seems to me strange enough. But that our pretensions, which are still higher in India than in Europe, should be allowed by these innumerable dar‍ skinned strangers, over whom we rule, strikes me as being still more extraordinary.

The Story of the Freedom Struggle

On 28 December 1885, Gokul Das Tejpal Sanskrit College in south Bombay played host to the first meeting of the Indian National Congress, an organization founded with the aim of obtaining a greater share in government for educated Indians. For many Indian children, Amar Chitra Katha's panels are the most vivid recounting of that moment the sun began to set on the British empire.

—Eds

VASUDEO BALWANT PHADKE STOOD LIKE A ROCK UNTIL THE JUDGEMENT WAS DELIVERED.

THE SENTENCE I PASS UPON YOU IS TRANSPORTATION FOR LIFE.

LATER WHEN HE WAS ALONE—

OH, MY COUNTRYMEN, YOU HAVE NOT DERIVED ANY BENEFIT FROM ME. I COULD NOT ACCOMPLISH MY TASK. PLEASE PARDON ME FOR MY FAILURES.

VASUDEO PHADKE WAS SENT TO JAIL IN ADEN, A BRITISH COLONY, IN THE MIDDLE EAST.

HE ESCAPED FROM THE JAIL ONLY TO BE CAPTURED AGAIN AND DETAINED TILL HIS DEATH ON FEBRUARY 17, 1883.*

ENLIGHTENED BRITISH OFFICIALS WHO WISHED US WELL WERE EQUALLY CONCERNED.

WHAT IF THE GROWING BAND OF EDUCATED INDIAN YOUTH JOINS HANDS WITH THE REBELS?

THEY WILL, UNLESS THEY ARE PROVIDED WITH A SAFETY-VALVE. A SAFE OUTLET FOR THEIR GROWING DISCONTENT.

ALLAN OCTAVIAN HUME, A SENIOR CIVIL SERVANT ABOUT TO RETIRE FROM THE SERVICE, CAME FORTH WITH A SOLUTION.

WHAT IS NEEDED IS AN ORGANIZATION TO PERFORM WHAT HER MAJESTY'S OPPOSITION DOES IN ENGLAND— POINT OUT TO THE GOVERNMENT ITS DEFECTS AND SUGGEST RIGHT ACTIONS.

WE DID HAVE SEVERAL ORGANIZATIONS AND NATIONALIST NEWSPAPERS, ALL STRIVING TO CREATE A NATIONAL AWARENESS. BUT—

NONE OF THESE STAND A CHANCE. THE GOVERNMENT WILL NOT ALLOW THEM TO GROW.

* TODAY AT SHIRDON, HIS BIRTHPLACE, STANDS A MEMORIAL PILLAR WITH A FLAME BURNING ATOP.

UNDER TILAK'S LEADERSHIP, OUR FARMERS REFUSED TO PAY LAND REVENUE AND DEMANDED WORK AND FOOD FROM THE GOVERNMENT. HE INITIATED THE CELEBRATION OF SHIVAJI JAYANTI. HE USED THIS AND THE GANAPATI FESTIVAL TO INCULCATE NATIONALISM IN US AND TO INFUSE US WITH THE COURAGE TO FIGHT FOR OUR RIGHTS.

SHIVAJI LOVED HIS COUNTRY. HE VALUED FREEDOM.

EVEN WHEN HE WAS ARRESTED ON CHARGES OF SEDITION, TILAK REFUSED TO APOLOGIZE FOR HIS WRITINGS IN THE KESARI * AND WILLINGLY WENT TO PRISON.

MY POSITION AMONG THE PEOPLE DEPENDS ENTIRELY UPON MY CHARACTER; AND IF I AM COWED DOWN BY PERSECUTION, I THINK LIVING IN MAHARASHTRA IS AS GOOD AS LIVING IN THE ANDAMANS+.

IN BENGAL, THE TORCH OF NATIONALISM WAS HELD BY SURENDRANATH BANERJI, BIPIN CHANDRA PAL, AUROBINDO GHOSH AND OTHERS. IN PUNJAB, LALA LAJPAT RAI BREATHED FIRE AGAINST BRITISH RULE. AND, WITH THE DAWN OF THE 20TH CENTURY, A NEW FORCE EMERGED IN THE COUNTRY.

"OUR EYES HAVE BEEN TURNED AWAY FROM THE GOVERNMENT; AWAY FROM THE HOUSES OF PARLIAMENT... AND OUR FACES HAVE TURNED NOW TO THE STARVING, THE NAKED, THE PATIENT AND LONG-SUFFERING 200 MILLIONS OF INDIAN PEOPLE, AND IN IT WE SEE A NEW POTENCY... AND IN THE TEEMING, TOILING, STARVING AND NAKED POPULATIONS OF INDIA, WE FIND POSSIBILITIES, POTENTIALITIES... WITH THE DECADENCE OF OUR FAITH IN THE FOREIGN GOVERNMENT AND IN THE FOREIGN NATION, HAS GROWN UP THIS HIGHER, THIS DEARER, THIS DEEPER, THIS MORE VITAL AND MORE DIVINE FAITH IN INDIAN HUMANITY".

IT WAS THIS NEW SPIRIT WHICH INSPIRED OUR STRUGGLE FOR FREEDOM IN THE YEARS THAT FOLLOWED.

* A NEWSPAPER FOUNDED AND OWNED BY HIM. + PENAL COLONY DURING THE BRITISH RULE.

First Ladies and Inferior Women

Gillian Tindall

The only woman associated with eighteenth-century Bombay whose name has been known to future generations was Eliza Draper. She it was who eloped, on the night of 14-15 January 1773, down a rope ladder into a boat from the Belvedere House on Mazagaon Hill; a sentimental cult grew up later about her fragile ghost, which was said to haunt the place. She was born in 1744 at Anjengo, 600 miles south of Bombay, where the Company had a small factory. She was sent to England to gain the kind of education that fitted a girl only for attracting a husband who would provide her with 'an Establishment'. She was returned to India at fourteen, and six months later docilely married Daniel Draper, an East India Company servant, twenty years older than herself. He had then been newly appointed Secretary of the Council, the job that Cleland had once held, and later became Accountant General. He is said to have been a 'noble and good-humoured man', but no doubt he and Eliza had little in common: she complained to a friend that 'our minds are not pair'd'. Two children were born, in 1759 and 1761. Eliza travelled back to England to be with them in 1765 to leave them there, in the British-India tradition which was already becoming established, and, while there, seems to have been ill: perhaps it was the thought of a return to Bombay alone. She was taken about in society, was flattered and called 'the Brahmine' and *la belle indienne* by the writer Sterne, among other people, who was himself more than old enough to have known better. She took seriously his suggestions that she had the makings of a literary lady

From *City of Gold* (1992).

a la Mrs Montagu and the Blue Stockings; in fact those of her letters which have survived show little trace of intellect or wit. One must suppose that she was pretty, in an oval-faced eighteenth-century way, and she is said to have played and sung charmingly. At all events, when she returned to Bombay, which was then admittedly provincial to the point of brutality, she found there 'a Dearth of everything which could charm the Heart—please the Fancy, or speak to Judgement'. More Madame Bovary really than Mrs Montagu, she solved her *ennui* by the drastic expedient of an elopement: it should be said that Daniel Draper, with whom she had ceased to share a bed, was by then carrying on an open affair with a maid. To a woman friend the day before, she wrote: 'My heart is full. The next 24 hours will, in all probability, either destine me to the grave or to a life of reproach . . . I had deserved a better, if chance but not counteracted the good propensities assigned to me by nature.' To her husband she wrote: 'I go, I know not wither, but I will never be a tax on you, Draper . . . I am not a hardened or depraved creature—I never will be so.' She added, in apparently unconscious bathos, 'The enclosed are the only bills owing that I know of, except about six rupees to Doogee, the shoe-maker. I have never meant to load myself with many spoils of your prejudice, but a moderate provision of linen has obliged me to secure part of what was mine, to obviate some very mortifying difficulties.'

The most incidental role of abducting lover in this carefully orchestrated drama was played by a Sir John Clark of the Navy; he was then in command of a frigate in Bombay and so was conveniently placed for carrying Eliza off by water. The liaison does not seem to have lasted much longer than the immediate need for it. Eliza sought refuge for a while at Rajahmandry with a 'kind uncle' called Tom Whitehall, relative of the Whitehall of Bombay who had sold the Company the property that became Government House in the Fort. Tom Whitehall may well have looked indulgently upon Eliza, for he himself was the father of many mixed-race children, but naturally the double standard applied in Anglo-India as in England. She later returned to England where, as Sterne had published his *Journal to Eliza*, she once again aroused a certain amount of flattering curiosity. From then on she seems to have declined, via a further self-conscious relationship with another old literary lion, the Abbe Raynal, and a less platonic affair with John Wilkes, the political pamphleteer, into relative obscurity and poverty; she died in Bristol at the age of thirty-five.

Her pathetic story is significant, not for the legend that accrued around it in nineteenth-century Bombay, but for the incidental light it throws on the East India life of the time. Eliza's flagrant behaviour made her an exotic oddity, but for Englishmen in India throughout the eighteenth century and into the nineteenth, unsanctified liaisons were the rule rather than the exception; the bibi-khana, the 'lady-house' in a corner of the compound, separate both from the main house and from the servant's quarters, was an accepted feature of many a European bungalow. It was inevitable: as late as 1800, European men outnumbered their female counterparts in Bombay by three to one, and many of those men would have spent virtually their whole adult lives in India. George Dick, for instance, who was the Governor of Bombay between 1793 and 1795, and whose memorial tablet is in St. Thomas's Church, came out as a writer for the Company in 1759 and remained in Bombay almost uninterruptedly until his death in 1818. What the tablet does not record is that for many years he kept a Mahratta woman openly in considerable state. Not till after 1806, when both the pay and the qualities required of a civil servant had been upgraded, and Company servants in Bombay were no longer allowed to trade on their own account, did society begin to be both more compartmentalized and more respectable; even so, there must have lingered in Bombay for many years longer old India hands who regretted the passing of the good-bad old days, the hubble-bubble and the bibi, the afternoon siesta, and the nights spent in drinking and cards.

Naturally all this unofficial activity left its result, in the form of a growing race of Eurasians. These, in Bombay, merged to some extent with the local Portuguese, themselves of mixed race, but they were not really acceptable to either the native community or the European, and became less so with time, as the image of the British as a separate ruling caste began to take shape. Ironically, the rise in standards of probity expected from the British, led initially to *less* real fairness and participation between different races. After 1791 Eurasians were no longer appointed to the Company's Civil, Military or Marine service, though those who were already there could stay. Colonel Skinner, born 1778, was the son of a British officer and a Rajput lady. In 1803 his mixed blood caused his dismissal, for a while, from the Company's Army, but he went on to found Skinner's Horse which was to become the crack cavalry regiment in India. He was a distinguished scholar and ended his career as a Companion of the Bath, though he in turn married an Indian lady and their large family were said to be 'quite black'. Charles Forjett, born in Madras about 1810, whose origins are obscure but who rose to become Chief of Police in Bombay in the 1850s and finally municipal commissioner, must have been a Eurasian, though by the mid-nineteenth century such a fact was no longer so freely mentioned: oblique references are made instead to his 'sun-burnt skin', his capacity to disguise himself as a native (very useful for gathering information) and his 'proficiency in the native tongues'. Forjett, nevertheless, after a lifetime in India elected to retire to England, where he built himself a large house at Hughenden in damp, green Buckinghamshire, perversely named Cowasji Jehangir hall after a prominent Parsi.

The fact that even these outstanding men suffered slights during their careers shows how unenviable was the position of the less gifted and socially prominent Eurasians, particularly as they were often illegitimate as well. Sons were sent to England to acquire the education of English gentlemen, but this, when unsupported by the appearance or the means, did them little good back in India once Company service above the level of clerk was denied to them. Half-caste daughters received, in theory, even fewer benefits, but with the prevailing wife-shortage many of them must, in practice, have managed to land English husbands and thus 'pass', at any rate in Bombay's rather mixed society. Others, at a lower social level, were the progeny of loose Indian women and common soldiers or seamen, and presumably many of these disappeared in turn into the developing red-light district of the native town. The vulnerability of such women, adrift in an Indian society which then, as now, provided security only within a close family and caste structure, is poignantly conveyed by a tombstone which stood for many years in Sonapur burial ground. It was that of

Captain Thomas Samuel Tydd of the Company's Army, who died, so the stone informed, in 1797, at the age of thirty-seven, after twenty years' service with the Company during which he had twice been wounded: 'He has left an infant daughter unprovided and her unhappy mother who had been cherished for some years by his bounty.' It seems an unusual message to put on a tomb, but perhaps the friend who paid for its erection was trying by these means to shame Captain Tydd's other acquaintances into 'doing something' for the girl and her child.

Gradually, with the decline of piracy and the improvement of ships, the number of women prepared to venture out from England increased. However, the route was still the long one round the Cape and was hardly undertaken lightly. Each passenger embarking on the six- or seven-month adventure was advised to bring for the voyage 'a sofa, with mattress, a pillow and a chinz covering for the day-time, a Hanging Lamp, a looking glass with sliding cover, swing tray, a chest of drawers in 2 pieces, a foul-clothes Bag, an oil cloth or carpet (this merely for the sake of Appearances), a bucket and rope for drawing salt water'—salt water was used for washing the person and the clothes, since fresh water was strictly rationed. In addition, it was suggested that a lady should bring hair powder, 'papillate paper', hartshorn, aromatic vinegar, aperients and cologne water.

Some of the women who ventured out complete with aperients, cologne and sofa did not live long to enjoy their destination. Elizabeth Rivett, a well-known beauty who was painted by Sir Joshua Reynolds and came out to India to marry the elderly General John Carnac, died in Bombay in 1780 at only twenty-eight; she is buried under the floor of the Church, and her brother, who added the Carnac name and monies to his own and fathered a future Governor of Bombay, is buried near her. Four years after Elizabeth Rivett's death a pretty twenty-three-year-old girl called Charlotte, niece of General John Bellasis whose name is remembered in Bellasis Road in Bombay, sailed there already engaged to marry Daniel Christie of the Bombay Engineers. (Mrs Bellasis herself had sailed out in the same way to marry her John a decade previously.) Charlotte's wedding was promptly celebrated, but she died two months later; a cart drawn by white oxen carried her body to the sad city of gold at Sonapur and the doctor who had attended her wrote an elegy to her in thirty-one verses. It is not necessarily true that in times or places where death is commonplace people become hardened to it.

Not all the women who came out to Bombay were already engaged. Charlotte's brother Joseph, who came out the following year, married a girl he probably met during the voyage. A Bellasis brother, George, married a girl who was one of seven good-looking but penniless sisters: these sisters came out to Bombay in turn to try their luck. The unwise exploits of one of his sisters-in-law compromised George Bellasis into fighting a duel with a young relative of Charles Forbes. He narrowly escaped with his life on the subsequent murder charge. It seems clear that by that date the old idea of women coming out to India expressly to seek husbands had been revived in an unofficial way, and for the whole of the nineteenth century it was to flourish under a thin veil of gentility that deceived no one. Not for another forty years, by which time the steamship route made matters so much easier, was Thomas Hood to write his satirical poem *Going to Bombay,* but there is a telling passage in an early work by Jane Austen, *Catherine, or the Bower* (c.1790) in which a penniless girl is 'obliged to accept the offer of one of her cousins to equip her for the East Indies'. Like Eliza Draper, she there marries a rich man twice her age, which one of her friends comments is 'no hardship'. Another, however, sees the matter differently:

'. . . to a girl of any Delicacy, the voyage itself, since the object of it is so universally known, is a punishment that needs no other to make it very severe.'

'I do not see that at all. She is not the first girl who has gone to the East Indies for a Husband, and I declare I should think it very good fun if I were poor.'

A Little Paperwork

V.S. Naipaul

It is 1964, and V.S. Naipaul arrives in India and confronts Bombay's bureaucracy in order to recover a couple of bottles of alcohol with which he sought to defy the Prohibition imposed on the state. In a similar situation, do not try his solution yourself.

—Eds

To be in Bombay was to be exhausted. The moist heat sapped energy and will, and some days passed before I decided to recover my bottles. I decided in the morning; I started in the afternoon. I stood in the shade of Churchgate Station and debated whether I had it in me to cross the exposed street to the Tourist Office. Debate languished into daydream; it was minutes before I made the crossing. A flight of steps remained. I sat below a fan and rested. A lure greater than a liquor permit roused me: the office upstairs was air-conditioned. There India was an ordered, even luxurious country. The design was contemporary; the walls were hung with maps and coloured photographs; and there were little wooden racks of leaflets and booklets. Too soon my turn came, my idleness was over. I filled in my form.

The clerk filed in his, three to my one, made entries in various ledgers and presented me with a sheaf of foolscap papers: my liquor permit. He had been prompt and courteous. I thanked him. There was no need, he said: it was only a little paperwork.

One step a day: this was my rule. And it was not until the following afternoon that I took a taxi back to the docks. The customs officers in white and the degraded men in blue were surprised to see me.

'Did you leave something here?'

'I left two bottles of liquor.'

From *An Area of Darkness* (1964).

'You didn't. We seized two bottles from you. They were sealed in your presence.'

'That's what I meant. I've come to get them back.'

'But we don't keep seized liquor here. Everything we seize and seal is sent off at once to the New Customs House.'

My taxi was searched on the way out.

The New Customs House was a large, two-storeyed PWD building, governmentally gloomy, and it was as thronged as a courthouse. There were people in the drive, in the galleries, on the steps, in the corridors. 'Liquor, liquor,' I said, and was led from office to office, each full of shrunken, bespectacled young men in white shirts sitting at desks shaggily stacked with paper.

Someone sent me upstairs. On landing, I came upon a barefooted group seated on the stone floor. At first I thought they were playing cards; it was a popular Bombay pavement pastime. But they were sorting parcels. Their spokesman told me I had been misdirected; I needed the building at the back.

This building, from the quantity of ragged clothing seen in one of the lower rooms, appeared to be a tenement; and then, from the number of broken chairs and dusty pieces of useless furniture seen in another room, appeared to be a junkshop. But it was the place for unclaimed baggage and was therefore the place I wanted. Upstairs I stood in a slow queue, at the end of which I discovered only an accountant.

'You don't want me. You want the officer in the white pants. Over there. He is a nice fellow.'

I went to him.

'You have your liquor permit?'

I showed him the stamped and signed foolscap sheaf.

'You have your transport permit?'

It was the first I had heard of this permit.

'You must have a transport permit.'

I was exhausted, sweating, and when I opened my mouth to speak I found I was on the verge of tears. 'But they *told* me.'

He was sympathetic. 'We have told them many times.'

I thrust all the papers I had at him, my liquor permit, my customs receipt, my passport, my receipt for wharfage charges, my Tourist Introduction Card.

Dutifully he looked through what I offered. 'No, I would have known at once whether you had a transport permit. By the colour of the paper. A sort of buff.'

'But what is a transport permit? Why didn't they give it to me? Why do I need one?'

'I must have it before I can surrender anything.'

'Please.'

'Sorry.'

'I am going to write to the papers about this.'

'I wish you would. I keep telling them they must tell people about this transport permit. Not only for you. We had an American here yesterday who said he was going to break the bottle as soon as he got it.'

'Help me. Where can I get this transport permit?'

'The people who gave the receipt should also give you the transport permit.'

'But I've just come from them.'

'I don't know. We keep on telling them.'

'Back to the Old Customs,' I said to the taxi-driver.

This time the police at the gates recognized us and didn't reach the car. This dock has been my own gateway to India. Only a few days before everything in it had been new; the sticky black asphalt, the money-changers booths, the stalls, the people in white, khaki or blue; everything had been studied for what it portended of India beyond the gates. Now already I ceased to see or care. My stupor, though, was tempered by the thought of the small triumph that awaited me: I had trapped those customs officers in white and that degraded man in blue.

They didn't look trapped.

'Transport permit?' one said. 'Are you sure?'

'Did you tell them you are leaving Bombay?' asked a second.

'*Transport* permit?' said a third and, walking away to a fourth asked,

'Transport permit, ever hear of *transport* permit?'

He had. 'They've been writing to us about it.'

A transport permit was required to transport liquor from the customs to a hotel or house.

'Please give me a transport permit.'

'We don't issue transport permits. You have to go—' He looked up at me and his manner softened. 'Here, let me write it down for you. And look, I will also give you your code-number. That will help them out at the New Customs.'

The taxi-driver had so far been calm; and it seemed now that my journey had fallen into a pattern that was familiar to him. I began to read out the address that had been given me. He cut me short and without another word buzzed through the thickening afternoon traffic to a large brick building hung with black-and-white government boards.

'You go,' he said sympathetically, 'I wait.'

Outside every office there was a little crowd.

'Transport permit, transport permit.'

Some Sikhs directed me round to the back to a low shed next to a gate marked *Prohibited Area*, out of which workers came, one after the other, raising their hands while armed soldiers frisked them.

'Transport permit, transport permit.'

I entered a long corridor and found myself among some Sikhs. They were lorry-drivers.

'Liquor permit, Liquor permit.'

And at last I reached the office. It was a long low room at ground level, hidden from the scorching sun and as dark as a London basement, but warm and dusty with the smell of old paper, which was everywhere, on shelves rising to the grey ceiling, on desks, on chairs, in the hands of clerks, in the hands of khaki-clad messengers. Folders had grown dog-eared, their colours faded, their spines abraded to transparency, their edges limp with reverential handling; and to many were attached pink slips, equally faded, equally limp, marked URGENT, VERY URGENT, or IMMEDIATE. Between these mounds and columns and buttresses of paper, clerks were scattered about unimportantly, men and women, mild-featured, Indian-pallid, high-shouldered; paper was their perfect camouflage. An elderly bespectacled man sat at a desk in one corner, his face slightly puffy and dyspeptic. Tremulous control of the paper-filled room was his; at his disappearance the clerks might be altogether overwhelmed.

'Transport permit?'

He looked up slowly. He showed no surprise, no displeasure at being disturbed. Papers, pink-slipped were spread all over his desk. A table fan, nicely poised, blew over them without disturbance.

'Transport permit.' He spoke the words mildly, as though they were words but words which, after searching for only a second in the files of his mind, he had traced. 'Write an application. Only one is necessary.'

'Do you have the form?'

'No forms have been issued. Write a letter. Here, have a sheet of paper. Sit down and write. To the Collector, Excise and Prohibition, Bombay. Do you have your passport? Put down the number. Oh, and you have a Tourist Introduction Card. Put down that number too, I will expedite matters.'

And while I wrote, noting down the number of my Tourist Introduction Card, TIO (L), 156, he, expediting matters, passed my documents over to a woman clerk, saying, 'Miss Desai, could you start making out a transport permit?'

I thought I detected an odd pride in his voice. He was like a man still after many years discovering the richness and variety of his work and subduing an excitement which he nevertheless wished to communicate to his subordinates.

I was finding it hard to spell and to frame simple sentences. I crumpled up the sheet of paper.

The head clerk looked up to me in gentle reproof. 'Only one application is necessary.'

At my desk Miss Desai filled the forms with that blunt, indelible, illegible pencil which government offices throughout the former Empire use, less for the sake of what is written than for the sake of the copies required.

I managed to complete my application.

And at this point my companion slumped forward on her chair, hung her head between her knees and fainted.

'Water,' I said to Miss Desai.

She barely paused in her writing and pointed to an empty dusty glass on a shelf.

The head clerk, already frowningly preoccupied with other papers, regarded the figure slumped in front of him.

'Not feeling well?' His voice was as mild and even as before. 'Let her rest.' He turned the table fan away from him.

'Where is the water?'

Giggles came from women clerks, hidden behind paper.

'Water!' I cried to the male clerk.

He rose, saying nothing, walked to the end of the room and vanished.

Miss Desai finished her writing. Giving me a glance as of terror, she brought her tall bloated pad to the head clerk.

'The transport permit is ready,' he said. 'As soon as you are free to sign for it.'

The male clerk returned, waterless, and sat down at his desk.

'Where is the water?'

His eyes distastefully acknowledge my impatience. He neither shrugged nor spoke; he went on with his papers. It was worse than impatience. It was ill-breeding and ingratitude. For presently, sporting his uniform as proudly as any officer, a messenger appeared. He carried a tray and on the tray stood a glass of water. I should have known better. A clerk was a clerk; a messenger was a messenger.

The crisis passed.

I signed three times and received my permit.

The head clerk opened another folder.

'Nadkarni,' he called softly to a clerk. 'I don't understand this memo.'

I had been forgotten already.

It was suffocatingly hot in the taxi, the seats scorching. We drove to the flat of a friend and stayed there until it was dark.

A friend of our friend came in.

'What's wrong?'

'We went to get a transport permit and she fainted.' I did not wish to sound critical. I added, 'Perhaps it's the heat.'

'It isn't the heat at all. Always the heat or the water with you people from outside. There's nothing wrong with her. You make up your minds about India before coming to the country. You've been reading the wrong books.'

The officer who had sent me on the track of the transport permit was pleased to see me back. But the transport permit wasn't enough. I had to go to Mr Kulkarni to find out about the warehouse charges. When I had settled what the charges were I was to come back to that clerk over there, with the blue shirt; then I had to go to the cashier, to pay the warehouse charges; then I had to go to Mr Kulkarni to get my bottles.

I couldn't find Mr Kulkarni. My papers were in my hand. Someone tried to take them. I knew he was expressing only his kindness and curiosity. I pulled the papers back. He looked at me; I looked at him. I yielded. He went through my papers and said with authority that I had come to the wrong building.

I screamed: '*Mr Kulkarni!*'

Everyone around me was startled. Someone came up to me, calmed me down and led me to the adjoining room where Mr Kulkarni had been all along. I rushed to the head of the queue and began to shout at Mr Kulkarni, waving my papers at him. He got hold of them as I waved and began to read. Some Sikhs in the queue complained. Mr Kulkarni replied that I was in a hurry, that I was a person of importance, and that in any case I was younger. Curiously, they were pacified.

Mr Kulkarni called for ledgers. They were brought to him. Turning the crisp pages, not looking up, he made loose-wristed gesture of indefinable elegance with his yellow pencil. The Sikhs at once separated into two broken lines. Mr Kulkarni put on his spectacles, studied the calendar on the far wall, counted on his fingers, took off his spectacles and returned to his ledgers. He made another abstracted gesture with his pencil and the Sikhs fell into line again, obscuring the calendar.

Upstairs again. The clerk with the blue shirt stamped on Mr

Kulkarni's sheet of paper and made entries in two ledgers. The cashier added his own stamp. I paid him and he made entries in two more ledgers.

'It's all right,' the officer said, scanning the twice-stamped and thrice-signed sheet of paper. He added his own signature. 'You're safe now. Go down to Kulkarni. And be quick. They might be closing any minute.'

Temples of Desire

Busybee (Behram Contractor)

Busybee a.k.a. Behram Contractor was a Bombay institution who wrote a column called 'Round and About'. Few other journalists could pull Bombay vignettes out of a hat with such regularity, and in a city where irregularity is the law and sophistication is the sine qua non *of survival, someone who writes every day and writes with a deliberate naivete was prized. A sampler of the Busybee style.*

—Eds

Excelsior may be old, very old, but the first movie house I remember having visited is Regal.

In those days the ushers used to wear black coats and looked like advocates at the Esplanade Court. These days they wear white jackets and look like waiters at Ambassador.

The picture, I think, was Jesse James with Tyrone Power (later there was *The Return of Frank James* with Henry Fonda). All I remember of it is Tyrone Power chasing a train on a horse.

There is also one other scene that I vaguely recall. The final scene, when he had retired from his bad old ways, winding a clock and shot down by a member of his gang. Somehow it always makes me think of Abraham Lincoln.

The other early cinema I remember is Edward. It is still there (at least it was there the last time I passed down Kalbadevi), tucked among second-hand book shops where you sometimes pick up bargains.

At Dhobi Talao, minus Metro and Liberty, there was the old Wellington. It had black curtains on the doors and ushers with torches in their hands.

From *Round and About*, a compilation of columns from the *Evening News* and the *Times Weekly* (1971).

The first picture I saw at Metro had something to do with Napoleon. Napoleon looked like a marble bust of the Napoleon we had at home.

Empire was the old Empire with the scent of the biryani from the adjoining Empire Restaurant wafting into the auditorium.

At Alexandra they used to run serials. There was one of Superman, in two parts, the first part ending with Superman plunging into the sea from the Brooklyn Bridge. (Will Superman survive? Come again next week.) I think he survived and went through twelve more reels the following week.

In Panchgani they used to have the tent in the summer. You sat on the grass and watched the Indian Tarzan swinging in the trees. (The following morning I borrowed all the Edgar Rice Burrough books from the library.)

A couple of years ago, when I was in Mysore, there was a cinema with a notice in the foyer saying 'Beware of Pick-Pockets.' I did not enjoy the picture as all the time I was worried about pick-pockets.

All of which makes me feel very old, as old as the Old Excelsior.

★

I think I saw *The Mighty Chang* at the old Excelsior that is being pulled down today.

A solid brown man with a single lock of hair on the top of his head, looking like the gentleman who keeps popping out of Aladdin's magic lamp.

There was a steel cable connecting the top of the balcony—the old balcony way up among the gods—to the stage and he swung himself across on his tiny pigtail.

I say I think I saw him because it was a long time ago and with age one often imagines things.

But I am definite about the *Marcus Show*. It was during the war years with the V for Victory signs plastered all over the town and Australian servicemen roaming about the streets.

There were three clowns and a gag about golf. Also a woman, dressed in black tights, swimming in a glass tank and looking like an octopus.

In those days when we were not bored with a lot of silly Russian and Czech films, a lot of George Raft films used to come to the Regal and Betty Grable to Eros. He was one of my favourites and I used to watch him sitting among the gods (it cost four annas then and it was a long climb to the balcony).

From above we used to throw things at the gentry sitting in the stalls.

There were a lot of pirate pictures, of Captain Hook and the Spanish Main (007 and the spy pictures had not come into fashion, though there was the Scarlet Pimpernel).

In later years, there was William Holden and *Picnic* (which I did not care for) and again William Holden and *The Bridge on the River Kwai* (which I saw twice, the second time in Baghdad where they yesterday shot a lot of army officers).

And now Excelsior is being pulled down and it may not be as regrettable as the pulling down of half the Tata Palace, but some things will be missed.

Things like scotch broth and Kobe steaks and a little place where you can sit in the afternoon and watch all the pretty girls in paper dresses.

Sitara: Dancing Tigress from Nepal

Saadat Hasan Manto

Manto's position as the chronicler of Partition is now canonical. But he was also capable of writing gossip and was a master of the innuendo. Even today, few film magazines would dare to note, as Manto does with calculated casualness, the manner in which K. Asif's pimples cleared up.

—Eds

As a writer, I have had to go through and overcome many difficulties but I have never felt more hesitant than I now do as I sit down to record my memories of the famous dancer and film star Sitara. To most, she was known as an actress who was a superb dancer, but I happened to have the opportunity to study her character, hence this piece. Sitara was a living case history and only a psychologist could writ-e about her as she deserved to be written about. Over the years, I have known and analysed many women but the more I learnt about her, the closer I came to the view that she was not a woman but a typhoon which did not blow in and out as typhoons do, but which retained its force and fury without showing any signs of weakening. She may have been a woman of average build but she was stronger than most people I have known. Had another woman suffered as many illnesses as she did, she could not have survived. Sitara was made of a different clay and was both brave and strong-minded. She never missed her morning dance exercises and spent at least an hour dancing as if there was no tomorrow.

From *Stars from Another Sky: The Bombay Film World of the 1940s* (1998).

Every morning, she would dance with bone-breaking vigour for an hour, but I never found her looking tired. She had amazing stamina and there was never a sign of fatigue on her face. She loved her art in the same total way as she loved her men. Even for an ordinary performance, she would rehearse for hours and give it everything she had. She always wanted to do new things. Her movements were swift and she was one of those restless people who cannot sit still even for a minute. She was always up and about.

She had two sisters named Tara and Alaknanda which made them into a female trinity. These three sisters were probably born in a Nepalese village and came to Bombay one by one to seek their fortune. Her sisters faded out long ago and there would be few who would even recall their names but in their time, they lived interesting lives. Tara had many affairs, including one with Shaukat Hashmi who was married to Purnima who later divorced him. Alaknanda passed through many hands and in the end settled down with the famous Prabhat Studio actor Balwant Singh. How long she lived with him, I do not know. Of the three sisters, only Sitara was able to make her mark. I hesitate to write about her because she was not one but several women and so many were the men with whom she had affairs that it would be impossible to deal with them all in one short piece.

Were the sisters to have a biographer, the book would run into thousands of pages. I have often been denounced as a writer of pornography. Those who do so never give me credit for refusing to write about smutty people, and God knows there are enough of them in this world. People in my view do smutty things either out of instinct or because of the surroundings in which they live. What comes instinctively to a human being can perhaps be kept under control if he tries, but if he is indifferent, then whom can he blame except himself?

Whenever I think of Sitara, I am reminded of a typical five-storey Bombay high-rise with many flats and rooms, all inhabited. It is a fact that she had the ability to be involved with many men at the same time. When she came to Bombay, she was with a gaunt-looking Gujarati film director whose name I do not recall but it was something Desai. They were probably married too. He was very good in his work but obstinate by nature, which earned him many rejections. I met him at a time when the Saroj Film Company was still in business but dying slowly. We became friends right away because he understood film-making and had a taste for literature. Sitara had just left him but he had few regrets because he told me that he did not have the ability to cope with a woman like her. She was then living with someone else but, off and on, she would come to see Desai. He would welcome her but never encourage her to stay long. There was no divorce under Hindu law. Desai and Sitara had had a Hindu marriage and despite her affairs with a succession of men, technically she remained Mrs Desai.

I am taking you back to the time when Mehboob's star was rising. He cast her in one of his movies and soon there was a roaring affair going on between the two of them. I won't write about it because only Ishrat Jahan known to movie-goers as Bibbo can do justice to this story. Mehboob was shooting outdoor in Hyderabad and despite his affair with Sitara, his routine was unchanged. He would offer his prayers with greatest devotion and make love to her with the same single-minded enthusiasm. Mehboob was completing a film at Film City Studio where P.N. Arora (later to make his mark as a producer) was the sound recordist. Fazal Bhai who was all-in-all at Film City had earlier sent Arora to England for training. The recording laboratory was under the overall charge of Seth Shiraz Ali. Mehboob was still carrying on with Sitara. But according to Diwan Singh Maftoon, editor of the famous journal *Riasat* she was also having it on the side with Arora. After the Mehboob movie was done, she moved in with Arora. Then there appeared on the scene the handsome Al-Nasir who had just arrived from Dehra Dun to become an actor. Because of his looks, he was given a role in a movie which also starred Sitara. It was only to be expected that he would get added to her list. In effect, besides Al-Nasir, she was maintaining relations with three other men all more or less simultaneously: her husband Desai, Arora and Mehboob.

Her fifth man was Nazir whose mistress, a Jewish actress by name of Yasmin, had recently left him. I don't know exactly how Nazir and Sitara met, but they instantaneously fell for each other. Nazir was a very forthcoming and open-hearted person. When we met, for instance, instead of shaking hands, he would shower me with the choicest abuse, his way of showing affection. He had a heart of gold and he was straight as an arrow. His affair with Sitara lasted for several years. Because of his strong personality, she temporarily gave up other men but it was not going to last because Sitara was not a one-man woman. Before long, she had fallen into her old ways with time for everybody: Arora, Al-Nasir, Mehboob and her husband. This was too much for a self-respecting man like Nazir who believed in maintaining a relationship faithfully, once it had been formed. Sitara was made of a different clay and even a man like Nazir could not keep her from hopping into bed with other men. His former mistress Yasmin was both very feminine and quite beautiful, but when she had told Nazir that she would like to settle down with a husband and a home, he whom many considered a hard man, had said to her in all sincerity that since they were not going to get married, she was free to marry whom she pleased. How that kind of a person could carry on with a woman like Sitara for so long always baffled me.

I first met Nazir at Hindustan Cinetone. It was a bad time for the movie industry. Many financiers had been bankrupted because of playing the stock market to make quick money. The original name of Cinetone used to be Saroj Film Company, and God knows what else before that. I had written a story called 'Keecha' which Seth Nanoobhai Desai had liked immensely. It is the sort of story which no producer would have been willing to film because of its theme which was sure to provoke the government's ire. Nanoobhai was a brave man and he had bought the story, but the project had remained incomplete because of other difficulties he had run into. I had specially written a character— that of a labourer—for Nazir which he had liked. On learning that Nanoobhai was unable to make that 'heretical' film, he had offered to buy the story and promised to film it no matter what it took.

Since Nanoobhai really liked the story, he had declined the offer. He had also in the meantime arranged the money, and the film, which was in the Gujarati language, had been completed and released, directed by Dad Gunjal. Nazir had been playing with the idea of forming a film company of his own for some time and being at a loose end since the end of his affair with Yasmin, he had concentrated on this project and managed to set one up. As far as I can remember, his first production was *Sandes*, followed by *Society* which starred Sitara. And that was when she had really got under his skin, though true to form, she had not stopped meeting her other lovers, especially P.N. Arora.

Here is an interesting story. After I left Bombay for a year to work for the All India Radio, Delhi, it was only natural that I would remain unaware of the gossip in Bombay. One day I ran into Arora on the street. He was walking with the help of a stick and his back was bent. He was always thin but he looked in extremely poor shape that day. I felt that he had difficulty even walking, as if there was no life left in him. I was in a tonga which I asked the driver to stop. Expressing surprise at his appearance, I asked him what was wrong. Almost out of breath with fatigue, he managed a faint smile and replied, 'Sitara . . . Manto, Sitara.'

Al-Nasir who lost his slim, upright and handsome figure after a few years, becoming fat and flabby, was a sensation when he came, with his fair, almost pink complexion, nurtured by the cool hill air of his native Dehra Dun. He was so good-looking that one could almost compare him to a beautiful woman. When I returned to Bombay from Delhi after receiving an offer from Shaukat Hussain Rizvi, I met him at Minerva Movietone. I just could not believe my eyes. His pink complexion had become ashen and his clothes hung loose on him. He seemed to have shrunk and all energy and strength appeared to have been squeezed out of him. 'My dear, what have you done to yourself?' I asked because I was worried about his health. He whispered the answer in my ear, 'Sitara . . . my dear, Sitara.'

Sitara was everywhere. I wondered if Sitara's only purpose in life was to infect men with pallor, from the England-trained Arora to the Dehra Dun-born Al-Nasir. So I took Al-Nasir aside and asked him to give me the lowdown on her. He said it was Sitara who had drained him out and he had come to a point where he knew that if he did not fight free of her and run, it would be the end of him. So one day, he had just hopped on a train bound for Dehra Dun where he spent three months in a sanatorium and recovered some of his strength. He said she had been writing him long letters in Hindi which he was unable to read, but added that he dreaded their arrival. He again whispered in my ear, 'Manto sahib, that woman . . . I tell you!'

Women like Sitara are rare, perhaps one in a million. She survived illnesses so dangerous that few other women could have scraped through them. She had determination and so formidable was her constitution that not once, but several times she successfully cheated death. Many thought that after such grave bouts with a host of ailments, she would lose her will and ability to dance, but they were wrong. She danced as she had always danced, in her later years as in her early youth, giving it everything she had. She would never miss her daily practice and she would have herself massaged every day. She always had two house servants, a man and a woman. The massage was always performed by the man. As for the woman, she invariably chose one who looked like an old-fashioned procuress.

Sitara was mostly to be seen in a fine muslin sari which left nothing to the imagination. It wasn't too pretty a sight. She never talked much but she had sharp eyes which noticed everything. When she was fifty-five, she had the agility of an eagle-eyed young woman. For a time she lived alone in Dadar's Khudadad Circle. Khudadad in Urdu means God-given and the truth is that her talent and her qualities were God-given. Nazir, who later got tied up with the actress Swarn Lata (whom he married), despite his tolerance and generosity, could only take so much of Sitara and no more. In the end, he gave up on her because she could never be satisfied with one man. I am told he had once stood in front of her with his hands joined together in supplication and begged her, 'Sitara, please let me go. I made a mistake and I am sorry for it and I want you to forgive me.'

Nazir used to rough up Sitara occasionally but she did not seem to mind. Perhaps she was one of those women who derive sexual pleasure from this sort of thing. There is an interesting sub-plot to the Sitara-Nazir affair. His nephew K. Asif (later he became a film-maker of note) was staying with his uncle when Sitara was living in the house. Asif was a big, strong man, still tender in years, who, as far as I know, had never known a woman in his life. He was keen on movies and curious to learn everything about them because he had ambition and he had come to know many film personalities, including actresses, since he had moved in with his uncle. He must also have witnessed what went on between Sitara and Nazir. A restless young man, he was raring to go and though Sitara may have appeared to him like a stone wall, she was the kind of wall which men like Asif would be challenged to scale.

Nazir's flat was off a courtyard in front of Ranjit Sudio. It had three rooms, one of which served as the office of his company, Hind Pictures. The place did not offer much by way of privacy, so it is to be assumed that young Asif must have witnessed, and certainly heard, what a man and woman do when they are alone. This must have been a new experience for someone whose knowledge of such things consisted of stories he had heard his married friends tell. His opportunity came one day when he actually saw 'action play' between his uncle and his mistress. It reminded him of a fight between two wild dogs who were trying to bite and tear each other apart as, frothing at the mouth, they carried on their savage encounter. A shiver ran down his spine. Man, he said to himself, was an animal, and love was a deadly encounter, but there was one difference. He wanted to be in just one such encounter himself. His body was young, sinewy and powerful, his blood warm; all he wanted was an opportunity to prove his manhood.

The talented but luckless Pakistani film director Nayyar was also living in Bombay in those days and staying with Nazir. He and Asif were the same age, both bachelors with wild and youthful fantasies. They would talk about women who were to be theirs in the future which stretched ahead. Whenever Sitara's name came up, they would tremble and feel transported to a world inhabited by demonic spirits. They did not know what a nymphomaniac was, nor could they have known that if, on the other hand, there were women like Sitara, the flip side of the coin was that there were others who were frigid like slabs of ice. They did not know then that Sitara was not faithful though she was Nazir's mistress. They did not know that she still made love to Arora, her husband Desai and Al-Nasir. But they did know why every other day there were scratch marks on Nazir's rhinoceros skin.

Sitara would be up at the crack of dawn and begin the day by dancing like a savage for an hour. Her drummer would get exhausted but not she. The earth would tremble under her feet as she completed her exercises. This was followed by an extended session with her masseur. Then she would bathe, put on fresh clothes and go to Nazir who would still be asleep. She would wake him up and make him drink a cup of milk or something else. That over, another dance would begin. Asif and Nayyar were aware of all this. They were still at an age when you look into empty rooms and peek through windows, when the slightest sounds makes you come to a standstill, when you try to read meanings into everything. Nayyar was slightly built compared to Asif and his sexual urges were also less headstrong than his friend's. Asif's body was full of the static of youth and raw passion which made him long to fell a woman like thunderbolt which falls on the earth's stony surface on a dark night.

Sitara would spend hours chatting to Asif. He felt less shy with her than when he had first come from Lahore, but he still could not muster the courage to touch her. He was terrified of his uncle's temper. However, there was one thing he was in no doubt about: Sitara was attracted to him. If he were to grab her wrist, she would come with him, no matter where he took her, even on a bed of stones on a dark, stormy night. Asif was restless. He did not want to wait. The two of them were like two trains which were programmed to collide headlong one day. This bothered him because he wanted the collision to take place today. He felt close to her but they were running on parallel tracks, near yet far. There was no physical contact. The two would talk as passengers riding on trains going in opposite directions do, only to move apart. Asif was waiting for that dark and stormy night when he would take the leap. Nazir in the meanwhile had become suspicious, and he was horrified. One day he screamed at Sitara and ordered her to pack up and leave. He also beat her up.

Sitara was after all a woman and after the violence and unpleasantness with Nazir, she did not have the strength to just walk out of the door. She wanted help but how could she ask for it? He was frothing at the mouth with anger because he knew what she was up to. That night he went into his office and slept here. Asif knew that his chance had arrived and he slipped into Sitara's room and rubbed her body where it hurt, then he helped her pack and took her to her Khudadad Circle flat in Dadar. Sitara thanked him for his kindness and encouraged by that, he took her hand and said, 'You don't have to thank me.' She did not try to free it and one thing led to another. And so it came to pass that young Asif joined the long line of men on whom she had cast her siren spell.

Sitara gave him the time of his life. Had it happened during the day, he would have surely seen stars in the sky, but it had taken place at night in the privacy of her flat at Khudadad Circle. Asif was smitten. 'Look,' he said to her, 'we should have a strong relationship, it is time you stopped going after other men. You should belong to just one man.' Sitara promised that she would not look at another man from that day on. Asif was happy and left as he was afraid his uncle might ask him where he had been. He promised to be back the next day. After he left, Sitara went to her dressing table, brushed her hair, put on a fresh sari, walked down to the street, hailed a taxi and gave the driver P.N. Arora's address.

Sitara hated my sight. I was editing the film weekly *Mussawar* in which I wrote a couple of satirical but amusing pieces about her. My column *Nit Nai* (the latest) and *Baal ki Khal* (splitting hair) were popular and always in good taste, but Sitara did not like what I had written; not that I cared because, frankly, there was nothing I wanted from her. It was also my effort, as far as possible, to keep well away from film personalities. When I wrote a rather naughtily embellished account of her quarrel with Nazir, she was besides herself with rage and was said to have abused me all day. When my spies gave me details of her affairs with Asif and I made indirect references to it in my column, she asked him to beat me, adding that if he didn't, she would hire someone to do it. She also asked him to have some other journalist attack me in his paper. Asif did nothing because he could take a joke; he just left Sitara to curse me to her heart's content.

Things between Asif and his uncle, meanwhile, had reached a rather delicate stage. Nazir was getting very, very suspicious about his nephew's movements. Asif was out of the house until the small hours and when he was asked where he had been, he would come up with one excuse or another. But excuses, no matter how good, run out in the end. Nazir had banished Sitara from his life and once his mind was made up, he never changed it. Sitara he did not give a damn about, but he was worried about his nephew whom he had brought all the way from Lahore so that he could make something of himself. He did not want him to fall into Sitara's clutches. He knew her well and he also knew that she fed on young men like Asif. She had a way with men. Most of the time, she did not even have to try; they just fell into her lap willingly and once there, found all escapes routes blocked.

Once a man caught Sitara's fancy, he had to be on call all hours of the day and night. Asif, therefore, had begun to be absent from home much of the time. Once or twice, Nazir asked him if it was Sitara who was the cause of his disappearances. 'Uncle, I can't even think of it,' Asif would say. Not that Nazir believed him. He was too old in tooth and claw not to know that this boy, his own nephew, was Sitara's latest acquisition. As for Asif, had it been a woman other than his uncle's former mistress, he would not have lied; but this was different. How could he tell his uncle that he was having an affair with his ex-mistress? Not only did Asif have no desire whatsoever to turn away from Sitara, he would not even have been able to, had he tried.

Nazir's anger was mounting, but slowly. He did not wish to act until he had caught the two in a compromising position himself. And one day, the opportunity came his way. I do not remember how Nazir caught Asif, but catch his nephew he did. Asif still swore that there was nothing between Sitara and him, but it was no use. Nazir's first impulse was to break every bone in their bodies, but thanks to the actor Majid (who came to Lahore after 1947), who was in his good books, he cooled down. Majid, on his own, had tried several times to warn Asif about Sitara and the dangerous game he was playing, but Asif was beyond advice. He was also foolish enough to believe that his affair with Sitara would remain a secret. Nazir may have had a temper but he was also a tender-hearted man. He had had a long physical relationship with Sitara. He did not want his nephew to fall in her hands because he knew it would do him no good. Even if Asif had not been his nephew, he would still have given the young man the same advice. Nazir, a man of great sincerity—although he gave the impression of being hard—was not happy with what he had done, rather not done. And he was nobody's fool; he was perceptive, and, what was more, he knew Sitara as few men knew her.

Asif began to get home earlier so as not to provoke his uncle's ire. Once he would leave, Sitara would make up her face, change and hop into a taxi to spend the rest of the night with Arora on whom the potions of Delhi's herbal medical miracle-makers had had a salutary effect. He had regained some of his old vigour and he no longer had the hollow-cheeked look. She had not given up her other old flames either. They—Al-Nasir, Mehboob and God alone knows how many others—remained on her 'active list'. Asif had reduced his visits because of his uncle, but he had not eliminated them. And how could he, even if he tried. Sitara was like a sorceress of old who turn their loves into life and stick them on the wall. In fairy tales, it always required a prince bearing a special amulet to break the spell and release the sorceress's prisoners. Was a prince going to come to Asif's rescue, because he was bewitched by one on whom even the most potent black magic could not have much effect? She was a fort that could not be stormed; so Asif continued to see Sitara and his relationship with his uncle kept worsening. By the way, after Nazir threw out Sitara, the famous musician Rafiq Ghaznavi had tried to make peace between them but without success. Once he invited Sitara, Arora and Nazir to his flat for drinks but despite his best efforts—he was a most persuasive conversationalist—he could not manage to change Nazir's mind. In the end, everybody left and Sitara spent the night with Rafiq, who kept assuring her that her time with Nazir was a thing of the past and she should accept it. That was the beginning and the end of his peace mission. It was also the first and last night she spent with Rafiq. One should wonder why. Was it that he had found her to be less than a perfect dancer and she had discovered that he was not the musician he fancied himself to be?

Sitara was perhaps the first woman in Asif's life and she had taken a shine to him. Nazir unfortunately caught them *flagrante delicto* one more time, but I do not know who got Asif off the hook this time. Some days later, I heard that Asif had disappeared from Bombay. Then I was told that Sitara was not to be seen anywhere either. When people asked, they were told that she had gone to a Hindu shrine. Had it been the annual Haj pilgrimage season, some wags would have quipped that Asif had gone to the holy land, but it wasn't. Then news came that both of them were in Delhi, were married and further, that Sitara had become a Muslim and taken the name of Allah Rakhi. One can imagine the effect it must have had on Nazir. Under Hindu personal law, there is no divorce. Once a woman is married, she is married for life. She can have a hundred men but she will remain the wife of the man to whom she first got married. Even if a Hindu woman changes her religion, she remains married to her original husband. From that point of view, Sitara may have become Begum K. Asif, but for all intents and purposes, she was still Mrs Desai.

Once the story was confirmed, I had a field day with it in my *Mussawar* columns. Every week, I would write about the newly-married couple in a cutting manner. When the two returned to Bombay after their honeymoon, Nazir was so embarrassed and angry that it is not possible to describe it in words. One day at the races I found Asif in a shark-skin suit with his arm around Sitara's waist. When he saw me, he smiled, then began to laugh. He shook my hand and said, 'Brilliant, the columns you are writing are most amusing, by God I say.' Sitara made a face and stood aside, but Asif paid no attention to her and kept talking to me for quite some time. He may have had little education but he had the ability to take a joke. In Bombay, word down the bazaar grapevine was that someone called Asif had married Sitara. In Bhindi Bazaar and Mohammad Ali Road, traditionally Bombay's Muslim-dominated localities, men would sit in Iranian cafes sipping and express satisfaction over the fact that a Muslim had married a Hindu and converted her to Islam. Most of these devout Muslims often happened to be ardent supporters of the All India Muslim League. Some would say that Asif should not allow this *sali* to appear in movies, others would say there was nothing wrong with it, as long as she observed purdah when she left home. Some cynics would declare, 'It is all a stunt.' Once I asked Asif if he had really married Sitara in a Muslim ceremony. 'What ceremony, what marriage!' he answered. Only God knows what the truth was.

Asif had no place of his own, so he was living in her flat and driving her around in her car. In Delhi, Asif had met a financier, Lala Jagat Narayan, and talked him into investing in a movie he wanted to make. He must also have taken an advance because he did not appear to be hard-pressed for funds. Asif had a lot of self-confidence and could get the better of even famous directors and writers. He had great native intelligence, and plenty of horse sense. When he became a director, he did not confine himself to the advice of a small coterie, as so often happens, but invited a cross-section of people to advise him, never hesitating to accept a good suggestion or idea.

I am reminded of a story which involves me. When Asif was making *Phool* and I was living in a flat on Claire Road, one day I heard persistent honking on the street. I came out on the balcony and found a huge car parked in front of my building. I had a first-floor flat and I bent over to see who the occupant was. It was Asif who stuck his head out of the car window and smiled. 'Come in,' I said. He opened the car door, said something to Sitara who was in the back seat and replied, 'In a minute.' The car drove off and a minute later, Asif walked in. He shook hands warmly and said, 'I want to read you my story.' 'I charge a fee as you know,' I said jokingly. Without another word, Asif walked out. I called after him and even ran out to the street but he would not return. All he said was he would come back when he had my fee. I felt ashamed of my bad joke, though I had been quite sure that he would take it in the spirit in which I had made it. When I told my wife what happened, she said it was silly of me to have said what I had. Asif, after all, was not a close friend and it was understandable that he had reacted the way he did.

Of course, I had not the least intention of injuring his feelings for expecting him to give me money. On the other hand, I really wanted him to narrate the story of his yet-to-be-made film to me. There were so many third-class directors in Bombay who had asked me to listen to their stories not once but twice and even thrice because they wanted my opinion. I had never asked them for money. I regretted having upset Asif. One day, there was a knock at the door. I opened it and found a man with an envelope which he gave to me and left. I had not even opened it when I heard a car honk on the road. It was Sitara's car. The envelope contained 500 rupees and a one-line note, 'Here's the fee. I will come tomorrow.' I was floored. Next day, Asif appeared at nine. 'Well doctor, have you received your fee?' he asked. I was speechless but I apologized and tried to return the money, but he would not take it. He sank into the sofa and said, 'Manto sahib, what are you thinking? This money is not mine, nor my father's, but the producer's. It was my mistake that I arrived without a fee because I wasn't thinking. I do not believe in getting things done free. You are going to waste your time, so it is only right that you should be paid for it. By God, that is what I believe. But let's forget about this nonsense and let me tell you the story.'

Without giving me an opportunity to answer, he sat down in a sofa and I took a chair facing him. I had never heard him tell a story and it was quite an experience. He rolled up the sleeves of his silk shirt, loosened his belt, pulled up his legs and assumed the classic posture of a yogi. 'Now listen to the story. It is called *Phool*. What do you think of the name?' 'It is good,' I replied. 'Thank you, I will narrate it scene by scene,' he said. Then he began to speak in his typical manner. I do not know who the author was but Asif was playing all the characters, raising his voice, moving around all the time. Now he would be on the sofa, the next minute his back would be against the wall, then he would push his legs against it and his upper torso would be on the floor. At times, he would jump from the sofa on to the floor, only to climb onto a chair the next minute. Then he would stand up straight looking like a leader asking for votes in an election. It was a long story, like the intestine of the devil, as the expression goes. After he finished his narration, we were silent for a few moments. 'What do you think about it?' Asif asked. 'It is trash,' I replied. Asif bit his lips, sat upright on the sofa and asked furiously, 'What did you say?' Had it been somebody else, he might have flinched, but I am not made that way. 'It is trash,' I repeated.

Asif tried his various conjurer's tricks to impress me but they had no effect on me. Also, I simply have no patience with loudness, which was one of Asif's characteristics. Finally, I decided to give it to him. 'Look here, Asif, I suggest you get hold of a big, heavy stone, place it on top of my head and hit that stone with a hammer, once, twice, thrice, and as long as you like. And by God, I swear I would still say that your story is trash.' Asif stood up, took my hand in both of his and said, 'By God, it is trash. I had only come to hear you say that.' I first thought he was joking but he was serious, so we sat down and began to think of improvements.

Asif and Sitara stayed married for quite some time, which reminds me of another story which predates my friendship with Asif and his relationship with Sitara. Asif had pimples on his face, which was associated with adolescence. I used to think that if youth was so ugly and painful, then may it please God not to bless anyone with youth. (I am thankful to the Almighty that he has never conferred such youth on me.) I used to dabble in herbal medicine and I wanted to do something for Asif's appearance. I also consulted a couple of doctor friends and one day I brought a handful of medicines for him, but they did him no good. But when Sitara came into his life, every pimple on his face disappeared.

Kamal Amrohi and I used to be colleagues at Bombay Talkies. I recall the time when we were trying to put his story, later filmed as *Mahal*, into final stage. One day I noticed a pimple on his face and thought nothing of it, but in a few days it became so painful that we felt something had to be done to rid him of it. 'I have a treatment that can't miss,' I told Kamal. 'What?' he asked. 'Do you know where Sitara lives?' I asked. 'I do,' he replied. 'All you have to do is go there, walk up the stairs right up to her door but under no circumstances are you to enter. There is your cure,' I said. Kamal was an intelligent man and burst out laughing. He knew what I meant.

Meanwhile, Sitara and Asif were living together in Mahim where I visited them several times. Their third-floor flat was the other end of a street facing the church on Lady Jamshedji Road. Asif had finished *Phool* and was thinking of making *Anarkali* which Kamal Amrohi had scripted for him, but he was not too happy with it and asked various people to give it a new twist, including me. I used to get to his place by eight in the morning where the door would be answered by an old woman wearing a thin muslin sari which always made me uneasy. She looked like an old Arabian Nights witch to me. It would go in and sit on the sofa. From the next room which was the bedroom, I would hear strange noises which sent a shiver down my spine. After some time, Asif would appear, smacking his lips. He used to be a sight, with his night shirt torn at various places and blue marks on his chest and arms, his hair dishevelled, and his breathing uneven. He would greet me casually and then fall in a heap on the floor. After some time, Sitara would send him a cup of custard which he would eat with undisguised reluctance. Then we would begin our work that was more gossip than anything. The two of them seemed to be doing well, though rumours spread that Asif was marrying a girl from his family and a date had been set and soon he would be travelling to Lahore with his friends for the ceremony.

I was busy when all this happened, otherwise I would have met him and asked what it was all about. I never got an opportunity until many days later. 'Well, I have decided to put an end to it and I will,' was all he said. He was in a car and I was walking. He had stopped and was in a hurry so we could not have a proper conversation. A few days later, I learnt that Asif had gone to Lahore with a large party of friends and a big wedding had taken place there where drinks flowed and dancing girls performed. Then I heard that Asif had returned to Bombay with his new bride and hired a portion of a house in Pali Hill, Bandra. I later found out that it was actually Nazir's house and he had vacated one half of it for his nephew. I am not sure what Sitara thought of it, but I do know that her visits to Arora continued. Asif had now begun to make preparations to make *Mughal-e-Azam* (completed several years after independence).

Then a most interesting development took place. Asif began to remain absent from home and it came to light that he was again spending his nights with Sitara. Consequently, the marriage failed. Nazir's grown-up son was also around at the time and one is not sure what exactly happened, but this much was known that Asif had stopped going home at night. There was unpleasantness and then we heard that a divorce was in the offing. All through this crisis, Asif kept meeting Sitara. It seemed they were together again. There were many stories in the market about Asif's new wife but I have no wish to go into them because I am not sure if they were true. All I know is that Asif had married in Lahore with great fanfare and brought his bride to Bombay, settled down in Pali Hill and in less than three months, the marriage was on the rocks. Who but Sitara could have been responsible for it? She was a woman of experience and knew how to make herself attractive to a man, rendering him useless for other women. That was how she weaned Asif away from his new bride and that was why he had come back to her. That woman Sitara had something other women lacked. Asif left his wife because she probably did not have the qualities that he had found in Sitara. Was it that she had left Asif with no taste for inexperienced virgins?

I have written this account and I know that it will not annoy Asif because he is a big-hearted man. Sitara, of course, would be angry, but after some time, she will forgive me because in her own way, she too is a big-hearted woman. In my book, she walks tall. I do not know what she thinks of me but I have always thought of her as a woman who is born once in a hundred years.

—*Translated by Khalid Hasan*

The Rajdhani Express to Bombay

Paul Theroux

It was at a railway station in Bombay that V.S. Naipaul panicked and fled, fearing that he 'might sink without a trace into that Indian crowd'. The story is told in *An Area of Darkness*. But I did not find Bombay Central especially scarifying; a closer acquaintance with it made me think of it as a place of refugees and fortune-hunters, smelling of dirt and money, in a neighbourhood that had the look of the neglected half of Chicago. The hurrying daytime crowds might have frightened me more if they had been idly prowling, but in their mass there was no sense of aimlessness. The direction of those speeding white shirts gave to these thousands of marchers the aspect of a dignified parade of clerks and their wives and cattle, preparing to riot according to some long-held custom, among the most distinguished architecture the British empire produced (cover your good eye, squint at Victoria Station in Bombay, and you see the grey majesty of St. Paul's Cathedral). Bombay fulfils the big-city requirements of age, depth, and frenzy, inspiring a chauvinism in its inhabitants, a threadbare metropolitan hauteur rivalled only by Calcutta. My one disappointment came at the Towers of Silence, where the Parsis place their dead to be eaten by vultures. This may strike a casual visitor as solemn barbarity, but it is based on an ecologically sound proposition. The Zoroastrian at the gate would not let me in to verify it. I had been brought there by Mushtaq, my driver, and, leaving, I said perhaps the stories were not true—I couldn't see any vultures. Mushtaq said they were all down at the towers feeding on a corpse. He looked at his watch: 'Lunchtime.' But he meant mine.

From *The Great Railway Bazaar* (1975).

After my lecture that evening I met several writers. One was Mr V.G. Deshmukh, a jolly novelist who said that he could not make a living by his pen. He had written thirty novels. Writing is the single activity in India that doesn't pay, and anyway this man wrote about the poor: no one was interested in reading about poor people. He knew, because the poor were his business.

'Famine relief, resettlement, drought prevention, under-privileged, anything you can name. It is a headache sometimes. But my books don't sell, so I have no choice. You could call me an organizer.'

'How do you prevent droughts?'

'We have programmes.'

I saw committees, position papers, conferences—and dusty fields.

'Have you prevented any lately?'

'We are making steady progress,' he said. 'But I would rather write novels.'

'If you've written thirty, surely it's time to stop.'

'No, no! I must write 108!'

'How did you arrive at that figure?'

'It is a magic number in Hindu philosophy. Vishnu has 108 names. I must write 108 novels! It is not easy—especially now, with this damned paper shortage.'

The paper shortage was also affecting Khushwant Singh's *Illustrated Weekly of India*. His circulation was 3,00,000 but he was about to cut it down to save paper. It was an Indian story: Indian enterprises seemed to work so well they produced disasters; success made them burst at the seams and the disruption of unprecedented orders led to shortages and finally failure. India, the largest rice-grower in the world, imports rice. 'Hunger is the handmaid of genius,' says the Pudd'nhead Wilson epigraph above one of the Bombay chapters in Mark Twain's *Following the Equator*, and truly India's hunger-inspired genius threatens to sink her. Every success I heard of convinced me that India, swamped by invention, was hopeless and must fall unless what I saw later that night ceases to exist. It is the simplest fact of Indian life: there are too many Indians.

Unable to sleep, I went for a walk. I turned left out of my hotel and walked a hundred yards past the brothels to the sea wall, counting the sleeping figures as I went along. They were stretched out on the sidewalk, lying side by side; some were on the pieces of cardboard but most slept flat on the cement, with no bedding and few clothes, their arms crooked under their heads. The children slept on their sides, the others on their backs. There was no sign anywhere of their possessions. I reached seventy-three and turned the corner, where down the road that ran next to the sea wall there were hundreds more—just bodies, no bundles or carts, nothing to distinguish one from another, no evidence of life. It is sometimes thought that these sleepers in the Bombay streets are a recent phenomenon; but Mark Twain saw them. He was on his way to a midnight betrothal ceremony:

> We seemed to move through a city of the dead. There was hardly a suggestion of life in those still and vacant streets. Even the crows were silent. But everywhere on the ground lay sleeping natives—hundreds and hundreds. They lay stretched at full length and tightly wrapped in blankets, heads and all. Their attitude and rigidity counterfeited death.

That was in 1896. They were more numerous today, and there is another difference. The ones I saw had no blankets. Hunger—*pace, Pudd'nhead Wilson*—is also the handmaid of death.

5:46, Andheri Local

Arundhathi Subramaniam

In the women's compartment
of a Bombay local
we seek
no personal epiphanies.
Like metal licked by relentless acetylene
we are welded—
dreams, disasters,
germs, destinies,
flesh and organza,
odours and ovaries
A thousand-limbed
million-tongued, multi-spoused
Kali on wheels.

When I descend
I could choose
to dice carrots
or a lover
I postpone the latter.

From *On Cleaning Bookshelves* (2001).

Elephanta

André Malraux

The town from which one reaches Ellora is Aurangabad, a Muslim city dominated by the tomb of Aurangzeb's wife, a rugged Taj Mahal amid rose-bushes that have gone back to nature, which reminded me of the archaeological museum at Autun, a kitchen-garden with Celtic steles and Romanesque statues growing among the artichokes.

The town from which one reaches Elephanta is Bombay.

Like Calcutta, Bombay, which was born in the nineteenth century, is not at all a modernized Indian town: it is a town as Anglo-Indian as Agra, Lahore and Aurangabad are Indo-Muslim. The Red Fort, from whose gigantic gateway a woe-begone camel emerged, the domes of marble and confectionery surrounded by woods full of squirrels, the Victorian Gothic building (inspired by what cathedrals?) bristling with outsize dentists' advertisements designed in the form of Sanskrit invocations, the dusty coconut palms overgrown with a jumble of old tyres—all this blurred into a single derisory backdrop as soon as one entered the sacred caves. Their link with the bowels of the earth suggested an entire subterranean India, secretly watching over the India of the villages, the animals, the processions of urn-carrying women, the majestic trees, while the towns, chimerical and theatrical, made ready to return to dust. The caves of Ellora reign over the area and unprepossessing plain which they overlook, while those of Elephanta seem hidden away in their island where the gulf shone with a Hellenic radiance beneath the gulls of the Arabian Sea. But they are all united in their sacred darkness. As soon as one entered Elephanta, the glittering ocean was borne away, like the towns, like the India of the British Raj, the India of the Moguls, the India of Nehru—all perishable offerings to the famous Majesty, the gigantic

From *Antimemoirs* (1967).

triple head of Shiva.

Photographs, and even the cinema, give no idea of the scale. These heads, fifteen to twenty feet high, are smaller than those of the Bayon at Angkor; but, colossal in comparison to the figures around them, they fill the cave as the Pantocrator fills the Byzantine cathedrals of Sicily. Like the Pantocrator, this Shiva stops below the shoulders without becoming a bust. Hence its disturbing aspect of severed head and divine apparition. It is not simply a question of its being 'one of the most beautiful statues in India', whatever meaning one may assign to the word 'beautiful'.

Here, recognizable at first glance, is a masterpiece of sculpture. A full face and two monumental profiles, whose planes (notably those of the eyes) are worthy of the very highest works of art in spite of a seductiveness which is more to do with the jewellery than with the faces.

But then there is Shiva, the cavernous gloom, the sense of the Sacred. This figure belongs, like those of Moissac, to the domain of the great symbols, and what this symbol express, it alone can express. This face with its eyes closed on the flow of time as on a funeral chant, is to the dancing Shiva of Ellora what the latter is to the *Dances of Death* of the South, and even to the fabulous figures of Madurai.

Finally, as with many of the works which make up the treasury of humanity's imaginary museum, there is the conjunction of the artistic effect of the work, its religious effect and another, unforeseeable, effect. The effect of the *Pharaoh Zoser* arises from the fact that the weathering of the stone has turned it into a death's-head, that of the *Winged Victory* from the fact that fate has devised the perfect mythical creature which men have looked for in vain in the angels: wings being the arms of birds, the *Victory* is perfect only without arms. The famous line that runs from the point of the breast to the tip of the wing was born of this amputation. The perfection (in this sense) of Shiva demanded the sacred gloom, the absence of a body, even a dancing one, the two profiles still embedded in the mountain, the mask with closed eyes— but above all the unique creation by which the Shiva of Elephanta is also the symbol of India.

In the neighbouring cave, they were chanting verses from the

Bhagavad Gita. It is familiar to all Hindus. It was recited during Gandhi's funeral wake, and during the fourteen hours of his cremation. Mysteriously in harmony with the subterranean temple, with the colossal Shiva, it seemed the very voice of this sanctuary to which it owed nothing.

> Then, standing in their great chariot drawn by white horses,
> Krishna and Arjuna sounded their sacred conches . . .
> And Arjuna, filled with deep compassion, spoke despairingly

The two legendary armies of India are face to face. The old king whom Arjuna is fighting against is blind. His charioteer has the magical power of knowing what is happening on the battlefield. He hears the dialogue begin, in the midst of the enemy army, in the chariot with the white horses, between Prince Arjuna and his charioteer who is Krishna and will become the supreme Deity. The Gita is divine speech reported by magic to a blind Priam enclosed in his darkness.

Arjuna looks at those who are to die, and Krishna reminds him that if the greatness of man is to free himself from fate, it is not for the warrior to free himself from courage. It is the fratricidal combat of the epics, and for us the Trojan sadness of Arjuna seems like the desolate echo of the voice of Antigone:

> Krishna, I see such omens of evil!
> What can we hope from this killing of kinsmen?
> What do I want with victory, empire,
> Or their enjoyment?
> How can I care for power or pleasure,
> My own life, even?
> The chanting voice was answered by another, as Krishna
> answers Arjuna in the poem.

> Your words are wise, Arjuna, but your sorrow is for nothing.
> The truly wise mourn neither for the living nor the dead.
> There never was a time when I did not exist, nor you, nor any

of these kings
    Nor is there any future in which we shall cease to be . . .

This chant began the Revelation which my companions knew by heart, accompanied in the darkness by the distant surge of the ocean and streaked with the cries of gulls: the song of the Deity who transcends, animates and destroys worlds, and of the spirit which transmigrates through bodies and souls, the Atman:

    Know this Atman, unborn, undying,
    Never ceasing, never beginning,
    Deathless, birthless, unchanging for ever.
    How can it die the death of the body?
    Worn-out garments are shed by the body:
    Worn-out bodies are shed by the dweller
    Within the body . . .

I had heard this last stanza in Benares. Here it had shed its funeral overtones; and what followed took on among these unseeing gods an even greater solemnity than among the funeral pyres:

    There is day, also, and night in the universe;
    The wise know this, declaring the day of Brahma
    A thousand ages in span
    And the night a thousand ages.
    Day dawns, and all those lives that lay hidden asleep
    Come forth and show themselves, mortally manifest:
    Night falls, and all are dissolved
    Into the sleeping germ of life . . .
    And all creatures exist within me:
    As the vast air, wandering world-wide,
    Remains within the ether always,
    So these, my wandering creatures,
    Are always within me . . .
    . . . I am Being and non-Being, immortality and death . . .

One of my companions answered the distant chant with one of the most celebrated verses of the poem, and his voice reached across the enormous pillars, muffled and yet carried by the low roof of the caves:

Who can kill immortality? . . .

For the chanting priests, was this response rising out of the silence as mysteriously natural as my wish for the poor couple at Madurai had been? They had fallen silent. At Benares, I had re-read the Gita. From its subterranean depths, from all that it owes to an earlier Brahmanism, there emerged dimly, like the figures in these caves, the divine sermon of love which Brahmanism scorned, and above all the cosmic stoicism to which the poem owes its fame. In the inexorable march of constellations which is the return to the source, man is united with god when he discovers his identity with Him and when he observes the Law, which is caste duty. Action is necessary, because the divine scheme must be fulfilled: it is not you who are about to kill your kinsmen, says Krishna to Arjuna, it is I. And action is purified to life if man is sufficiently in communion with God to offer it up to him as a sacrifice.

> . . . Because they understood this, the ancient seekers of
> liberation
> Could safely engage in action . . .
> There is nothing, in all the three worlds,
> Which I do not already possess;
> Nothing I have yet to acquire.
> But I go on working, nevertheless . . .
> Realize that pleasure and pain, gain and loss, victory
> And defeat, are all one and the same: then go into battle . . .

For my companions, this famous moment was an eternal moment. Yet the sculptures all around me in the shadow, and the Gita itself, expressed not so much the sacred stoicism of the last verses as the communion with God into which the metaphysical austerity had transformed itself: the mystique which Brahmanism, like Buddhism,

Christianity and Islam, had discovered. Even if the verses of communion had not been recited in another cave, the metamorphosis of faith would have been present here as palpably as it is in St. Peter's in Rome when one remembers our cathedrals there. India is obsessed by the image of the ever-changing waters of the changeless rivers, and the successive souls of its religion passed before Shiva as did its ancient armies before the sacrificial pyres. The Old Testament of the Upanishads has become the New Testament of the Gita. In the depths of time, there was the hymn to Kali:

> Thou, Mother of Blessings,
> Thou, terrible Night, Night of delusion, Night of death,
> We greet thee.

And, well after Elephanta, the parable of prayer:

'I pray in vain,' said the daughter of the disciple of the Master. 'What do you love best in the world?' 'My brother's little child.' 'Retire and meditate on him alone, and you will see that he is Krishna. Only love can cure the blind.'

The meditation of the colossal heads of the *Majesty* on eternity and time, twin prisoners of the Sacred, also seemed like a meditation on the destiny which guides religions from veneration to love as it guides mortals from birth to death—but beneath which there remained an inviolable permanence. If the Bhagavad Gita is present in so many holy places, it is because it expresses this; like the *Majesty*, it is India. Gandhi had tried to translate it. The greatest of the Renouncers of modern times regarded action carried out in the spirit of surrender to his God as the supreme form of renunciation. 'My devotion to my people is one of the aspects of the discipline I impose upon myself in order to liberate my soul. I have no need to seek refuge in a cave: I carry my cave inside myself.'

> Certain is death for all who shall be born,
> And certain is birth for all who have died . . .

Night falls on the dead of the final combat, after the eighteen-day battle. The few survivors have withdrawn into the forest to die there as ascetics. The patient birds of prey are waiting, and among the fallen swords glittering in the moonlight, monkeys like those accompanied me at Madurai touch the eyes of the dead with puzzled fingers.

Girls were passing by outside, each with a red flower in her hand. The gulls of Oman still wheeled across the sparkling gulf. A motorboat took us back. Bombay, a crazy bazaar that thinks itself a town, rose little by little above the water, and we made our way towards the enormous archway of the Gateway to the East. Once it watched over the English steamships like a marine temple over a war-fleet. Today, ours was the only boat to berth there—back from the India of eternity. On the waterfront, atomic reactors glittered . . .

On the Waterfront

Chirodeep Chaudhuri

Talking Heads

Duke Ellington

The jazz pianist and composer Duke Ellington visited Bombay as part of a US State Department tour in 1963 that took him through large swathes of Asia. The trip was immortalized in his musical travellogue The Far East Suite, *which features the tunes* Bluebird of Delhi (Mynah) *and* Agra. *Sadly, the only impressions of Bombay he recorded were diaristic rather than melodic.*

—Eds

I arrive in Bombay a day ahead of the band and check into the Taj Mahal Hotel. They offer me a choice of suites. The first I look at is the Honeymoon Suite, way up on the top floor facing the Arabian Sea. It is actually a duplex, the bedroom on the upper level having wide-open windows in every wall. They were not built to have glass in them and they stay open all the time. Birds are flying in and out of them. I don't know what kind they are, whether they are bats or eagles, but they are kind of large and probably a little far out for *un petit carré* like me. Another drawback is the fact that the bathroom is on the lower floor, and this is the cause of my definite decision to decline the suite. Imagine me going down a flight of spiral stairs in the middle of the night on my way to the bathroom!

They show me a couple of other suites, and I settle on one not so high up and far out. I am told that yet another mistake was made in the building of this hotel, and that the entrance, the main façade, and magnificent garden face the city rather than the sea. I forget the name of the architect, but they say that when he came and saw what had happened he committed suicide. Great stories you hear in the East.

Being a chronic room-service type, I ring for my room boy right

From *Music Is My Mistress* (1973).

away and start inquiring about available food. I begin by reciting my favourites and get all the way down to chicken, but he responds to every item by shaking his head side to side. Although I am right here on the sea, he shakes his head again when I mention fish. Not knowing any better, I wind up eating lamb curry for four days, after which I discover that shaking the head from side to side means 'Yes.'

I go for a ride one day along the crescent-shaped drive by the bay that is known as the Queen's Necklace, because of the way it looks at night when all the lights are on. On the way up Malabar Hill to see the Hanging Gardens, we stop and get out of the car for a photographer who wants some pictures of me in a local setting. A man comes by to watch what we are doing. He has two little boys with him, his sons. This man is black, the blackest man I've ever seen in my life, and he has the most beautiful face I've ever seen. It is pure, completely positive, showing absolutely no sign of any susceptibility to any degree of negativity. There are no lines and no signs of anything in his face but innocence and virtue. I am told that they are members of the Hindu caste known as Untouchables.

There are a lot of people, too, who look like the Strayhorn* family in this land, where so many races and religions are represented. I find the diversity endlessly fascinating. India is one of the oldest civilizations in the world, and the mixing of different strains and the coexistence of different races has long been a source of wonder to foreigners. Indians explain their land as a kind of wall in which the windows are always open to receive fresh breeze. Its enormous population can roughly be divided today into four groups—Indo-Aryans in the north; Dravidians, the main, original stock (shorter and darker), in the south; Mongolians, most in the northeast; and primitive tribes in relatively isolated hill and jungle areas. The West has also left its mark on India, in one way or another, from the time of Alexander the Great's invasion right up to the long period of British domination.

There is a terrifying storm one day, and I sit and watch it through the window as it rages over the Arabian Sea. It is the greatest exhibition of its kind I've ever witnessed. Lightning blazes, thunder roars, rain

---

* The pianist Billy Strayhorn was Ellington's arranger.

deluges down, and after the storm there is the most extraordinary sunset. The whole sky over the Arabian Sea is cerise.

When I am strong enough to appear on stage, I am still too weak to do more than fifteen or twenty minutes, so I play only the medley and Billy Strayhorn plays all the rest of the concert. At a little reception afterwards, I learn of the black market for tickets. A lot of musicians write and telephone complaining about the impossibility of buying tickets. All musicians are brothers in arms and it distresses me terribly that they could not get in to our concert, so we go about the business of readjusting the conditions. I insist that from now on, no matter how limited the space all musicians are to be admitted.

There are always surprises in Bombay. Harry Carney tells me that when he went down on the beach he saw I don't know how many turtles. They say some grow to weigh as much as three or four hundred pounds. When the eggs are laid, the mother digs holes or trenches deep in the sand and buries them for the purpose of protection, but large packs of dogs that roam the beaches dig them up and eat them. The baby turtle's chance of survival of being hatched and born, is only 2 or 3 per cent hereabouts.

To the City of Bombay

(Dedication to 'The Seven Seas')

Rudyard Kipling

The Cities are full of pride,
Challenging each to each—
This from her mountain-side,
That from her burthened beach.

They count their ships full tale—
Their corn and oil and wine,
Derrick and loom and bale,
And ramparts' gun-flecked line;
City by City they hail:
'Hast aught to match with mine?'

And the men that breed from them
They traffic up and down,
But cling to their cities' hem
As a child to the mother's gown:

When they talk with the stranger bands,
Dazed and newly alone;
When they walk in the stranger lands,
By roaring streets unknown;
Blessing her where she stands
For strength above their own.

(On high to hold her fame
That stands all fame beyond,
By oath to back the same,
Most faithful-foolish-found;

Making her mere-breathed name
Their bond upon their bond.)

So thank I God my birth
Fell not in isles aside—
Waste headlands of the earth,
Or warring tribes untried—
But that she lent me worth
And gave me right to pride,

Surely in toil or fray
Under an alien sky,
Comfort it is to say:
'Of no mean city am I!'

(Neither by service nor fee
Come I to mine estate—
Mother of Cities to me,
But I was born in her gate,
Between the palms and the sea,
Where the world-end steamers wait.)

Now for this debt I owe,
And for her far-borne cheer
Must I make haste and go
With tribute to her pier.

And she shall touch and remit
After the use of kings
(Orderly, ancient, fit)
My deep-sea plunderings,
And purchase in all lands.
And this we do for a sign
Her power is over mine,
And mine I hold at her hands!

Scenes from a Life

Dosebai Cowasjee Jessawalla

Dosebai Cowasjee Jessawalla was the daughter of Meheribai Guzdar, the first Parsi woman to receive an English education—or so Dosebai claims. Be that as it may, the story of her life is full of interesting details even if it seems almost completely alienated from post-1857 India. It can also be banal, repetitive, snobbish and sycophantic, reflecting the foibles of her times and her class.

—Eds

After the wedding festivities were over (around 1848), my mother and I retired for a time to Walkeshwar, Malabar Hill, where we lived in a tent. This being the first time for a Parsi family to sojourn under canvas, many visitors drove out to see us and satisfy their curiosity. We continued to live in our tent, till a small bungalow, my mother had in course of erection, was completed. We were the first Parsis to settle in Malabar Hill. In time, we made the acquaintance of our European neighbours, who were as astonished at our advent as if we had come from another world. While living at Malabar Hill my younger brother and I were attacked by cholera and, as no medical assistance was to be at hand in those days in the remote locality, we were moved to our house in the Fort, where, by the timely assistance of our physician, we recovered. Had it been otherwise, people would not have been slow in laying the blame on our distant abode. In the treatment of this terrible disease, our doctor had strictly enjoined us not to drink water, but being unable to endure our intense thirst, we contrived to elude the vigilance of our attendants and drank copiously of some water which had been left standing in the empty room for two months. With the deepest gratitude to almighty God we remember our miraculous escape from this premium paid to death.

From *The Story of My Life* (1911).

★

Another irksome and senseless mode of gratifying one's friends and relations was that of sending trayfuls of sweetmeats on the monthly or annual ceremony for the dead. These sweetmeats were very troublesome to prepare and therefore the first recipient would discharge her obligation to another friend by sending them on to her, she in her turn would despatch them to another and so on, the original trayful of sweets sent off early in the morning would be seen knocking about from door to door till even considerably past midday. My friends, contrary to my urgent request, insisted on sending questionable benefits to my far-distant bungalow at Tardeo. As the tray-loaded consisted of a variety of viands over which the priest had performed prayers, only Parsis could partake of them, but they reached us at a late hour and were considerably wanting in freshness; they, therefore, went usually to fill the belly of a cow or other domestic animal. To avoid all this, I ultimately made it a rule to decline with thanks such presents, although at the risk of offending the donor. It is gratifying, however, to note the steady decline of such stupid customs.

★

The year 1870 was a memorable one for India, for it marked the visit of an illustrious guest, H.R.H. the Duke of Edinburgh. The news of his advent was hailed with delight by Her Majesty's loyal subjects and fitting arrangements for the reception for the first time of one of her children were at once set on foot. Government resolutions were issued requesting the people to whitewash their houses, observe cleanliness throughout the city and make a suitably display, all which they cheerfully did as they were eager to behold the benign features of the sailor-prince. Accordingly, after visiting other cities, His Royal Highness came to Bombay, where an august assemblage of feudatory chiefs and princes had gathered to pay their respects to the Queen's son. On this occasion, Parsi women, casting off their awkward reserve, were seen threading the streets and entering into the spirit of the day, and I who had for a while taken leave of gaiety returned to it now with fresh zest. I first saw His Royal Highness from the balcony of a Hindoo temple near Byculla Bridge as the royal procession was passing along Parel Road and the next time when he was going to visit an Indian prince, the Thakore of Bhownuggur, who had taken up his temporary abode in a bungalow adjoining ours. On this occasion several other Indian ladies and myself stationed ourselves at the gates of our compounds, presently the carriage of His Royal Highness and the Governor of Bombay came slowly along. On seeing us, Sir Seymour Fitzgerald saluted, His Royal Highness with his wonted courtesy raised his hat and returned our salaams, while I fervently invoked benedictions on him and his gracious Mother.

★

In June 1871, I lost my beloved daughter Baiai, after one day's illness from diphtheria; she was two years and a half old, but so healthy and precocious as to have been always taken for double her age. This equally sad and sadder blow plunged me into inexpressible grief and I could only derive consolation from the thought of the immutable will of an all-ruling Providence and instability of earthly joys. As an antidote to my grief, my husband took me for a change of air to Sewree, my daughter Gollbai and her children bearing me company. The love of my dear little granddaughter did much to alleviate my grief. My son-in-law and cousins used frequently to visit us; two of the latter (Manockjee's sons) were ready-witted and jovial, and in this agreeable company, I in a measure 'steeped my sorrows in forgetfulnesss'. On account of its airy and pleasant situation, Sewree is now and then resorted to by pleasure-seekers, but it has no permanent residents. Every variety of fish and in the freshest state, such as is very seldom to be had in Bombay, is here obtainable. There are two or three bungalows for the occupation of Customs House officials, also a large cemetery for the Christian population of Bombay, where I used frequently to go in the evening stillness. The general aspect of this small suburb is refreshing and calming. After a stay of a month and a half, I returned to Tardeo.

★

On the 4th April of this year, Mr and Mrs Albert Sassoon gave a splendid ball to Sir Seymour Fitzgerald, the then Governor of Bombay, to which my daughter and I were invited. The only other Parsi ladies present were the two daughters of Judge Manekjee, who from their early years had accompanied their father wherever he went. Before this none of the Parsi ladies are known to have taken part in a ball, but on this occasion my daughter better known as Mrs D.D. Cama, danced just like a European lady. She was therefore the first Parsi lady who publicly took part in dancing and this constituted a novelty in the eyes of both Indian and European. The fact was widely commented upon in the European and native journals, the former of which were all in favour of the movement and gave us their hearty congratulations. Some of the native newspapers vehemently condemned the innovation and sarcastically criticized my daughter's conduct, while private individuals lodged complaints with my father-in-law characterizing our conduct as scandalous and indecent. My aged relative at first regretted these proceedings, but on my explaining to him the merits of English society, he showed himself content and said, 'Nothing but rank envy could put such a dubious interpretation upon such an innocent pleasure.'

★

In November, the new viceroy of India was expected in Bombay and a grand Durbar was to be held, at which the native princes and chiefs were requested to be present. Magnificent tents were erected on the Esplanade for the occasion and Bombay wore a gay appearance. Besides the Rajahs, some influential natives were honoured by invitations from the government. My husband, daughter, son-in-law and I were present, in this august assemblage, and it was gratifying to note the admission of Parsis for the first time into such a grand state ceremony, though their number did not exceed ten. Neither Mrs Ardeshir Wadia, who was ever prone to criticize my movements, nor any of her family was present on this occasion. All the princes and chiefs, heartily responding to the invitation, were there, bearing costly presents. The Begum of Bhopal was also amongst them, but veiled, and she was then and there invested with the order of G.C.S.I. by the Viceroy, by command of the Queen.

On the 19th November Sir Albert and Lady Sassoon gave a splendid ball in honour of Lord Northbrook, the Governor-General. Amongst guests were to be seen representatives of several sections of the native community, such as Parsis, Banias, Memons and Purbhoos. Nevertheless there were no other native females present, but my daughter and myself. We were kindly encouraged by the English, who assured us that if we would lead the way hundreds would soon follow. We were always treated with the utmost kindness and consideration, both by ladies and gentlemen; indeed our presence in their midst seemed to give them pleasure.

'Son, Eat Your Fill'

Daya Pawar

My father worked in the dry dock in Bombay. I used to call him Dada. Even today, my own son calls me Dada. I don't like the idea of his calling me Daddy or Papa. That would be like a foreign cactus grafted on a native prickly pear.

What was I saying? Oh, yes. In those days we stayed at the Kaavakhana. A ten-by-twelve room. An indoor tap. A common latrine. My mother, grandmother and uncle's family lived there too.

You won't find the Kaavakhana in a map of Bombay today. In those days, the tram that started from the 'Khada Parsi' statue would pass the corner of Foras Road and go towards Girgaum. Aji—my grandmother—remembered seeing a horse-drawn tram. She used to tell us her memories. So when I was small, I would see vividly how the horse must have pulled the tram over the bridge, how he must have foamed at the mouth. The Nagpada area began at the end of the bridge. It was in Nagpada that the Kaavakhana stood. Today there's a massive six-storey building there. At one end of the Kaavakhana there was Chor Bazaar. On the other, was Kamathipura. At the Golpitha was the red-light district. And beyond it was the Kaavakhana which could be reached from either side.

The Mahar community lived in little islands in the surrounding areas. They were all from the Ghats, gathered together from Sangamner, Akola, Junnar, or Sinnar. Around them lived Christians and Muslims.

The Mahars' living conditions were wretched. In each little cubby-hole, there were three or four sub-tenants. In between them were partitions made of packing-case wood. In those wooden boxes were

---

An extract from 'Baluta' included in *Poisoned Bread: Translations from Modern Marathi Dalit Literature* (1992).

their entire world. The men worked as porters. Some went to work in mills and factories.

The women were not kept in purdah. On the contrary, they slaved even more than their men. However much a drunken husband belaboured them, they would look after him, even pander to his addiction. Their occupation was to collect rags, papers, broken glass, iron and bottles in the street, bring them home, sort them out all night, and go and sell them in the morning. Just nearby was the Mangaldas market where trading in cloth took place. These women would gather the paper swept out of those shops. Each woman had her own appointed shop. There would be fierce quarrels about who should take the rubbish from which shop. And the shop assistants would be bribed in small coin.

Some women washed the saris of the prostitutes in the nearby brothels. Some would cook bajri bhakris and barbaat for the whores who were bored with eating kheema and bread. An occasional quarrelsome brothel customer would demand one of these women. At such a time they would with difficulty guard their honour, fragile as glass, and escape him.

There was another special thing about the Kaavakhana—a club attached to the area. An almost open one, in front of the big hall, made of matting walls with a tarpaulin roof. It was this club itself that was called the Kaavakhana. White men, Jews, strapping Arabs—occasionally a Black among them—such were the rich men who gambled all day in the club. Their games were varied. Cards, poker, billiards. We used to stand and watch that game of billiards through a crack in a closed door, see them pushing around those shining, coloured balls with a smooth-slipping stick.

The men in our tenement never played that game. It was imprinted on their minds that it was not a game for the poor.

We never saw the rich men in this club going to work. They loitered there from morning to midnight, drinking tea without milk. There was another drink they would take to, one made of cocoa beans. They called it 'kaava'. We used to wonder what joy those Jews, red as carrots, could get from drinking that black, bitter brew.

Talking of Jews reminds me—they had a strange ritual method of slaughtering the chickens. A Jew killing a chicken never cuts its throat clean from side to side with a knife. A chicken with its throat half-slit would be thrown into the maidan in front of us. It would spout blood and desperately flap its wings. We couldn't bear to watch such cruel games. This butchery would go on all the time next to the huge Jewish synagogue that was on our road to and from school, our hair leapt on end when we saw it happen . . .

Sometimes, the club was a nuisance to the neighbourhood. We could never tell when there would be a riot, when chairs and vessels would be thrown about. All day long words such as 'satta', 'race' or 'betting' would fall on our ears. These men had dealings in thousands of rupees right there where they sat. Some would be fake, some genuine.

When we children, all of my age, woke up in the morning, we would be asked what we had dreamt of in the night. If we had dreamt of fire, that meant a particular number, if water, then another. This would be the topic of conversation in the morning. In this 'China-betting game', one anna was a sufficient wager. All the adults in the house took part with enthusiasm. Even the mad man lying on the footpath, a heap of dirt on his body, had his worth in the game of 'satta'. Meanings would be read into whatever gestures he made. Someone's fortunes would bear fruit as a result, and the mad man would be respected as an auspicious man.

Adjoining the club was a horseshoe-shaped tenement with a tiled roof. That is where we used to live. Around us lived the four hardworking sons of my grandmother's elder sister. My father's brother was called Jaba, and these four uncles were named Rabha, Naba, Shiva and Kaba. I called one of them Tatya, another Baba. One of them pulled a handcart, another was a porter. At first only my father worked in the dock. Then he stuck them on there with him one by one.

Aji, my grandmother, worked in the dog's dispensary at Byculla. A sahib who knew her had done her this favour. The dogs of the gentry used to come there for medical treatment. Her work was to give them their milk, clean out their dirt, bathe them with soap. I sometimes went to the hospital with Aji. I used to love the newborn puppies, and felt like just sitting and watching them. I enjoyed hearing the slurping, sucking sounds they made as they drank milk out of a wide china dish. I felt like hugging them close to me. But I didn't dare touch them, for fear of what the sahib would say.

There was a real little island of our relations in the Kaavakhana. A man pulls his coat close about him in a strong wind, they say. In the same manner, these relations lived close to one another. Their mutual love and hate were limitless. From their quarrels you would think that these people would never again see each other's faces; that they would scatter far apart in that great metropolis. But nothing like that actually happened. Their condition was like that of beans that are uprooted together when their vine is uprooted from the earth.

When these people came here to stay, a large building opposite was vacant. But because they didn't want the bother of climbing up and down the stairs, they chose this low-tiled tenement, which had probably been a stable in the past. Even today, I am amused at their ignorance.

Of course, there may not have been just one reason for what they did. Their business was gathering the rubbish of the whole of Bombay. Who would have let them stay in a flat in the building opposite, if that was their trade?

But for that reason, what a hell they lived in! and how many of my growing years did I spend there! Almost all the rooms leaked in the monsoons. All night long, vessels and pans would be put down in spot after spot. It was hard to know when sleep finally came to us across the music of this jal tarang.

At first I was the youngest child in all the houses about us, and was petted a great deal. If I made the excuse of a headache and stretched out on the quilt, at once a bright yellow malpua from the Irani restaurant across the way would appear in front of me. And at once my headache would stop. They used to make fun of my illness in the house. But no one would scold me.

One pay day . . . Dada and Tatya got paid the same day. I threw a tantrum for a suit and boots. I don't think I was old enough to wear them. I was probably seven or eight years old. But I cried and screamed.

At last they take me to Pila House. I see such huge, shining, glass-front shops for the first time. They buy me a woollen jacket and pants and shiny black boots. I can't even wait till I get home; I change my clothes right there in the shop. I don't know what Dada feels as he watches me. A photograph of all of us is taken that day.

I preserved that photograph for a long time. But in these twenty-five or so years of house-moving within Bombay (after the fashion of the scorpion whose house is on his back), somewhere in that confusion the photograph has been lost. Today I feel as if a priceless treasure has been robbed. A rare photograph of Dada and Tatya. That is the only memento I have of them. But even that memento is lost to time.

I can still remember Dada's face. Dada was dark as black wood, tall and skinny. His clothes were spick and span. A crisp white mercerized dhoti of good quality. A woollen jacket. A high black cap of the 'Gandharva' brand on his head. He had a good smile, and when he laughed, a speck of gold shone on one tooth. He could neither read nor write. But for the photograph, he had bulky volume on his hands, and a pen was clipped to his coat pocket.

Tatya was princely in his bearing. His hair was neatly combed back. He was up-to-date in all he did. At one time he used to engage in gymnastics. He placed with stick and sword, and could fight with a lathi. He could halve a lemon with ease with a sword and a stick. Around his neck, on a black thread, he used to wear an amulet for strength.

My grandmother was a simple soul, a fund of anecdotes. Her name was Devkai. She had lost her husband at an early age, and borne her widowhood with great courage. She had scraped and scraped to bring up her two sons. If one asked her:

'Aji, when did you come to Bombay?' she would look off into the distance and reply:

'It was like this, son. Your grandpa Bhaga died of drink. Your pa was just knee-length. Tatya was a baby. They were very hard on us in the village. Our turn used to come for the Mahars' duties. There was no grown man in my house. So my relations, too, used to be cruel to me. The widow should call out the village proclamations, they said. She should be asked to guard the village gate. She should help carry the carcasses of dead animals. If any one in the village died, we had to go from village to village, come rain or shine, and give the news. These were the jobs of the Mahars.

'Once the Patil sent me to cry out a proclamation in the village. It was the Holi season. There was smallpox in the village. The cart of the goddess Mariai was going in procession to the next village. The Mahars used to pull it. If it was stopped at that time, the smallpox would increase. So the Patil told me to cry this proclamation in the village: "Don't stop or delay the cart." I took the stick with bells in my hand and was going round shouting the proclamation. And there was young Kondiba, sitting on threshold of Vithoba's temple. I don't know what whim he had. Maybe he wanted to make a joke of me. He stood in my way and said: "Catch hold of this Mahar woman. Tie her up in the square. Has she gone mad? She's quite happily saying, 'Don't fry or fuck.' " A crowd had gathered. Some were laughing. Some were furious with me. I fell at the feet of the villagers. I swore earnestly about what proclamation I had really been crying out, but they wouldn't listen. My husband's cousin heard about it in the Mahar quarter. He was little respected in the village. When he came, the villagers finally let go of me. I couldn't sleep all night. I thought hard. I didn't want to stay at that place. I took my two sons and came to Bombay, and lived under the protection of my sister.'

Aji could remember no names earlier than her father-in-law's. We read many people's genealogies in books. The many-branched family trees of others are written in histories. But I don't know any names earlier than that of my great-grandfather's. They say that the names of people's ancestors are preserved in the books of the *pandas* and other Brahmins at place of pilgrimage. But would my ancestors have gone to such pilgrim centres? If they went at all, they would have gone to Khandoba at Jejuri.

Aji has remained embedded in my memory for another reason. When the breadwinner of the house sat to eat, Aji used to sit by him till he finished, stroking his back and repeating, like a refrain, 'Son, eat your fill.'

While Dada was the breadwinner, and brought home his pay, Aji used to sit next to him. After Dada, came Tatya's turn. He once came home royally drunk. When Tatya sat to eat, Aji's refrain went on, 'Son, eat your fill.' Tatya grew wild with rage that day, he threw his thali angrily into the courtyard in front of the house. All the food fell into the dirt. He said furiously: 'Will you say it again: "Eat your fill, son?" Am I a little child?'

For two or three days Aji was quiet. But her habit never left her. Later, when I grew up and started working and bringing home the cash, Aji used to sit by me as I ate. She used to stroke my back and mutter, 'Son, eat your fill.' My eyes would swim with tears.

Today Aji is dead and buried. When I sit to eat I remember her. Her words ring in my ears. If you think of it, Aji never knew a moment's happiness all her life. But today I wonder how harsh reality had not ground out the gentleness and affection in her nature. Old people like Aji and her generation are vanishing fast. I see around me only people with mercenary motives and bitterness in their pocket.

—*Translated by Priya Adarkar*

Muharram in the Mohalla

Sameera Khan

On the tenth day of Muharram, Imamwada Road in the heart of Dongri, awakes to the sound of knives being sharpened. Metal rubbing against metal, the air reverberating with the whirring and hissing of the knife-grinders' wheel, the men pedalling furiously to prepare one more blade for its grim fate.

On any other morning, the scene here is quite different. The kite shops in the area, decorated with large kankauwas and vivid spools of manjha, are opening their doors for business; steam is pouring out of the dingy Irani hamam at the corner and the blue-tiled newly restored Moghul Masjid is deserted after the bustle of the early morning Fajr prayers, except for a few old men who habitually lounge at its doors.

But on the tenth day of the first month (Muharram) of the Muslim lunar calendar, an especially sacred day called Ashurah, the atmosphere on this narrow street is more sombre. Kite shops have given way to pedlars of knives, daggers and sharp blades tied to chains. Roadside stalls sell religious books and souvenirs, including prayer lockets and sword-shaped pendants. Dark colours, ceremonial flags and flowers shroud the many sabils, the makeshift charity water stands that are set up during the first ten days of Muharram to dispense free water and sherbet to the thirsty. Some of these stalls arrange seating around a hired television set tuned in to the special Muharram discourses put out by local cablewalas.

By ten in the morning, the community kitchens have already started operations in the by-lanes off Imamwada Road. Wood and coal fires are stoked and huge dekchis—which can feed hundreds—are readied to cook either a simple meal of dal-chawal or a nourishing khichda (with wheat, mutton, mixed lentils and spices). On this day of mourning and fasting, no food is cooked in Shia Muslim households. Instead, when the fast is broken in the early evening, everyone will share the food from the community kitchen.

However, all this activity is merely a prelude to what unfolds at noon—the grand passion play of Imam Hussain enacted by local Shia Irani Muslims. Year after year—and by some historical accounts the performance of the passion play in Mumbai is at least a century and a half old—the drama and pageantry of the event never fails to move the faithful to tears. The grisly fate of the Imam is a reminder that truth and goodness may not always be victorious, but they are still worth the fight.

★

Ashurah has pre-Islamic significance but it is the events of a brutal day in AD 680 that give it a special importance, particularly for Shia Muslims. Muharram commemorates the martyrdom of Hazrat Imam Hussain, the younger grandson of Prophet Mohammad. While journeying from Medina, via Mecca, to Kufah, Imam Hussain was brutally killed along with members of his family and seventy-two others on the plains of Karbala (Iraq), by the troops of Yazid, son of Muawiya, the Umayyad ruler of Syria.

Yazid, known for his depravity and despotism, was keen to inherit the Caliphate from his father and thus wanted an oath of allegiance from Hussain. When Hussain refused, Yazid's army intercepted him and his companions at Karbala, on the western bank of the Euphrates river, and over a period of ten days tortured them to death. They starved the camp of water and then attacked it on the tenth day, killing most of the women, children and men in a most gruesome fashion. While Imam Hussain's elder son, Ali Akbar, was slashed to pieces, the younger son, Ali Asghar, a mere baby at the time, was pierced by an arrow as he lay in his father's arms. His daughter, Sakina, died of dehydration. Hussain himself was speared to death, beheaded and his head carried off, impaled on a lance.

Although Imam Hussain's death at Karbala occurred more than 1300 years ago, for Shia Muslims the tragedy comes alive annually through the observance of Muharram. The first ten days of Muharram, sometimes even the whole month and the next, are observed with grave solemnity, with the tenth day being a special day of prayer and mourning.

In Mumbai, public observances of Muharram still tend to remain largely confined within certain core areas, mainly the Shia neighbourhoods of Bohri Mohalla, Bhendi Bazaar and Dongri, all part of the larger old Muslim quarter of the main island city. During Muharram, these are the centres of much activity and ritual. Each Shia group—Dawoodi Bohras, Khojas, Shia Ithna-Asharis (the Twelvers) and the Irani Muslims—follows its own traditions with regard to the observance of Muharram and sometimes even participates in each others' rites.

On and around Raudat Tahera Road in Bohri Mohalla, where the Bohras set up sabils, there's a smell of tuberoses in the air. The flowers are used along with lights and coloured cloth to decorate the water stands. Some of these have specific religious themes and they all compete for the title of 'the best decorated sabil' on the tenth day. Usually every building society in the area contributes to the sabils, with young children taking charge of dispensing rose and khus sherbet from earthernware pots.

On the same street, tazias or miniature representations of the tomb of Hussain are lined up by the Shia Ithna-Asharis on the tenth day. People gather to pay obeisance to the tazias, tying red-and-yellow threads to them asking for the Imam's protection all year round. In Pala Galli, which is a portion of Samuel street in Dongri, the Khojas set up their own sabils and tazias, fashioned of paper on bamboo frames.

For most of the month, each Shia group organizes the majlis, or mourning assembly, where the day-to-day events relating to the battle of Karbala and its tragedies are recounted and remembered. Several ceremonial processions are held on the seventh, eighth, ninth and tenth days of Muharram as a mark of respect and support for the dead Imam and his family. The mehendi juloos on the seventh day, for example, commemorates the death of Qasim, son of Hasan, who was betrothed to the daughter of Hussain. Processionists carry trayloads of mehendi, fruit and lit candles from the BIT chawls, near J.J. Hospital, to Imamia Masjid on Mirza Ali Street in Dongri.

But certainly the most impressive demonstration of religious zeal and fervour is the enactment of an extended passion-like Persian drama about the events of Karbala by the local Irani Shia Muslims. In a by-lane off Imamwada Street, stands the Amin Imambada, the oldest Irani Imambada in the city. Till the early 1960s, this was also the only school in Mumbai where Persian was the language of instruction and Iranis across the city sent their children to study here. Now, the dilapidated school, under a process of renovation, only runs till kindergarten. But on the main day of Muharram, this is the place where the Irani Shia community gathers in strength to enact a story that still manages to stir the deepest emotions and rouse the strongest feelings among the participants.

★

There is an air of expectancy surrounding Amin school this Muharram morning. Almost everyone is dressed in some shade of black and walking around barefoot. Others like me wear their slippers up to the gates of Amin school and then quickly take them off and wrap them in a plastic bag. Though the passion play only starts at noon, most people come as early as nine o'clock to find suitable seating.

Men stand below while women and children are herded to the top floors of the building, on to the balconies and parapets that surround the central courtyard of the school where the main play is staged.

This year I've managed to squeeze in with a group of Irani women on a broad balcony overlooking the main scene of action. It is a large family of sisters, pregnant cousins, grandmothers and young children. All the women have covered their heads with black chaddars or dupattas. Bags filled with popcorn and tetrapack drinks for the children are unpacked; collapsible stools and folding chairs are set up for the elderly; the others settling on to rolled-out dhurries and blankets. Some bring out prayer books and prayer beads. Many others choose to catch up on family news.

This is the day when Irani Muslim families from all across the city, and even outside, come together to witness the annual ritual enactment of the battle of Karbala. The passion play, or as the Iranis call it, the shhabi, attracts several hundred people on the tenth day of Muharram.

Non-Irani Shia Muslims—irreverently referred to as 'Indians' by the Irani Muslims, many of whom have lived in India for over three to four generations—also join in and the place gets crammed quite early.

One Muharram, I had to squat on the edge of a narrow cement ledge looking down on the play. Little boys sat on the wall behind me, their feet dangling over my head. This was the seating reserved by a friend a week prior to the enactment, with a bedsheet confirming the reservation laid out on the spot the night before.

By the time the maulvis, usually visiting priests from Iran, enter the Amin courtyard to start the proceedings, the crowd is large and restless. People are now peering from neighbouring roofs and balconies as well. The maulvis walk around the schoolyard, at the centre of which is an empty water tank, reciting in Farsi prayers and lamentations on the death of Imam Hasan and Imam Hussain.

Suddenly the drummers start a reverberating beat. Men in red uniforms and with blackened faces rush in with bamboo sticks. They are led by a general in a battle helmet and armed with a whip. Obviously these are Yazid's men. They start hitting the gathered spectators and mourners. The audience becomes participants in the living drama.

As the crowd fights back, the scene changes. Now men wearing black outfits with green shawls enter bearing the alams or standards of Hussain. The alams, made of large pieces of cloth, are usually mounted by a crest, the most common form of it being the panja—or the sacred open hand emblematic of the five pure members of the Prophet's immediate household. Dressed with red roses and white lilies, the alams are held aloft for all to see. Yazid's men attack the men of Hussain. Swords are drawn and step-by-step the battle unfolds.

The drumming becomes louder; the clash of the cymbals joins in. Horses carry in the faithful. Palanquins bearing the women in Hussain's party are brought in and attacked by the men in red. A cradle is carried in, a visible reminder of the baby son of Hussain who was killed in his arms. There is a sudden flurry of activity and then a sharp intake of breath as several chubby Irani babies, dressed appropriately in green baba suits, are tossed in the air by Yazid's men invoking the memory of Ali Asghar. Collectively, mothers and babies shriek. An Irani woman by my side, who has kindly accommodated me within her family, explains that it's a matter of pride for Irani families to have newly born babies participate in the annual play.

Meanwhile, on the sides of the courtyard I see groups of shirtless boys and men gradually gather together for the matam, the mourning rituals. Some beat their chests in grief, calling, 'Ya Ali, Ya Hussain'. Others hold a bunch of chains to which freshly sharpened blades have been attached and swing them in the air, now over the left shoulder, now over the right, striking their backs and drawing blood. A few go a step further and perform the qamaa—using a short dagger to make cuts on the top of the forehead. It all seems very organized and the men seem particularly trained for it. I see one agitated youngster, not more than twelve years of age, wanting to perform the qamaa being stopped by some older men as he isn't quite ready to perform this form of matam.

In one corner, a group of men perform the Bushari matam. The working-class Bushari Iranis originally came from Bandar Bushar to Mumbai in the mid-1800s. The men hold the belts or hands of each other and with a slow rhythmic shuffling of feet, they move in a circle while beating their chests. The grace of the act makes it reminiscent of a folk dance.

The crowd seems to have got thicker. The Irani woman next to me, who has taken it upon herself to educate me on the finer points of the ritual, now points out the familiar faces in the crowd. 'That one in black, who is part of Hussain's army, is Ali Asgar, the television star. He has come here every year since he was a child.' You recognize him as Kamal in *Kahaani Ghar Ghar Ki* and wonder if enacting the passion play year after year pushed him towards a career in acting. 'There's Dr Ali, the physiotherapist, and that one being beaten is a computer engineer,' she adds. And I guess somewhere in the middle of this medieval play-acting are also the men who run the many Irani cafes and bakeries across the city.

By now almost everyone is striking their left breast with their right hand and chanting aloud the names of the martyrs with sorrow and reverence. Some of the women wail and weep, berating the mercilessness of Yazid. Red welts rise on the chests and backs of the men inflicting injuries on themselves with the chains. Many wounds bleed and a nauseating stench of sweat and blood fills the air. I think to myself, the real battlefield must have smelt something like this.

The Irani women around me seem dismayed at the blood letting. A woman who has witnessed similar mourning rituals in Iran tells me that the men participating in those rituals are never bare-chested— they always wear white shirts during the matam. 'They beat themselves with a bunch of chains but they use no knives or blades. So while their backs turn black-and-blue, there's no bleeding,' she explains. 'Arré, you want to give your blood for Hussain, go to a blood bank,' sneers a woman loudly behind me. Some more women join in the jeering.

As the drama below continues, it is clear that Hussain's faithful have now lost the battle. The flower-bedecked alams are now stained with red colour, to depict the blood of the fallen martyrs. Similar red colour marks the single white horse that trots in, signifying Duldul, the empty mount of Imam Hussain after his martyrdom. Such a horse is usually included in the ceremonial processions that mark Muharram. A coffin, pierced by swords, is then brought in. Lifted by several men on their shoulders, it circulates the courtyard along with a few red-stained doves. The drumbeats have got louder and the wails of the crowd get drowned in its reverberation.

As the alams leave the courtyard, the passion play ends. Tears are dried and the crowd starts to stream out. The family around me has come well-prepared. Thermos flasks are quickly taken out of bags and the women pass out plastic cups in to which cool badam sherbet sprinkled with *sabza* seed is poured. Soon they will move to the nearby Moghul Masjid to pray.

By the time I reach outside, the street seems even more congested. I'm still to recover from the emotional fervour and high energy that I have just witnessed. The death of Hussain now seems like a personal blow. What am I responding to? Is it the story itself—the death of the Imam but the continued immortality of goodness and faith—or is it just the power of drama, of retelling a story so realistically that it can't but move you? Year after year, I'm sure many visitors to the shhabi have a similar experience.

In 1877, James Maclean in his 'A Guide to Bombay' wrote about Muharram and mentioned the passion play. 'In a compound of the old Imambara . . . a passion play is performed in which all the incidents of this tragedy—mournful rites to observe the death of Hoosain, who was killed at Kerbela by troops of Moawiyah, the Caliph of Damascus—are dramatically represented, from Hoosain's parting with his family, to his death,' wrote Maclean, adding that the 'place was so packed—no room for one more man to fit in. Circle in centre staked off with ropes and in it band of half-naked men formed a ring, each grasping with the left hand the belt of his fellow man; leaving the right hand free—At a signal, they sang and shouted and whenever the name of Hoosain was mentioned they slapped their breasts with their palms. In short time, their breasts became like raw flesh and blood squirts out.'

Maclean goes on to describe the howling and wailing—'Little girls employed in representing the children of Hoosain mourning for their father seemed overcome with real grief, beating themselves etc . . .' Maclean concludes that the show was 'very impressive'.

As I walk down Imamwada Road, the community kitchens are in full swing. The smells emanating from them bring me back to ground and to the realities of a hungry stomach. In the evening, the last of the Muharram processions will leave from all Shia masjids in the area for the Rehmatabad graveyard in Mazgaon. Here, the flowers decorating the alams will be finally laid to rest. The juloos will disperse for the final time till it comes together again the following year.

*

Till about three decades ago, the Irani Shia population in Mumbai was around 20,000. Many resided in and around the inner city areas of Dongri and Char Nal. Today only about 3000 Irani Shias live in the city, most of them in the suburbs. While some moved back to Iran in the years before the revolution, others have shifted out in more recent years to Hyderabad and Pune.

When the Irani Muslims first came to Mumbai—in the last years of the eighteenth century—they were referred to as 'Moghuls', a term then used in Bombay to describe Muslims from West Asia in general, and in particular Shia Muslims from Persia. Of course they had no connection with the Moghul dynasty, which had its antecedents in Central Asia and ruled much of northern India for about 200 years since the early sixteenth century. But as the Irani Shias spoke Farsi (Persian), the court language of the Moghul kings, it became customary to speak of them as 'Moghuls'. Also, in Bombay it served the purpose of distinguishing them from the Parsis who had already come to the Indian coast as settlers.

The first Irani Muslims came from Shiraz. They were traders who came to transact business in India, eventually settling down to exporting tea and spices from India to Iran and running successful shipping lines. Later came the Busharis, working-class Iranis, who usually worked for the Shirazees. It was only in the early 1900s that the drought-hit farmers from the province of Yezd came to Bombay. Many of them started tea-shops on the Bombay roadside, which later became the legendary Irani cafes and bakeries of the city. Most managed to acquire store space at street junctions and corners quite cheaply as traditionally these were considered inauspicious locations by Marwari businessmen.

For Mumbai city at large, the Muslim Iranis—and also the Zoroastrian Iranis—have always been synonymous with the chai and *brun-maska* serving Irani restaurant at the street corner. But for Mumbai's local Muslim population, especially the Shias, the coming of the Irani Muslims meant a lot more. After all, it was they who brought much innovation and change in the observance of Muharram in the city. It is commonly acknowledged that the very public Shia juloos during Muharram in Mumbai was, in fact, started by the Irani Muslims.

As Jim Masselos says in his essay on the Bombay Muharram, in the late 1820s the Shia Muslims from Persia introduced a new feature to Muharram—the procession of horses through the streets of the inner city. On these horses were placed 'arrows and swords so as to appear as if they were pierced by them . . . also placed were the image of the sacred head of Imam Hussain . . .' This was accompanied by loud lamentations and beating of the breasts.*

---

* From *Change & Custom in the Format of Bombay Mohurrum during the 19th and 20th Centuries*, South Asia, Vol. V, No. 2, December 1982.

The Persian-inspired horse procession caused several clashes between the Sunnis and the Shias, with Muharram henceforth being a tense time for law and order in the city. Prior to the horse processions, the Sunnis—mainly Konkani Muslims—led their own street processions of tabuts—models of the tombs of Hassan and Hussain—during Muharram and the local Shias held the majlis within their own Imambadas.

The Shia Iranis also brought the Persian passion play about the events of Karbala to Mumbai, with some of the earliest performances recorded in the mid-1800s when the first Aga Khan, leader of the Khoja Ismailis, arrived in the city with a band of Persian soldiers. Till today, in a corner of Dongri, the age-old Persian drama or shhabi, a social as much as a religious tradition, has been kept alive by the Irani Shias, a spectacular reaffirmation of their continued presence within our midst.

Like the Iranis, several other Muslim communities have made Mumbai their home over the last 400 years. Every group has added to the shaping of the heterogeneous identity of the Mumbai Muslim. For historically, the Muslims of Mumbai, currently an estimated 17 per cent of the city's population, have never been a single entity. As Rafiuddin Ahmed, a prominent Muslim of the time, pointed out in a letter to the editor of the *Times of India* in 1908, 'the most essential fact to be learnt about the Mahomedan community of Bombay is that there is no such community. There are various communities in this city which profess this religion.'

The 1901 census of the city listed some fourteen different categories of Muslims in the city, including the Arab, Bohra, Baluchi, Egyptian, Julhai, Khatri, Khoja, Memon, Moghal, Pathan, Sayyad, Shaik, Sidi, Turk and a further category of 'unspecified'. Many of these continue to live and work in Mumbai, each occupying a particular section of the old Muslim quarter, commonly referred to as a mohalla.

What makes the Muslim mohallas of Mumbai interesting is their diverse blend of languages, sects, customs and cuisines. Indeed, the Muslims of Mumbai constitute one of the most heterogeneous Muslim groups in the South-Asian subcontinent: From the working-class weavers of Madanpura to the trader-class Bohras and Khojas of Bhendi

Bazaar and Dongri, from the Konkani-dominated Jama Masjid to the Halai Memon-led Minara Masjid, with Gujarati-speaking neighbourhoods and Urdu-tongued localities where Sunnis rub shoulders with Shias.

The key to understanding the Mumbai Muslim is to understand his or her mohalla. For here, every street corner has a different story to tell, each by-lane a new character to present, every neighbourhood distinct from the other, every identity has more to reveal. Sometimes it just depends on the time of the day, the change of the season, or the waxing and waning of the moon.

Like on the tenth of Muharram, when all paths lead to Imamwada Road.

The Rage of the Marathi Manus

An Oral History of the Rise of the Shiv Sena

Meena Menon and Neera Adarkar

*The Shiv Sena, the militant right-wing organization led by Bal
Thackeray, is today fanatically anti-Muslim, but in its early years, the
target of its hate campaigns was the South Indian community of
Bombay. This extract from the authors' forthcoming book on the
social, political and cultural history of Bombay's textile district examines
the rise of the Shiv Sena in the late sixties and seventies.*

—Eds

In August 1960, a cartoonist named Bal Thackeray, known to the
Maharashtrian populace as the son of Keshav Sitaram 'Prabodhankar'
Thackeray, a prominent leader of the Samyukta Maharashtra movement of the
late fifties and early sixties, published the first issue of the magazine Marmik
(meaning sharp or trenchant). The chief guest at the launch was leading
Congressman Y.B. Chavan, who later became chief minister of Maharashtra.
Marmik, attractively produced, always featured a full-page Bal Thackeray
cartoon on its front page. The language was satirical, the content light and easy
to read.

  In 1965, Marmik began to publish statistics of the Marathi and non-
Marathi population in Bombay. Later, it added weekly lists of top officers in
Bombay's big businesses and bureaucracy. It was clear that the majority of these
were South Indian; very few Maharashtrians featured among these names.
The list ended with the terse one-liner: Vacha aani thand basa (Read and be
silent). The magazine was bold, provocative and it became immensely popular
with the Maharashtrian youth, especially the unemployed. Soon, youngsters

From *A Hundred Years, A Hundred Voices*, to be published by Seagull
Press in late 2003.

were furnishing their own lists to Marmik.

Bal *(also Balasaheb) Thackeray and the youth organization he set up, called Shiv Sena, rode on the powerful linguistic and regional sentiments generated by the Samyukta Maharashtra movement—the post-Independence agitation for the creation of the linguistic state of Maharashtra and the inclusion of Bombay city in the state as its capital. The Left played an important part in the movement—the majority of those who came out on the streets were workers lead by communists—and this had led to the belief that the quality of life of the urban masses would improve, that there would be jobs for all. The agitation did succeed in winning Bombay as the capital of Maharashtra state, overturning a plan to make it the capital of a bilingual state that would include Gujarat. But the leaders of the Samyukta Maharashtra struggle failed to increase employment opportunities. It was left to* Marmik *and* Thackeray *to exploit the frustration thus generated among the educated Maharashtrian youth and middle class in Bombay.*

Yeshwant Chavan *(seventy), one of the founders of Lal Nishan Party, a breakaway group of the Communist Party of India (CPI)*: 'The break-up of the Samyukta Maharashtra Samiti created the ground for the growth of the (Shiv) Sena. The failure of the Left to respond to the aspirations of the working class gave the Sena the opportunity to come out as supporters of the unemployed youth of Bombay. They took an extremely anti-communist stance and hence got the support of the Congress. They started mobilizing unemployed youth. They were not prosecuted even if they indulged in acts of violence. Their demands might not have been justified but that was the situation, which was developing in other parts of the country as well—Tamil Nadu, Bengal, everywhere. In cosmopolitan Bombay there should be some reservation for Maharashtrians, but the Sena's actions against North and South Indians were not justified. It broke working-class unity.'

Kusum Randive *(seventy) belongs to the well-known Randive family who dedicated themselves to the communist movement. She joined the communist party in 1944.* 'I remember Comrade Lalji Pendse saying that if we do not take up the issue of unemployed youth, now that we have Samyukta Maharashtra, we cannot claim that we have succeeded in the agitation. Subsequent events and the growth of the Shiv Sena, which capitalized on this problem, have vindicated Pendse.'

Shahir Sable, seventy-seven years old; popular singer and producer and director of folk theatre work whose 'Garja Maharashtra Mazha' *became one of the most popular songs in Maharashtra*: 'Earlier, everyone spoke Marathi in Bombay. Today you have to speak in Hindi. That is the tragedy of the Marathi language. There was a working-class culture here in Girangaon, and it was in Marathi.

'I have been writing and singing since 1947. My songs have been broadcast on All India Radio, and many of them have been cut as records. When Congressman Ramrao Adik started an organization called the Maharashtra Hitwardhini on the issue that the Marathi manus (the Marathi-speaking populace) was being displaced from Bombay, I enrolled. One Chavan from a local gymnasium also started a six-month debate in the pages of the *Loksatta* newspaper on why the Marathi manus was still backward. We also drafted a petition and approached the then chief minister, Vasantrao Naik. But then I could see that the Congress was not really interested in the issue, so I left. I told Adik that Naik must have thrown our petition into the trash basket . . .

'I have known Balasaheb Thackeray's family for years. His father, Prabhodhankar Thackeray, was opposed to communalism. When Bal Gangadhar Tilak held a meeting in Pune, Prabodhankar went there and threw eggs on him because he was opposed to Tilak's Brahminism . . .

'When *Marmik* started, I sang in the programme organized by the Maharashtra Hitwardhini. *Marmik* ran a series titled Vacha aani thand basa . . . (It) highlighted the fact that the Marathi manus was relegated to jobs like coolies or peons while the clerical and management jobs went to others . . . (Then) Bal Thackeray started the new slogan Vacha aani utha (Read and arise). And the Shiv Sena was formed.

In June 1966, Marmik *published a twelve-point oath for a new youth organization called the Shiv Sena (the army of Shivaji), a name coined by Thackeray's father, Prabodhankar. The name was well chosen, since the warrior-*

king Shivaji was the most popular folk hero in Maharashtra's history. On 30 October 1966, on Dussera day, Thackeray called a public meeting at Shivaji Park in Dadar to launch the Shiv Sena, in which he exhorted youth to come forward to support Maharashtra. The response was tremendous. During the rally itself, thousands of youngsters signed up as members. The stated programme of the Sena was social, not political—in fact, Thackeray went on record to say that rajkaran (politics) was gajkaran (an infestation of ringworm). The Sena's slogan was 'Justice for the Marathi manus' and their emblem was a snarling tiger.

Dinoo Randive (seventy-two), leading Marathi columnist and an active member of the Socialist party: 'Bal Thackeray was not active in the Samyukta Maharashtra movement, (but) his father was. At the time, Thackeray was working as a cartoonist in the *Free Press Journal,* and his cartoons were being fanned out to six-seven journals. He used to sign as 'Mava'. I was then running a weekly, *Samyukta Maharashtra Patrika.* The committee decided that we must have a contribution from Bal Thackeray . . .

'After Thackeray's differences with the *Free Press Journal,* he and four-five people, S.B. Iyer, one Hariharan, George Fernandes . . . left the paper and started their own daily, *News Day.* The paper survived for barely one or two months. Thackeray had to do something, so he started *Marmik.*

'During the Samyukta Maharashtra (movement), he was closer to the communists. At that time, Thackeray's house was like the Samyukta Maharashtra Kriti Samiti's unofficial office because everyone would assemble there. He was sympathetic to the communists then. We thought *Marmik* would be a pro-communist weekly . . .

'The Left leaders had promised that after the formation of Maharashtra, all our problems would be over. And what was the main problem of Maharashtrians? Unemployment. Economically, Maharashtrians were very weak, the situation was so serious that at a book release function . . . Chief Minister Y.B. Chavan, in 1961 I think, said, first in Marathi and then in English, Bombay is the capital of Maharashtra, but it is dominated by others. We have not been able to give it a Marathi imprint.

'At that time, Acharya Atre's daily *Maratha* was selling like hot cakes. I'm told that Atre himself had said that though a Marathi state had been formed, the Marathi people had no role to play in it, that we had to launch some organization . . . (like the Shiv Sena that Thackeray started later) . . . Atre was not capable of taking his own stand, he was always leaning on others. The communists prevented him from forming such an organization, probably because it would spoil Bombay's cosmopolitan atmosphere.

'What was Thackeray's first call? Why are we unemployed, he asked. Because people are coming from other states and are getting all the jobs—like the hotels run by the Shetty community from Udupi, Karnataka. Bombay boys are not even getting the job of waiters in these hotels. When he heard of the anti-Hindi agitation in Tamil Nadu, he said, if they are anti-Hindi, we are also anti-South Indian. He went on about South Indians, but he didn't give such a call against Gujaratis, even though they were economically dominant. Actually, most of the South Indians were employed with the Central government, not the state government . . . The communists were right that the Sena's formation would lead to sectarianism.

'Shiv Sena was formed on Dussera day, which is an emotional day for Maharashtrians. The Marathas used to start their campaigns on Dussera. The (first) meeting was also addressed by Ramrao Adik . . . Thackeray said, "I want the Tatas, I want the Birlas. These communists want to liquidate them but they are giving us jobs." He (also) said, "This country needs a Hitler . . ." From Hitler, he went on to the prostitutes in Bombay city—"In Bombay, the goondas must be Marathi, the prostitutes must be Marathi, the bootlegger must be Marathi, in every field there should be Maharashtrians."

'(I remember) one Samant had written a book on Hitler. Thackeray purchased 500 copies for free distribution. Later, the writer of the book was accused of plagiarism and that left Thackeray looking very foolish indeed!'

The lists continued to appear in Marmik, *but now, the line below read:* Vacha ani utha *(Read and arise). The edge of the campaign sharpened against South Indians. The time to act was near.*

The huge support generated by Thackeray's call was not just spontaneous. Before the rally, Thackeray had held a public meeting in Ganesh Gully in Lalbaug, in the mill area, the success of which was a sure indicator of the way things would go for the Sena. To prepare for the Parel meeting, Thackeray had campaigned hard in the area. He had held several meetings in the gymnasiums and mandals (neighbourhood associations) in Girangaon. It was here in the working-class Marathi heartland of the city that he created his militant mass base. For the middle classes, he concentrated on Dadar and Girgaum, the predominantly Maharashtrian middle-class localities. The Sena encouraged their activists, especially the middle-class youth, to do community service. This service was from its inception, a trademark of the Sena, and the mainstay of the strong, rooted and cadre-based organization that (Thackeray) created.

Bal Nar (forty-eight), is a mill worker who was retrenched from Piramal Mills. He was one of the founder members of the Band Girni Kamgar Sangharsh Samiti (Closed Mills Action Committee): 'Balasaheb used to move around in the lanes and by-lanes of Girangaon to mobilize support for his organization. He held meetings at the Modern Mills as well. Wherever young people like us called him, he would come. People were not in awe of him as they are today. "Justice for the Marathi manus"—that was the slogan, the inspiration before us.

'We could see it all before our eyes—the street vendors, the traders were all outsiders, Madrasis, Gujaratis, Telugus. They would not treat us with respect, they would do dadagiri and they were organized. No one could oppose them. As the Shiv Sena grew, some of them got beaten and started behaving with respect . . . We had no political knowledge then, our response was emotional. As time went by, we became more aware. In those days jobs were an important issue. I was in that morcha to the Air India office, demanding jobs. We beat up the general manager, Lal . . . the boys did well, he will remember it all his life. He was dragged from the lift up to his cabin, and he was beaten all the way. This had its effect; Maharashtrians were recruited. Incidents like these convinced the youth that the Sena stood up for Maharashtrians.

'Our first shakha pramukh (branch leader) of Lalbaug was Ramesh Labde. He set up a shakha in Modern Mills, a small makeshift place built over a gutter, like a urinal. We would sit there. Ramesh was an educated man, a Hindi teacher in a Christian school on Arthur Road. He was smart, he could pick up people; he knew who would be useful. The rest of us knew nothing about politics. We were in school then, and we would all roam around with Labde. When we wanted to organize Shiv Jayanti, we would collect two or three rupees each from the local baniyas. We told people about 80 per cent reservation for Maharashtrians, about the Belgaum Karwar border issue[*]: "Belgaum Karwar Maharashtracha, naahin kunacha baapacha! (Belgaum Karwar belongs to Maharashtra, not to anybody's father)." That way, we built the organization and the shakha.

'Then the Sena participated in the municipal corporation elections. We campaigned for Labde. He lost by just forty-nine votes. The Congress won the seat. Balasaheb came for the street corner meetings (when we were campaigning), Pramod Navalkar too . . . We also used to go to Balasaheb's house at Kalanagar in Bandra to meet him. And he would come down to meet us.

'There was no corruption in the Sena then. I know that in 1970, our shakha had just 4000 rupees. All mostly from membership of one or two rupees each and contributions for Shiv Jayanti from local black marketeers, like the liquor and matka owners. Shiv Jayanti emerged as an important festival because of the Sena. The party also became more visible because of their participation in the traditional Ganeshotsav festival. The Sena placed their cadres in the Ganeshotsav Mandals, which also helped the organization. Another issue we took up was the issue of name boards on the shops. If they were not written in Marathi, we smeared them with tar. Balasaheb asked us to do that.'

R.S. Bhalekar, fifty, ex-Sena goon: 'My father worked in Morarjee Mills. My father was a member of the Girni Kamgar Union and he collected union dues in the mill. As children we organized morchas during elections for the CPI . . . I was attracted to the Shiv Sena although my family was with the Left.

---

[*]   Belgaum Karwar is a disputed region on the border of Maharashtra and Karnataka.

'We had a club where we played khokho. We brought Balasaheb Thackeray to this gully before the Shivaji Park rally in 1966. Sahib was not a big leader then. He would collect people around him and explain that we should not enter politics. People gathered, funds were raised, and then he took his next step. He fought the corporation elections.

'We were attracted because he was doing something for the Marathi *manus*. Though my father was firm on his (communist) stand, he said to me, do what you want. We thought, this man is doing the right thing. Some parents also become his followers, thinking he would do something for their children. I got brainwashed. His speeches had a lot of affection, love. He was like our Krishna Desai*.'

Bal Khaonekar, fifty, general secretary of the Girni Kamgar Sena: 'My father was a freedom fighter. I joined India United Mill No.1 after being retrenched from China Mill (Standard Mills) in 1968. When I joined the Labour movement in the seventies, the communists were leading it. Krishna Desai was our leader. I was attracted to activities like demonstrations and morchas.

'When we were out of work, we were also attending meetings of the Shiv Sena. Workers of the Bhabha Atomic Energy Commission told us how the Sena had helped find jobs for the unemployed Marathi youth. Then, Marathi people were held in contempt in Mumbai. It was Balasaheb who took up the issue of the Marathi people through *Marmik*. From the lists of people in public and government organizations that were published in *Marmik*, we could see that all the jobs were going to non-Maharashtrians. That is why people were attracted to Balasaheb. There was a spontaneous response to his first public meeting in Shivaji Park. There, he told us that when the states in India were reorganized on a linguistic basis, the Marathi people got Bombay, but there were still no jobs for Maharashtrians here . . . This is how we were mobilized.

'Balasaheb was interested in art and sports, and developed contact with the vyayamshalas (local gymnasiums) . . . Balasaheb was confident

---

* Popular communist leader based in Girangaon who was later murdered.

that the movement would grow through activities in the cultural field. That is why he concentrated on capturing the vyayamshalas and with their help, he held local meetings in the chawls, in small halls and the maidans of Girangaon where he propagated his views. He held a meeting in Ganesh Gully Maidan at Lalbaug on the eve of the Shivaji Park meeting where the Shiv Sena was launched. This meeting and its press coverage were responsible for the huge response to the Shivaji Park meeting.

'My father was a Congress supporter, so naturally he opposed the thinking of the Sena. He was initially opposed to my involvement with the Sena, but when I got a job through them, he too began to see their point of view. All the people of Lalbaug were with the communists at first, then they began to support the Shiv Sena. I joined the Left movement when I was young, but it did not provide jobs. This was their drawback. No political party except the Sena bothers about providing a livelihood. That is the difference between the Left and the Right . . . And what's wrong with setting up batatawada* carts? Some people make fun of them, but how many families survived because of this. (In any case) Balasaheb was not saying we should involve ourselves only in the batatawada trade. He wanted Marathi people to enter mainstream businesses and professions . . . I was among the Sainiks who took the oath in Shiv Sena Bhavan. I don't remember the other points, just that we swore that we would buy only from Maharashtrians.

'Festivals like Ganeshotsav and Shiv Jayanti were being celebrated for years, but it was the Sena which gave them a social content and made them more grand and colourful. The Sena opened shakhas in every area, and their work was 80 per cent social work and 20 per cent political. The activities included health camps, vocational guidance camps and eye camps. Local people would also bring their grievances to the shakhas. In fact, the first shakha was established in Lalbaug. The communists had a base there, then the Congress and then the

---

* The Shiv Sena instituted a scheme for unemployed youth to operate carts selling a popular Maharashtrian snack—batatawada, which is a mashed potato fritter.

Praja Socialist Party. But it was the Sena which identified with the Marathi manus and his problems; which shared his joys and sorrows. The Sena corporators and MLAs had a deep bond with the Marathi sections. Managements in offices and factories were asked to provide employment to Maharashtrians. This and the social programmes won the confidence of the local people.'

Fire

Arun Kolatkar

This fire   This one laughing   This is yet another
What shall I do with it   Where shall I keep it
Shall I set it   to the house   to the door   to the world
What will it cook   where will it spread
This torch   where shall I throw it
This fire   must be obeyed
This fire   wear it on your head
Become a torch dance

Come, let's play
Light my cigarette
Fire my engine
Leaven my bread
Cook my stew
Condense my soul
Boil my blood
Bend my steel
Melt my gold
Bake my brick
Crackle my mustard
Burn my corpse
Fling my arrows
Helter skelter
This fire   This one laughing   This is yet another
I am the toppling Ravana   I am charcoal   I am charcoal
This is the Dussera

From *The Literary Endeavour* (1986-87).

This fire   Flames flames   This bonfire
Broken window   I'm a smashed door   This bonfire
          This bonfire   This bonfire
Limping chair   I'm a table on crutches   This bonfire
          This bonfire   This bonfire
Running fence   I'm a beam escaping   This bonfire
          This bonfire   This bonfire
Flying cupboard   I'm a warehouse being looted   This
     bonfire   This bonfire   This bonfire
This world without tunnels   This house of wax
Helpless   Helpless   Fire engines   Sandbuckets
          Water tanks

You are fire   I'm ash
You are today   I'm cash
You are yesterday   You are fire   You are tomorrow
You are fire   You are now   You are before
          You are after
You are flower   I'm stalk

You are matchhead   I'm matchstick
You are sacred fire   I'm holy man
You are fire   Ask   Take
I'm smoke   I'm smoke   I'm smoke

I am myself sacrificial fire   I am the host   I am the altar
          I am the priest   I am the fire   I am the sacrifice
The fire itself   is ignorant
I sacrifice   I sacrifice   I sacrifice

Your mane will catch fire   Be careful
Your tail will burn   Take care
Come my lion   Make a compromise
Jump   through   this burning hoop
From here to there   and again   from there to here
This fire shaped lie a zero   This freedom to burn is daily

This whole circus   is you alone
Rajabai Tower   The Gateway   The Taj
The Majestic Hotel
These buildings   beasts   foxes   tigers   wild boars
This jungle   moulded   this clear   darkness
These vultures
You are hearth   neighbouring   fire
Scatter the city   make them wait
Rajabai Tower   The Gateway   The Taj
The Majestic Hotel   Churchgate Station
The Town Hall   The Victoria Terminus   The Regal
          The Eros
Detached Immobile

Keep burning   please   for my sake
Keep   me   warm
Terrify   this   city
Otherwise   these buildings   will tear me   and devour me
This city   stays as is   because of you   or else   or else

Terrorize   the city   the museum
Be   a neighbour

—*Translated from Marathi by Dilip Chitre and Mick Fedullo*

Doongaji House

Cyrus Mistry

Act 1 Scene 1

PERIN, *a plain-looking girl in a long dumpy frock, is seated at the round marble-topped table. A few moments later,* PIROJA *enters from the kitchen with two plates of French beans and two knives, and joins* PERIN *at the table.*

PIROJA: Take care to peel the threads off both sides. This house is full of fusspots.

(They work silently; then PIROJA *puts down her knife and fans herself with piece of cardboard.)*

Ohoho! What heat. Unbearable heat.
PERIN: Terrible heat! Will the rains be here by next week? I wonder!
PIROJA: No sign of rain.
PERIN: Landlord said anything about your new wire fittings?
PIROJA: Two years since our wiring rotted. I've grown so used to this lamp, I think it will hurt my eyes if we ever get back our lights. But I miss the fan.
PERIN: If you were to keep the windows open, at least!
PIROJA: The house would be coated in dust in five minutes. These buses pass right under our noses now; people can look straight in. Ever since they cut the footpath to widen the road.

(As if in confirmation of her grievances, a loud bleating of horns mixed with general traffic noises.)

From *Doongaji House*, a play in five acts (1991).

PERIN: Next week, my Mummy will be sixty-three.

PIROJA: *Depdin Roj*?

PERIN: *Sherevar* . . . Just think, Piroja Aunty . . .

PIROJA: What?

PERIN: First your Rusi went away to Canada. Then Fali went away to Chikkalwadi. The Bogdawallas and their children moved out lock, stock and barrel. Who's left in the building now? Only old people.

PIROJA: Looks like the landlord's just waiting for our wickets to fall, one by one.

PERIN: Old oldies. Except Avan and myself, who else in the building is below sixty?

PIROJA: That's if we are not all buried together, one of these days.

(Looks up at the ceiling, apprehensively.)

PERIN: Remember? How we used to play on your landing! Racing up and down the stairs till late in the evening, till you would shout to us to go home! *(Tunefully)* L-O-N-D-O-N, London!

PIROJA: Hmm. Every step I take on the staircase now makes my heart quake. The boards feel like they'll give way any day.

PERIN: After dinner, we'd bundle ourselves into your large soft bed and play rummy. Everyone, Mummy, sometimes Hormusji also, if he was not too busy with his books and papers! *(Giggles)* All the children would fight to sit next to him. He'd pretend to be very absorbed in his cards, but slyly he was tickling whoever sat beside him. The way he would wag his big toe!

PIROJA: I think the vegetable-man has really cheated me today. Just keep the bad ones aside, Perin. I'll throw them at his face when he comes tomorrow.

PERIN *(after a pause)*: How boring everything has become! Everyone's left. Shall I say something, Piroja Aunty?

PIROJA *(slightly irritable)*: What is it?

PERIN: Sometimes I think it's for the best that Fali changed his mind about marrying me. Even if it was at the last minute.

(PIROJA throws her a contemptuous glance and continues working.)

You don't know the kind of talk that's flying around Chikkalwadi. Comes home late every night, reeking and really gives it to her. First he makes her squeal, then he makes her whimper. Keeps up the neighbours till one in the morning, with his swearing and shouting. I heard the tenants have put out a petition to the Panchayat to have him evicted.

PIROJA: Stop jabbering! You know the tiffin-man will be here at eleven. If I make him wait one minute, he starts shouting and runs away.

(PERIN *bends her head obediently and concentrates on trimming the beans. But* PIROJA *is uneasy. When she speaks again, her voice is charged with an emotional urgency.*)

I know. He broke off with you a week before the wedding. He went and married Jal Talati's ayah instead. He drinks. He smokes. He gave up a good job and became a matka-bookie instead. I know everything! *(Bitterly sarcastic)* Everyone used to say, 'Pirojamai, you are really blessed with such beautiful bright children.' Actually, they couldn't bear to see it. They were burning with jealousy. How well he played the piano! His father talked of sending him to Germany, Vienna. Suddenly he picked up a stick and smashed everything around him. See his state now.

(*Turns on* PERIN, *a flash of anger.*)

Why do you moon about the house all day, like a parrot that's losing its feathers? Why don't you go out and find someone else, while your flesh is still unwrinkled?
(At this moment, we hear HORMUSJI's *voice humming* La Marseillaise *off-stage. His singing and his approaching footsteps grow louder, then stop abruptly. He has become aware of the two women in the living-room. He tries to sneak into the bedroom unnoticed by* PIROJA. *He raises a finger to his lips cautioning* PERIN, *who has seen him, not to give him away. He is half-way across the stage, when—*)

PIROJA *(aggressively)*: Ah, back already? So early where have you been roaming?

HORMUSJI *(sighs)*: Yes! This heat is really something outside. No sign of the rains at all!

PIROJA: Is that so? *(to PERIN)* Saw his foxiness? What question I ask and what answer he gives. *(Shouts)* Say at once! Where were you?

HORMUSJI: What's the need to roar like that? Just went down to Mayrose for a cup of tea.

PERIN *(incredulous)*: Uncle! You never like tea!

HORMUSJI: Be quiet! Whole day you sit and butter her up.

PIROJA: She'll say whatever she wants. *(Rising from the stool)* Let's see since when you became a tea-lover? Open your mouth!

HORMUSJI *(backing away)*: Am I a child or what?

(A slight scuffle ensues, in which HORMUSJI tries to turn his face away, but PIROJA manages to catch a whiff of liquor in his breath.)

PIROJA *(striking her forehead)*: Saw? From this hour in the morning he begins scorching his throat. This is poison for you, poison! Dr Lalkaka has warned you thousands of times. When you are flat on your back, your liver all chewed up and rotted, then don't expect me to bring the bedpan to your cot.

HORMUSJI: Okay, so it's poison: I'll die. Few days I have left; let me live those in peace at least?

PIROJA *(mimicks)*: Okay, so I'll die. Spoken like a brainless ass!

PERIN: Uncle, why don't you be reasonable? Piroja Aunty worries so much about you.

HORMUSJI: *Chaal*, shut up! I'll drive you out of the house this minute.

PIROJA: Shall I remind you what happened to your friend Dinshah Kanga? When you went to his bedside in those last days, you came away dripping with sweat. *(Mimicks)* 'Piroja, Piroja, now I have seen so much, now I will never touch a bottle again.' Before his *uthamna* was done, you had started again. *(Pauses for breath)* As for that great friend of your downstairs, I wouldn't say any better fate awaits him: Darabshaa: *Salo* loafer!

HORMUSJI: Just now you were talking about me; now you've gone on to him?

PIROJA: Whatever is the truth I will say it. Of course he is giving you encouragement. He is two steps ahead of you. Hmph. Wanted to be a schoolmaster, it seems. Are you listening, Perin? Flask in his coat-pocket, and he would suckle at it every half-hour. One-two pegs, before every class, like a newborn babe! *(Turns to Hormusji)* But he is a bachelor, Hormusji. Even if he locks himself in the bathroom and gargles with carbolic acid there is no one to ask any questions. If something happens to you, who is going to pay the hospital bills?

HORMUSJI: Say. Say more. Say whatever comes to your mouth.

PIRJOA: Who would believe this man is approaching seventy? Have you given your wits a scrubbing and put them out to dry or what?

HORMUSJI: Bas? Finished? Say some more. Cast your spells. *(Darkly)* I hope every word comes true. In those days who would have believed that this would be my state today? *(In a tone of mock puzzlement)* 'Hormusji?' they would have asked, 'Which Hormusji?' *(Utter disbelief)* 'Hormusji Pochkhanawalla! Na, na, not possible, heh, heh, not possible.'

PIROJA: Come, baby. Better light the primus. Once Hormusji starts his theatrics, there will be no interval for hours.

(PERIN is too engrossed.)

HORMUSJI *(theatrically)*: One crate would be delivered here every week! Tell me if it is not true! Tell me if I lie! Scotch, cognac, vodka! Whatever you want, ask, and you shall have it. Today, to get two pegs of rotgut from that mad Irani in the bar, I have to fight tooth and nail, how many gallons of my liquor has he drowned? Forgotten? Lost count? Because I have lost my wealth, I have to listen to these words today from you, from my friends, from everyone. But I did not lose it! Ah! Correction! I was cheated out of it. Swindled. By one who had my own mother's blood in him.

PIROJA *(tensely)*: For whose sake these long-winded recitations? We have heard the story many times before.

HORMUSJI *(raises his voice)*: You shut up! I am talking to myself. I am mad!

PIROJA: Okay, talk. I am busy with my kitchen. *(To PERIN)* Are you coming or no?

(PERIN reluctantly follows her into the kitchen. HORMUSJI, calmer now, ruminates over the past, a certain bitterness in his voice as he talks, now addressing the audience, now only to himself.)

HORMUSJI: What made me do it, I wonder!? To this day, I still think about it. What made me offer him that job? For that matter, why did I ever let him set foot in my house, knowing his nature!? And why did I trust him in the end, when sickness preyed upon my senses. Blood is thicker than water, they say. Sometimes it curdles, and then it is so thick you could slice it with a knife. That's what he did to me. He ripped me up. Hacked me, and then fled. My own step-brother Sohrab. I had this strange illness, which nobody could diagnose. Rest, rest, take rest, they all said to me. So I went to a sanatorium and rested for three months. When I came back, I found the ice-cream factory closed. Heavy debts. Our cycle shop, which used to hire out bicycles lying in heaps, mangled! But worst of all, my bookshop . . . the bookshop which belonged to my father, and to his father before him. He had sold the bookshop! Rare volumes, priceless manuscripts, disposed off for a song, by a callous boor who could not even have guessed at their value. It was too great a blow for me! Too much!

PIROJA *(emerging from the kitchen)*: Don't add too much chilli powder.

HORMUSJI *(snaps)*: What's that?

PIROJA: I am talking to Perin. What are you getting excited about?

(She has come out only to take something from the table, and goes back into the kitchen.)

HORMUSJI: Sohrab never returned from Bangalore. With all the money he had accumulated at my expense, he built a house there, for himself and some bazaar slut he had taken for a wife. But there is, after all, a Justice that governs our Universe. And swiftly it took its course. One month after Sohrab moved into his new house, he suffered a paralytic stroke. Three weeks later, he was dead. His son, Cawas, has grown up now. Must be twenty-eight/twenty-nine.

(PIROJA comes out again, issuing final instructions to PERIN about the cooking, and settles into the easychair. Hearing HORMUSJI's last sentence, she shows a sudden interest.)

PIROJA: You told me he was doing very well for himself?
HORMUSJI *(stiffly)*: So I heard. And do you think he will be able to eat his ill-gotten wealth? He will choke on it.
PIROJA *(reasonably)*: But Hormusji, he seems qu'te a nice boy, really.
HORMUSJI: Who?
PIROJA: Why, Cawas. Remember he sent us such a lovely card last Papeti.
HORMUSJI *(mutters)*: Tricks. All tricks. I should have sued that family long ago.
PIROJA: We are the only family he has left, poor boy. May be he wants to make up in some way for what his father . . . May be, if he comes to Bombay . . .
HORMUSJI: I will spit on his face, if he dares to show it.

(But HORMUSJI is suddenly transported by the memory of a verse from Shakespeare, and he declaims, gravely, introspectively.)

'Ingratitude, thou marble-hearted fiend more hideous than the sea-monster, when thou showst thee in a child . . .'

(A subtle change of mood takes place in HORMUSJI. He chuckles.)

Major Bamji, heh, heh Major Minocher Bamji. How he taught us Shakespeare. How he instilled in us a love for the great Bard of Stratford . . . *(to PIROJA)* Well? I may have put my wits out to dry, but at sixty-nine the memory is still giving good service, eh?

(Sings)

'Then sing heigh-ho the holly, this life is most jolly,

Most friendship is feigning most loving mere folly . . .'

(Playfully) Say something? Some words of praise for an old wretch?

PIROJA: Very good. We'll announce it in *Jame* tomorrow.

(PERIN comes out of the kitchen.)

PERIN: I've put the flame slow. The beans are nearly done.
PIROJA: Just pass my specs, dear, and the newspaper.

(PERIN gives them to her.)

Haven't had a moment since morning, even to glance at the Deaths column!
HORMUSJI *(sarcastically)*: Going? So soon? Sit a little longer!

(PERIN puts her tongue out at HORMUSJI, on her way to the door. He raises his foot comically, as if aiming a kick at her. When she is gone and the old couple are alone, HORMUSJI suddenly looks very tired, drained. He takes off his jacket and hangs it on the back of the easychair; then asks, gravely):

Anyone we know?

(PIROJA shakes her head mutely. He takes off his shirt as well and hangs it. Then sits on a stool and begins unlacing his shoes.)

I have a memory that never fails me. I am not boasting, Piroja. It is my special curse. When I think of old times, I feel so brittle . . . Worn . . . I feel I could just pluck the fingers off my hand and toss them away. Then my toes, my nose, my ears, my tongue . . . till at last nothing remains, but a thought that rankles. How things have changed in the last few years.
PIROJA: Not few, Hormusji. Things changed nearly thirty years ago.

HORMUSJI *(bitterly)*: I don't care. Whatever followed has only been an endless desert for me. Do you remember those days, Piroja? When Rusi was only five or six, and Fali was still learning to walk?

(PIROJA *turns a page of the newspaper and continues reading.*)

Things were so cheap then, we had plenty of money. Every evening, coming home from work, I'd pick up something ... those eclairs from Monginis? Pineapple cake! Liqueur chocolates!

(PIROJA *puts down her newspaper, drawn into the web of nostalgia herself. Now she and* HORMUSJI *speak associatively, without really talking to each other*)

PIROJA: Everything was cheap. Eggs five annas a dozen. Only later, after Avan was born, they went up to fourteen annas. Everything started going up then. And never stopped.
HORMUSJI: Yes, Avan. How much she has changed too! What a cheerful, spritely little devil she used to be.
PIROJA: You gave us all the comforts. You called me your Queen Sheba of Princess Street. But you never had time for me. Only your drinking-mates, your precious books!
HORMUSJI: A most talented child, Avan. At school she won essay competitions. Two of her poems were published in *Kaiser-e-Hind*.
PIROJA: I had to look to others for companionship.
HORMUSJI: Now she does not write anymore. She has become so serious, so sullen. As if she is carrying some secrets inside her, something she will not share.
PIROJA: Sohrab left so suddenly for Bangalore. Not a word from him. Then the news of his death. Then everything fell apart.

(*A long silence*)

HORMUSJI: Is there no letter from Rusi this month also?
PIROJA: No letter.
HORMUSJI: How can it be? I have a feeling that postman is behind

this. Spiting us for not giving him his Diwali *bakshish*. Let him come
next time.

PIROJA: You think he has no better work than to steal your son's
letters?

HORMUSJI: You don't understand these people, Piroja. They've
got completely out of hand. They think it is their Raj now. Was a time
when they would bow and scrape to us. If a Parsi got on to a bus, they
would rush to offer him a seat. Today, walking down the street, they
make fun of you. '*Bawaji aya. Parsi bawaji ko dekho.*' Sometimes I just
feel like taking a horsewhip and flaying them! But those days are
gone. The Parsis of old are all gone. This is a generation of schoolgirls.
See in our own family. We have a good example.

PIROJA: Okay, enough now. Less said the better.

HORMUSJI: How can I keep quiet? How low he has stooped! These
people who don't even wash their arses after shitting . . . he's married
one of them.

PIROJA *(shouts)*: Didn't I say enough?

(*Another long pause ensues. Street noises fade-in, fade-out.*)

HORMUSJI: If only we could get away from here . . . If only Rusi
would just sponsor us.

PIROJA: What plans you make, Hormusji!

HORMUSJI: Why, don't you want to go?

PIROJA: To Canada? At one time I did. Now my bones feel too old to
carry me such a long way. Go now? To die there?

HORMUSJI: Yes. Yes, even that I would not mind . . . To meet Rusi
. . . to see the big cities . . . the snow. You know Piroja, I've never sat in
a plane.

PIROJA: Read his letters. I always say: if you want to be blind, all you
have to do is shut your eyes.

HORMUSJI *(reluctantly)*: It is strange. Always the same letter. Is this
a letter? 'Hi folks, how's everything out there? I'm fine. It's freezing
out here, but everything is centrally heated so it's quite pleasant. Bye
for now, Your loving son Rusi.' Is that a letter? God knows. God knows
what he is doing there. But I'll tell you one thing, Piroja, see this.

(HORMUSJI extends his right palm.)

Travel to a foreign land is very definitely in my fortune line. Besides
. . . no, never mind.

PIROJA: What?

HORMUSJI: No. Nothing. You'll laugh at me again.

PIROJA: Say? Say?

HORMUSJI *(in a hushed, reverential tone)*: Some months ago, I saw
Dhanjishaa Bapasola. He told me . . .

PIROJA: Dhanjishaa Bapasola! *(starts laughing)* At this rate you'll go
crack!

HORMUSJI: See. You're laughing. Don't laugh! I don't like it. Besides,
I am not the only one who has seen the spirit of Dhanjishaa Bapasola.
Darabshaa has seen it. Also old Burjorji.

PIROJA: One is a drunk who will agree with anything you say. The
other is half-crazed with age.

HORMUSJI *(sadly)*: After all these years, Piroja, you still do not
understand me . . . Poor Dhanjishaa. No one understood him either.

PIROJA: Go in and lie down. You've talked enough for one day.

HORMUSJI: No one in the whole building. Hardly anyone ever
spoke to him. Sometimes for weeks on end he would not be seen at all.
But once in a while, a housewife caught a glimpse of him on the
landing, saying his prayers, or down by the well doing his *kashti*. And
she would run, panting with excitement to the other housewives in
their kitchens and announce Dhanjishaa Bapasola is still alive.

PIROJA: And where was Burjorji?

HORMUSJI: I am talking about more than sixty years ago. Burjorji
and his wife moved in much later. At the time, there was only
Dhanjishaa upstairs. With his six dogs.

PIROJA: Six dogs!

HORMUSJI: Mongrels he had picked up in the streets, grown
ferocious from being chained all day.

PIROJA: No wonder the neighbours hated him.

HORMUSJI: One day, I was on my way home from school when I
saw a tall willowy man standing at the top of the stairs.

(The ghostly figure of BAPASOLA, gnarled with age, wrapped in a voluminous white sudrah *and flowing white pyjamas, appears on the elevated part of the stage, glowing dimly in the darkness. The figure on stage never speaks. His lines, spoken backstage, are amplified and booming with echo. The rest of the stage is dark.)*

BAPASOLA: HORMUZ! HORMUZ!

(Sounds of footsteps. A small boy of eight or nine in school uniform, carrying a satchel, approaches from darkness the aura of light surrounding BAPASOLA. Hesitantly, he climbs the steps leading to the platform.)

HORMUSJI *(in darkness)*: I wondered where he could have learnt my name, and faltered up the stairs.

(BAPASOLA bends down and whispers something in the boy's ear. He puts his arm around his shoulder and leads him out of the light into darkness.)

That day I found out that under his gruff exterior which everyone feared lived a very kind and loving man. He took me into his house and told me not to be afraid.

(The boy and BAPASOLA appear in another part of the stage which lights up. The boy puts down his school-bag.)

The furniture was old and dusty, and it made me sneeze. *(The boy sneezes: Aachoo!)* The six dogs were lying in a row, quiet and drowsy, as if they had been drugged. He told me their names and made me pat them on the head: Bruno, Caesar, Cerberus. *(The boy bends and cautiously caresses each of the dogs.)* Then . . .

BAPASOLA: HORMUZ
HORMUSJI: He said to me . . .
BAPASOLA: Do you know why everyone in this house hates me? Do you know? *(The boy shakes his head slowly, from side to side)* because I hate them! Men and women. I hate them both! But I love dogs . . . and

little boys . . . These have not yet been corrupted by Ahriman's forces!

(BAPASOLA *bends down and begins unbuttoning the boy's shirt and helps him out of it. The boy takes out a white hanky from his pocket and places it on his head. Then he begins untying his* kashti.)

HORMUSJI (*still in darkness*): Then he made me say my *kashti* prayers because he wanted to check if I was really a good boy.

(*The boy is now holding his* kashti *outstretched between thumb and fingers.* BAPASOLA *kneels, embraces the boy tenderly and kisses his forehead. Then, in an amplified whisper*):

BAPASOLA: Tomorrow night, when everyone is asleep, come quietly to my door and knock thrice. I will let you in and show you such wonders that even when you are old and ready to die, you will not forget the great Bapasola.

(*The light on* BAPASOLA *and the boy fades out, and now* HORMUSJI *is in the spotlight.*)

HORMUSJI: The next night, trembling with excitement, I got up when everyone was asleep, and made for the front door. But as my luck would have it. I stumbled over the servant sleeping in the passage. He screamed in fright and woke the whole family. After that, a strict check was kept on my whereabouts, constantly. Only a week later, something happened which shook everyone in the building out of their wits. At sunset, one evening, the old man was seen doing his *kashti* at the well. Then suddenly, without warning, everyone heard a loud—SPLASH (*Silence*) . . . That was the last they saw of him. His body was never recovered. The well was boarded up forever that night, the dogs in his house howled and howled, till the dogs in the street joined in, and all of Dhobhi Talao knew that Dhanjishaa Bapasola was dead.

(*Stage lights fade in to show* PIROJA *again, stretched out in the easychair.*

She has been a silent spectator to HORMUSJI's story. Though she appears not to be listening.)

But was that really the last we saw him? He was a very holy man. On certain nights, when the moon is only a slit in the sky, the Good Spirit of Dhanjishaa Bapasola appears at the well. He is seen in a long white *sudrah* that touches his knees and spotless white pyjamas. He can be heard doing his *kashti* late into the night, cracking it like a whip that can put the fear of God in the meanest and lowliest of devils!

(The high drama of HORMUSJI's tale is rendered anti-climatic by a suppressed giggle from PIROJA, which abruptly grows into unrestrained laughter.)

HORMUSJI (*contemptuously*): Don't jeer at things you can't understand! It is a boorish trait.

PIROJA (*provokingly*): I never said I don't believe in spirits. But the spirits that linger behind are unhappy, or evil. Good souls travel smoothly.

HORMUSJI (*snaps*): Watch what you say! There may be higher reasons.

PIROJA: Such as?

HORMUSJI: To aid those mortals it has known in its earthly life.

PIROJA: Meaning you?

HORMUSJI: Yes. Perhaps even me. (PIROJA *laughs again*.) You have no imagination, Piroja, no will to live. You think our condition will never change for the better. But how do we know what life holds in store for us? Avan is still young!

PIROJA: Avan?

HORMUSJI: Yes. Avan.

PIROJA (*mysteriously*): Yes. How do we know? How do we know anything?

HORMUSJI (*puzzled*): Why? What do you mean?

PIROJA: Nothing. Nothing.

HORMUSJI: Cheer up. Cheer up, Piroja. Never be a pessimist in life.

(*He collects his shoes and socks, his coat and shirt.*)

I think I'll go lie down for a while.
(*He starts humming the* Marseillaise; *then suddenly stops short, as he remembers something.*)

Guess who I met today? Kelso! My old school buddy. The first thing he asked me was, 'Remember the *Marseillaise*?' (*Laughs.*)
PIROJA: Now! What is it again?
HORMUSJI: Our French teacher, Father Gaston. He had this long thick beard he was very proud of. You could tell by the way he stroked it. 'Fr Gaston has bugs in his beard!' By God, he was wild. He spent two hours trying to make us confess who had written these words on the blackboard. In the end he gave up and said, 'For this grave insult, each of you shall write out the French national anthem 500 times.' Guess who had written that line on the blackboard.
PIROJA: How do I know? Must be you.
HORMUSJI (*terribly amused*): Me and my friend Kelso.
PIROJA: No shame to boast about it at this age?
HORMUSJI: Kelso can never remember the words beyond the first verse, as for me, I would be able to rattle it off even on my deathbed.

(*He begins singing lustily, shoes and all still in his hands.*)

Allons enfants de la Patrie, Le jour de gloire est arrivé.
Contre nous de la tyranie,
L'etendard sanglant élevé.

(*At the culmination of the first verse, a rude knocking on the front door tapped out in the beat of the songs martial rhythm. The old couple start. There is a shocked silence, before* HORMUSJI *drops his clothes and shoes and goes to the door. It is* FALI *who enters swaggering.*)

FALI: *Kem?* Some song and dance party in progress, Dad?
HORMUSJI: You!
FALI: Who do I look like?

PIROJA: For six weeks you didn't show your face. We didn't know if you were dead or alive.

FALI: Mummy I'm so busy, you have no idea. Whole day, no time even for a gulp of water.

PIROJA: How come?

FALI: I am expanding my business. Too much work.

HORMUSJI: Business? We know what kind of business. Sitting here we get all the news.

PIROJA: Is it true they are going to evict you?

HORMUSJI: Of course it's true. They will throw him and his ayah out on the footpath. Why shouldn't they? Its a Parsi colony. Not for *dheras* like—

PIROJA: Bas! Go in and rest now, will you? You've talked enough for one day.

FALI: No fighting, no fighting please. Actually I'm in a bit of a hurry. I just stopped by to give Daddy a tip.

HORMUSJI: What?

FALI: A number. A sure bet for tomorrow. Put a little something on it, make a few hundred bucks . . .

HORMUSJI (furious): A number! Besharam! Not enough that you degraded yourself, you now come to your own father with a tip?

FALI: Now, now. (*To* PIROJA) See how he behaves. (*Tauntingly*) As if Hormusji Pochkhanawalla has never betted on a matka number before.

HORMUSJI (*very emotional*): I? Matka number? You monster! Because I am old you think you can talk to me any way you like? I've eaten the ghee of earlier days. I'll remove your whole set of teeth— I'll—!

(*He rushes up aggressively, but* PIROJA *intervenes, speaking firmly but kindly, as if to a child.*)

PIROJA: Sit down. Sit down. Sit down at once.

HORMUSJI (*appeals*): This boy has cut off our noses. I can't show my face to half of Dhobhi Talao—(*starts coughing and clutches his chest. Backs down and sits, muttering:*)—His happiness will come only when he sees me dead. That is his one mission in life . . .

(HORMUSJI *holds his head in his hand. A pause, during which the metallic grating sound of someone roller-skating on the floor above begins to be heard. First faintly, then louder and faster. FALI and PIROJA seem not to hear at first but it is making* HORMUSJI *visibly tense.*)

PIROJA: And how is—Lucy?
FALI: She's okay.
PIROJA: What stories I hear about you . . .
FALI: Stories? . . . Mumma, in from one ear, out the other. Malicious people will talk. Why bother?

(The noises have grown louder. HORMUSJI *can't take it anymore. He rushes to the window and yells:)*

HORMUSJI: How are we to live here? Burjorji Bonesetter! Stop it at once!
FALI: What! That buddha is still alive?
PIROJA: He's eighty-four now, and still a proper nuisance. If he breaks a bone at this age, he'll never leave his bed alive. Stop it, Burjorji!

(Gradually the noise comes to a halt.)

Everytime he starts roller-skating, we have to shout some sense into his head. Sometimes he won't even listen, he'll go on.
FALI: Poor fellow. *Jara . . .? (Makes circular gestures in the region of his temple, to say: screw-loose)*
PIROJA *(nods)*: Ever since that night . . .
FALI: I remember. But that was ages ago.
HORMUSJI: What difference does it make? The pain remains.
PIROJA: *Dhandar* and *Kolmi no patio*. The little one's birthday, they were feasting. But the prawns must have been very old or not properly cleaned. All three of them were poisoned. And poor Burjorji the only survivor of his daughter's birthday dinner. Since then, everyone in the building has stopped eating prawns.

FALI: If you're going to die, you can die of pomfret as well.

(For some reason, this statement angers HORMUSJI again.)

HORMUSJI: Spare us your philosophy! If you think you're smart, go! Look at yourself in the mirror. See what you've made of yourself. . . If I had all the opportunity I gave you as a father, where would I have been today. At sixteen I was LTCL in violin. Old Arthur Furtado used to call me Homi Heifitz! But fate was against me, my family responsibilities too many . . . And look at you. I gave you everything— leisure, comfort, the best teachers, the best piano in Bombay. And all you could make of yourself is a contemptible matka bookie.

FALI: And suppose I wanted to be that? Did you ever ask me if I was even interested in music? Come to think of it, we haven't heard you play in a long time. Where's the old Stradi? Come on, Dad, give us a performance.

HORMUSJI: If two strings were not broken—*(livid)*. He's trying to make fun of me He's trying to taunt his old father. Tell him to get out, Piroja! I can't stand the sight of him!

(HORMUSJI hurriedly wears his shirt and jacket again.)

PIROJA: Now, now. What do you think you're doing?

HORMUSJI: Better still, I'll go myself.

PIROJA: You're not going anywhere.

(HORMUSJI ignores her and wears on his socks determinedly, when there is another loud knocking on the door. FALI answers. It is DARABSHAA. He is about the same age as HORMUSJI, slightly taller, plump and effeminate.)

DARABSHAA *(gasping)*: Hormusji! Hormusji! Hormusji!

HORMUSJI: What has happened, Darabshaa?

DARABSHAA: It's the heat. It's gone to everyone's head. The city is in ferment. Rioting may break out any minute, who knows? Bloodshed!

PIROJA: He's drunk, if you ask me.

DARABSHAA: I swear, I swear I'm sober. I heard it just now on my transistor. You can use my ice-box. Fill it up with foodstuffs. Tomorrow, who knows, nothing may be available in the market.

FALI: Rubbish! Old wives' gossip!

(DARABSHAA is stunned by this verbal assault. But a moment later, he starts grinning foolishly, obsequiously.)

DARABSHAA: Pardon me son, pardon me. You must know better, of course. Heh, hey, anyone can see I'm an old buffoon, heh, heh, what do we know, Hormusji? We must watch this younger generation. Watch how they will sweep us off our feet and into the gutters of—

HORMUSJI: Talk sense, Darabshaa. Get a hold on yourself. What's all this about?

FALI: I'll tell you. It's nothing serious. Last night two Maharashtrian boys were stabbed in a fight. Some political thing. They were members of that group—Yuvak Sangh or something. So their gang retaliated. Some shops in Null Bazaar were looted. A few windshields smashed. Some Muslim fellows were beaten up in random. That's all. No one's going to bother you.

DARABSHAA: There. Bravo. How well put. What did I tell you, Hormusji? This generation understands things much better than we ever could. We old dodderers will mumble and fumble, but they will come straight to the point. Of course, I'm only speaking for myself.

HORMUSJI: Shut up.

DARABSHAA: Sorry, sorry . . .

HORMUSJI: This is serious. No laughing matter. In 1921, when the Prince of Wales came to Bombay, the same thing happened. Parsis vs. Hindus. A few shops looted, a few of our women molested . . . before we knew it, it had spread through the whole city and we were fighting to save our lives. What a licking we gave them! Remember, Darabshaa?

DARABSHAA *(also animated by these memories)*: I was only eight years old, Hormusji. But I remember, my father and uncles were up on the terrace, singling out the Hindus one by one . . . *(Pretends to take aim with a rifle.)*

HORMUSJI: We even poured pots of boiling water on their backs. In three days they were on their knees, begging for mercy . . . But those days are gone, Darabshaa. This is a generation of sissies. The blood has been polluted. *(HORMUSJI slips into his shoes.)* I'm going out with Darabshaa now. Don't say anything, Piroja. I'm really angry today . . . Oh, but before I go . . .

(He goes into the bedroom and comes out a moment later, carrying a large airgun.)

Take this. Keep it with you.

(PIROJA, taken aback, only reluctantly accepts the gun from HORMUSJI's outstretched hand.)

My grandfather's. Only an airgun, but it can kill a man.
PIROJA: Giving me a gun and going loafing yourself?
HORMUSJI: No arguments please, no arguments . . .
FALI: I'm going too. If you want to put something on that number you know where to find me.
PIROJA *(anxiously)*: Don't go, Hormusji. Darabshaa can sit here with you. You never know. It may be dangerous outside.
HORMUSJI *(already at the door)*: Don't worry, Piroja, Don't worry! Never fear for Hormusji! Ha! *(Recites)* 'Danger knows full well that Hormusji is more dangerous than he! We were two lions littered in one day, And I, the elder and more terrible . . .'

(The three men troop out laughing loudly. Suddenly everything is quiet. PIROJA is alone now. She walks slowly towards centrestage, looking worn-out, still carrying, the airgun limply in her hand. Softly, at first, the noise of roller-skating begins again. It grows louder. PIROJA's voice is full of anger and despair, as she rushes to the windows and screams:)

PIROJA: BURJORJI!
    (BLACK-OUT)

Licensed to Kill

Manjula Sen

Early 1974. The young worker in the canteen of the Bombay-Goa steamer service was happy. He was going home to get married. Bombay would no longer be lonely. He smiled at the thought of the ten tolas of gold he had laboured to buy on his mother's instructions. Back in a remote village in Karnataka, his mother awaited her eldest child. But the day of the wedding came and went. Her son never returned.

Praful Bhosale. Daya Nayak. Pradeep Sharma. Vijay Salaskar. Hemant Desai. Prakash Bhandari. The encounter cops of the Mumbai police force, licensed to kill. Their targets set them a notch higher than their colleagues, yet they teeter dangerously on the tightrope, under a constant barrage of flak. Members of an elite corps or vigilantes—take your pick depending on your moral tilt—they inhabit a twilight zone. They wage war in the shadowlands of the underworld, collecting scalps, keeping secrets and blandly rewriting the rules along the way. Their survival code is Dumasian: modern musketeers with grim jobs, they live by the motto of 'All for one and one for all'.

These men were once engineers, bank clerks and unskilled labourers. They are the children of mill workers, English literature professors and railway officers. To venture into their minds requires you to suspend personal convictions; put on hold moral and ethical judgements. For the men who inhabit this world are convinced that the only good gangster is a dead gangster.

Even as this article was being researched, Police Commissioner M.N. Singh announced that the administration would replace the word 'encounter' with the word 'operation' to describe the task these men perform. He formally discontinued and reconstituted some of

---

A version of this first appeared in *Man's World*.

the encounter cells, launched departmental enquiries into some alleged excesses and transferred some of the members of 'encounter club'. But while the semantics may have changed, in the murky world of dons and deaths, the cut and thrust stay the same.

The special-task force of Mumbai's crime branch employs an argot that reflects its unique moral and functional yardsticks. The people other policemen call a khabri, what you and I define as an informer, the encounter cops call a dost, a friend. They never kill, they 'neutralize'. An operation is not what happens in a hospital, it's a shoot-out between cops and gangsters in the crowded streets of the metropolis. In this life, bhai—brother—is not a sibling but a mafia don. 'Shooters' are the gunmen on the other side. And 'encounter cop' is a self-explanatory tag earned by policemen who don't mingle with the rest of the force but compete among themselves.

★

The encounter cops work in the Crime Branch through so-called Central Intelligence Units attached to police stations around Mumbai. The CIU network handles high-risk areas such as organized crime, shoot-outs and high-profile cases. Its members are recruited from the ranks for their daring and intelligence. They must have an inherent relish for this particular kind of sleuthing, and a nervy cop can refuse to join. CIU members don't get any special training but it is their job to do their homework, know their targets and hone their detection skills. Although they are attached to individual police stations, these units are likely to keep to themselves and during an operation, few people know anything—not even the other cops in the station.

In this world of distorted mirrors, bonding becomes the way to outshine one's peers—bonding with informers, that is. Informers are the eyes and ears of the men for whom an 'encounter' often is the first meeting with a man whose corpse will soon allow a name to be struck off the most-wanted list. 'It's a competitive field. Informers must approach *you*. To get some benefit, you must bond. The key is secrecy about their identities,' explains Inspector Praful Bhosale of Ghatkopar police station. 'It's a long process. You must inspire confidence in them, treat them like family members. Sometimes information comes by fluke. Like cricketers, who cannot always deliver on the field, no informant can constantly deliver information. Even if there is no information from a person for two months, you must help him. If they need money around Diwali or Id, we give them money from our Secret Service Fund.' The identities of informants are kept secret even from the top brass. So, too, are the details of an operation. Most of the cops don't use new informers, preferring to depend on the tried and tested.

As they marshal their information and resources, teams are built. Competition between the tough-nosed cops is intense. In addition to knowing how gangsters function, they also know each other's styles of operation, their quirks and strengths. 'Who have you met so far?' asks the spiffily dressed Inspector Pradeep Sharma. As I list his colleagues, he curls his lip and proceeds, deadpan, to match each name to a particular style with wicked accuracy. Prakash Bhandari, assistant inspector, guffaws appreciatively.

Bhosale of Ghatkopar police station elaborates, 'We know our sources. Our teams are very secretive, very professional. We get to know the cops who would be a risk to us. We don't let them get into our groups. The sneaky ones also keep their distance from us. If they try, there are supervisors to control them.' Even participating officers don't know the details of an operation until the very last moment. While the rest of the world carries one mobile phone each, these men are usually armed with three: one for normal use and the other two meant only for calls from their informants that could come any time of the day or night. Only when they're flush with information do the encounter cops strike.

Information is a matter of life and death and Bhosale's junior sub-inspector, Hemant Desai, makes frequent forays to the five-storey police lock-up in Ghatkopar to identify faces, accumulate data and store it away for future reference. 'Knowledge is power so we keep adding knowledge. And we keep analysing it,' Desai explains.

It is the ordinariness of their backgrounds that makes these men unnerving. Most of the cops I met are Mumbai boys who went to colleges, like Ruia College or Somaiya, in middle-class strongholds.

What was it that allowed them to kill in so detached a manner?

★

Encounter deaths have their origins in Mumbai's rapidly-changing crime scene of the 1980s, when various gangsters were battling to fill the vacuum created by the retirement or deaths of the old-time operators such as Karim Lala, Haji Mastan and Yusuf Patel. The nature of the Bombay crime itself was changing. While the old timers smuggled gold and electronic goods, the new men branched out into extortion, real estate and film financing, activities for which cash transactions were key. While the old-time gangsters didn't pose a threat to the average Mumbaikar, the new toughs proved to be dangerous to the man on the street. The cops arrested many gangsters, but the situation didn't seem to improve. Even new laws like the Terrorist and Disruptive Activities (Prevention) Act proved unable to keep these men in jail because Dawood Ibrahim, Chhota Rajan and Arun Gawli employed the best lawyers to defend their men. Thugs who had been arrested after painstaking investigation would be bailed out in no time and back to their old rackets.

It got so frustrating for the cops, according to local folklore, that they decided that these gangsters were better off dead than in jail. So began the city's long affair with 'encounter' deaths. Newspapers would get press releases describing the shoot-outs in the chillingly detached vocabulary 'encounter specialists' employ to describe the time they drew first blood. Consider this account by Inspector Pradeep Sharma, M.Sc (organic chemistry) of the first 'target' he 'neutralized'. (He has notched up seventy encounter deaths since then.) In his words: 'Subhash Kanchi Makarwala hailed from Solapur. He was involved in thirty-six gang-war murders. He had even terrorized a Bollywood actress by forcing his way into her house to live there. He had been arrested just once, in 1984, so there were no pictures of him. His drunken boast was that only the special operations' squad could nab him, not cops from the crime branch. On 6 May 1993, I was tipped off that with his brother, he was visiting a particular place. At 6.45 p.m., we waited for him at the end of the alley. I was carrying a carbine, he an

AK-56. As their car nosed down the alley, we switched on our headlights blinding them. They reversed at full speed. I sprayed thirteen bullets in him. Bahut danger aadmi tha par usko fire karne ka chance nahin diya. (He was a very dangerous man but I did not give him a chance to fire.) Till date they don't know who the police informant was.'

Or this tale by sub-inspector Daya Nayak, who has killed fifty-nine gangsters so far: 'My first shoot-out happened during my first posting. It was the 1996 New Year's Eve. I was with the Juhu police station. Most of the police were on bandobast duty. There was a robbery in Juhu that night. I rushed there, fired at two robbers and saw blood. I thought I would lose my job. I had only been there six months. But DCP Satyapal Singh appreciated it and I also got good headlines. Kehte hain dhoondne se Bhagwan milega, to criminal kyon nahin? (It's said that if you search enough, you will even find God, so it's possible to find a criminal, too.) My greatest success was when I killed Sadiq Kalia, one of the best shooters of Chhota Shakeel. He killed his own brother-in-law to pass the entrance test to the gang. I cornered him in the Dadar flower market. I was shot in the left thigh, he fired six bullets but I got him finally. I have killed so many now—I don't remember.'

In the early days, the 'encounters' made front page news in the daily newspaper. But slowly, they began occurring with such regularity that they are now dismissed in a paragraph in the inside pages—if they're mentioned at all.

★

Bhosale, one of the first detection officers to tackle organized crime, is slight and deceptively soft-spoken. His office is a cul-de-sac in the Ghatkopar police station. The station squats on the edge of the arterial L.B.S. Marg, which threads together the eastern suburbs of Vikhroli and Ghatkopar. This is where Bhosale grew up.

These pockets of Mumbai were also the heartland of the underworld in the eighties and nineties and Bhosale could very well be a historian of the city's gangland. What are faceless names to you and me are familiar adversaries to him. There was Chotta Rajan in Chembur,

Ashok Joshi in Kanjur Marg, K.T. Thapa in Bhandup, Lalsingh
Chavan in Vikhroli—the last two were municipal corporators who
were later gunned down by rivals. These eastern suburbs were where
the shooters were concentrated. From there, the Dawood gang
provided the financial impetus while Chotta Rajan led with muscle
power. Bhosale's first posting, at the Vikhroli police station, was
opportune. That year, ganglord Chintya, alias Chintamani
Shivshankar, became a morgue statistic after an encounter led by
Bhosale. This is how he recalls the event. 'It was 1987. Chintya aka
Chintamani Shivshankar was a big-time operator in Vikhroli. I was
chasing him with three or four of my constables. It happened so
naturally. He was alone, there was a long chase, cross-fire and he was
shot. It was my first encounter death. In those days encounters were
not so frequent. There was a mixed reaction even among my
colleagues. Some even said that I was inviting trouble for myself by
taking on organized gangs. Other officers, and the people of Vikhroli
whom Chintya had troubled a lot, appreciated my actions.'

Bhosale is quick to share the limelight with his protégé, Desai.
Desai lived in the same suburbs as Bhosale but did a seven-year stint
as an engineer at Mahindra & Mahindra and Air India before taking
the competitive examinations and joining the police. He worked at
the TADA court for three years till 1996 and then was sent to Nagpada
police station in central Mumbai, where he participated in his first
encounter operations, led by Inspector Vijay Salaskar. A deputy
commissioner recommended him for the crime branch and he became
part of Bhosale's team at Ghatkopar.

Desai's English is fluent. His sentences run like entries in a logbook
as he describes some of the twenty encounters he has been in. In
Desai's view, even an intelligent criminal is only a bully. A bully because
he attacks from behind, a bully who hits easy targets, a bully who
never takes risks. 'Why be afraid of bullies?' he asks. What thrills him
most about the job is recovering rare handguns, pistols and stenguns.
'They are rare, sometimes they cost as much as Rs 1.5 lakh,' he says.
He is always armed. 'There are stenguns and AK-56 in our vehicles,
but we are also exposed because the handguns are tucked into our
holsters.'

Of all the encounter specialists I met, Vijay Salaskar had the best office. Located on Bandra's Tony Carter Road, it looked out onto the sea. His room was compact, but he was officer enough to get an assistant to take out his diary from his briefcase next to his chair. The son of a professor, Salaskar's mentor was a former deputy commissioner of police, Arvind Patwardhan. Salaskar sailed through his application exams and joined the force as zonal sub-inspector. He has been from the narcotics cell, to the crime branch, to anti-extortion.

'The ordinary police look at criminals. We concentrate on organized crime and go after the gangs all over India,' he explains. His score is twenty-two encounters, thirty-two people dead, according to the last page of a red diary that he keeps. 'I go on adding the details. I have been asked so often that I have started writing them down,' he says. So does the encounter become a habit? 'Every encounter is an experience to remember; can't be routine,' he replies. His first independent encounter death was Virendra Singh, a flour-mill owner from Jaunpur, UP who had turned dacoit. 'He had twenty murders to his name. In 1986, he came to Bombay and began extorting money. One day, we found out he was holed up in Malad. With two constables, I went and knocked on the door. He started firing unexpectedly and we were too stunned to even dodge. Only luck protected us. We fired back and killed him. I got the President's Gallantry Medal,' he recounts.

While Bhosale is the recorder of underworld lore and Salaskar is the finicky hunter, Inspector Pradeep Sharma is the smooth sharpshooter in the 007 mould. Lithe with thick hair, he sports a fat gold watch and a gold kada and wears a navy shirt showing some chest. His large office is like a doctor's waiting room in its neatness. The office has an aircooler and photographs of Shirdi Saibaba and the goddess Lakshmi. The youngest child of an English professor from Dhulia, Sharma entered the Nashik Police Training College in 1983. He was a detection officer in 1990 when he shot dead two gangsters on the job. 'I wanted to apprehend them. I was the only one carrying a gun and I shot them when my constable was attacked. There was a lot of publicity. My seniors like Ramamoorthy and A.A. Khan, then commissioner and deputy commissioner, expressed their appreciation. I was transferred to the crime branch immediately,' he says.

Of all the men I met, Daya Nayak had the most dramatic life story. Born to a family of modest means in Karnataka, Nayak didn't own a pair of shoes until he got to the tenth standard. His education in the local municipal school went as far as the number of classes it had—seven. His widowed mother worked in people's homes but despite her doggedness she could not afford to send him to the high school in the next village. Instead, he was sent to Bombay on a half-ticket that cost Rs 90. Nayak worked at an eatery in Versova whose owner his family knew. The Sahu family, who were Nayak's neighbours, noticed that the shy boy was always alone and asked why he did not study. When he explained he did not know the local language, they told him about a Kannada-medium school in Goregaon, two train stations away. The hotel owner gave him time off for classes. In all the years he went to Goregaon, he never bought a ticket.

'I used to earn Rs 700 plus tips. I had to send Rs 500 to the village,' he remembers.

Nayak got 88 per cent in his twelfth standard examination. In the Koli basti (fishermen's colony) in which he lived in Versova, the corporator gave out prizes to all those who had done well in school. For the first time, Nayak realized that there was an advantage to studying. By this time, his brother had joined him in Bombay and the two started hawking tea and vada pao from a cart. Today when he goes back to the basti, they still call him the chaiwala sahib.

In 1991, he learnt about competitive exams for state-sector jobs and sat for as many as he could. He passed six, including those for a position at the State Bank of Hyderabad, for inspector of sales tax, and for Air India traffic inspector. He also got a call for an interview and physicals for the police force. His brother was sure it was pointless to attend, as they would want money. Instead, he got through with flying colours, scoring 194/200 in the interview and a full hundred marks in running. 'Tum 100 per cent sub-inspector ho gaya,' his PE examiner assured him, even before the interview.

★

Through their careers, these men have averaged fifty deaths each.

They notch them up in little diaries and large notebooks. Their contempt for their adversaries pumps them up like a testosterone cocktail and choice expletives roll easily off their tongues. 'Look at how Chhota Shakeel dresses,' says Sharma. He gets up and curves his arm to his chest. 'He does not even come to my shoulder. Have you seen what he wears? A shiny maroon shirt, red trousers, shoes with six-inch heels! How can one fear them?' This is not an honourable feud. Their adversaries do not earn either their respect or their fear.

'We are not scared of dying, then why should we be scared of Dawood?' shrugs Sharma's lieutenant, Prakash Bhandari.

In graphic detail, Nayak recalls the afternoon when Chhota Shakeel called on his mobile. 'He began to abuse me. I listened for a minute and then cut in saying, "Sahib is not in. I am the constable speaking. Call after ten minutes." I went and asked my boss, Pradeep Sharma, "Shakeel is calling up." He said, "Speak to him." And so I did. Shakeel abused me. For the next ten minutes, I abused him back two-fold. It is my job to abuse, I told him. You have not killed anyone personally; you get others to do that. I have killed sixty people. I know how people die, I taunted him, and you call yourself bhai!'

Nayak wraps up this lesson in gangster studies saying, 'That is what organized crime is; you don't do it yourself. Bana banaya dukaan chalaana koi badi baat nahin hai. (It's no big deal to run an already-running business.) I have confidence that he can't shoot me. I told Shakeel, "If you do, in Bombay, we will not leave you. If you touch my friends, wife, relatives, my men, an innocent person, we will kill yours." '

What about their security when not on the job? Aren't they scared for their own lives, or the security of their families? All of them are armed to the teeth and are constantly protected by even better armed body guards. They take the usual precautions of not frequenting public places, or travelling by the same vehicle very often. Their families are also provided extra protection, though there seems to be some kind of understanding among criminals that targeting a cop's family would result in instant retaliation. 'Our families are here, so are theirs,' says a cop. 'Where will they go?'

★

There are unanticipated encounters sometimes but most operations are the culmination of much planning. Many of the shooters are brought in from the northern states because a spate of encounters dampened local recruitment in Mumbai. These uneducated men barter life for throwaway prices. They are the arms and legs of the bhais. Chhota Rajan and Chhota Shakeel don't kill each other's shooters apparently. Salaskar speaks clinically, 'Gangs operate through shooters. They can only create fear through them. Once you arrest the shooters, you weaken the gang.'

The stake-out begins. Patience is a virtue in this business. Salaskar maps out his approach to an operation. 'Gathering information and planning is the most important part. Laying the trap is the most exciting. To find out that Dawood is staying on the ground floor is most important. I believe in targeting gangs. So Naik and Gawli in South Mumbai, Chhota Rajan and Chhota Shakeel in Bandra—ek ek aadmi ko kaun dekhne baithega, gang ko thokna chahiye. (Who is going to bother pursuing them one man at a time? Slam the gang instead.)'

His strategy: Go after the big criminals, patiently, consistently. Work slowly. Study their associates, family backgrounds, habits, prospective hideouts, weak links. 'We send our informants to identify, confirm, then we decide which situation is less risky. The situation should be in our favour. No catch is worth police casualties,' Salaskar says.

Execution, he says, is not half as exciting as planning. After months of planning, there is the chase. 'We sometimes know the face. An encounter is often the first meeting with that person. We try to confirm that with our informants it is the same person. Yes, there is a danger that we might get the wrong man for, very often, I don't know if the target is reaching for a hanky or a revolver.' The hanky is a reference to the death of an innocent businessman killed by the Delhi police, who thought he was carrying a gun. 'They did not identify him properly,' Salaskar shrugs.

Innocent people killed? Well, too bad. In the melee of an operation, sometimes it is the company you keep that is the end of you. 'When we act on a tip that XYZ gangster will be at a particular spot and things get out of control, we don't have time to find out if the guy he was talking to was just an acquaintance or an accomplice,' is their chorus. They are awfully sorry if indeed an innocent person died, but, excuse me, there is little time for politeness here.

Cold-blooded? All in a day's work. Apocryphal stories abound. There was the mobster who refused to die after the cops riddled him with bullets. His persistent rattling breath had a rookie cop throwing up until a seasoned cop stepped back into the room and, with one shot at point blank range, put the gangster out of his misery. Or the 'good cop' who cajoled a gangster into spilling all his information, while chatting with him about his girlfriend, and shot him mid-sentence.

But talk to the cops about these and other tales of summary killings, such as those shown in the film *Chandni Bar* or the television show *Bhanwar*, and their reactions range from denial to derision.

'Why should we deliberately kill someone?' asks Bhosale. 'A dead gangster is of no use,' he says. As Nayak explains patiently, 'If we jail him, we can get information about their plans, their gang members. The public does not understand that. There are a lot of people we have successfully arrested and got them convicted too. Why doesn't anyone talk about that?' Salaskar admits there is apprehension. 'When someone runs from the police, I tell him to surrender. Many don't listen, don't believe me. They think, 'Why is Sahib saying this? It must be a ruse.'

In a gesture that may appear rather morbid to some people, Salaskar often calls on the families of those he has killed. 'I always feel bad for these criminals, even hardened criminals. I often visit their wives and parents. I have even helped a criminal's family after he died. While they are alive, the families have power, money, everything. After they die, no one turns up even for the funeral. The gangsters leave money with friends who don't go and give it to the bereaved family. Sometimes the families don't even know what their sons or husbands are up to,' says Salaskar. Like the gangster from Mira Road who would take a briefcase and leave for office every morning at 9.30: his wife thought he was an executive. Another wife confessed that she knew her husband was a gangster. He had approached the gangsters for help in a property deal and then got sucked into their world.

Bhosale tells of a Chhota Rajan shooter killed in an encounter, an Iyer boy from Chheda Nagar in the northern suburb of Chembur, whose parents thought he was working in Africa, from where he claimed to be calling. When his parents discovered the truth, they refused to claim the body. 'Not even for last rites. They disowned him. I felt so bad for them. But these gangsters often have upright parents like this.' According to him, there are many parents who know the truth about their gangster sons and refuse to accept their money.

In the twilight zone, the warring sides are sometimes mirror images distinguished only by state sanction. It is rumoured that the Dawoods also extend welfare to families of cops killed in encounters. But the lures that attract men to the ranks on each side are a little different. The cops say that young men are drawn to the underworld because of gang loyalty, the idea that membership will bring them more respect and finally, the assurance that the gang will look after his family if the man is killed. The personas of individual gangs and religious identity also play a role. The dons, they say, can be honey-tongued talkers. 'Chhota Shakeel very sweetly calls his boys 'beta' and Chhota Rajan calls his boys 'raja'. The boys never so much as see their faces but offer them so much loyalty. That and money gets the boys in. Once they commit the first crime, they're hooked,' sighs Bhosale.

On the other side, several of the cops can recall their early fascination for the uniform, the regulation dark glasses, the bikes and the media headlines. The glamour of it has long since dimmed, though. Continually looking death in the face, always living life on the draw and being preached at by squeamish colleagues and indignant human rights' activists, the moral prism of encounter cops is determined almost entirely by the end game—job satisfaction. That is what spurs them on when they are taken off the front pages.

'It is not a job for the faint-hearted. Real life is a hundred times worse than *Satya*,' says a cop. Says another, 'You must want to do it. The pay is the same, the risk is far greater.'

Wanting to do it must be the key because ambition can't be. Most encounter cops are drawn from the state police cadre, so they can never dream of becoming the police commissioner, a position reserved for recruits from the national cadre. 'In our police system, there are no out-of-turn promotions. Promotions are seniority-based, not performance-based,' one of the police inspectors says. There aren't even internal exams that will clear the way. Instead, the highest they can hope to rise is the rank of assistant police commissioner or perhaps deputy police commissioner.

★

No wonder then, that the chase becomes all-consuming. The stubbornness to see that the backbone of the mafia is broken has its rewards in the shape of government honours, media recognition, public support and prize money. 'What motivates me is *zidd*,' says Bhosale. Fully aware of their vulnerability to vested interests who seek to use and discard them, these cops know how to manoeuvre their way about their jobs. Ultimately, they know their targets so intimately that their war on the mafia almost becomes personal, each officer with his own catch-list.

'Lafde ka kaam hai par mazaa aata hai. (The work is hazardous but it is fun),' says Bhandari, the assistant police inspector who works with Sharma. 'There is no saturation point in this job. In any case, one is not going to live for 150 years. Death is certain, so why fear death. People fear God because they can't see him. It is the same with Abu Salem and other gangsters: they operate from so far, you can't see them. Let them come here . . .'

Yet, fame of this kind is a double-edged sword. 'Sometimes, I get called by other police stations to scare an accused into talking. They are told, "This guy shoots people." It may work but I don't like that label,' says Nayak. But with names like Chhota Shakeel's Sadiq Kaliya and Simon and Chhota Rajan's Vinod Madkar and Parvez Siddiqui on his score card, it is a reputation that can come in handy.

Mumbai's encounter cops have killed nearly 300 people over the last four years. The officers feel their efforts have paid off. Extortion has declined, the scale of crime has come down. The results could be even better, these cops say, if it wasn't for interference from seniors. Says a high-ranking officer at the police headquarters, speaking on the condition of anonymity, 'Our biggest headache is the seniors.

They want results but then whine that these encounter deaths are not good. But they can't replace us because no one will take our place. There are no takers for detection work.'

Warming up to his theme, he continues, 'According to me, arresting gangsters doesn't work. In a city of one crore people, how many gangsters will you lock up? Arresting them, seizing their weapons, detaining them—all these are temporary measures. Also, there is acceptance from society now for these deaths. People have begun to feel that it is OK for the police to fight fire with fire. There is moral support now. Even crime reporters start questioning if there are no deaths.'

Isn't that tantamount to vigilantism by trigger-happy cops?

'I wouldn't know about that,' he says.

The moral dilemma is sometimes acknowledged, but mostly it is skirted. These cops believe that Mumbai has its own peculiar rhythm, its own peculiar underworld problem that calls for its own peculiar solution. What works for the rest of the country does not work here, they claim. 'Lawmakers live in a different world. They have no idea of Dharavi or Sion. The lawmakers' world has cars, clubs, advocates, committees. Try taking someone out of the congested maze of a basti without handcuffing him, as these lawmakers want us to do,' says one cop bitterly. Adds Sharma coldly, 'Human rights is for gangsters, for Dawood, and Abu Salem, and Chhota Rajan. I don't see any human rights' activist visit the family of the small restaurant owner who was killed by gangsters. We see what happens to the common citizen.'

What about lawlessness and mob violence that often go unchecked by the police? Or political terrorism? Or those who get off with the help of fancy lawyers or legal loopholes? It makes no difference. These cops wage their own war, though sometimes they have to bow down to VIP pressure until the heat dies down. They know which political party is backing which gangster or if the government wants to use Chhota Rajan to neutralize Chhota Shakeel or Dawood. These cops know who is making appeals based on religious identity and why. It does not affect their scheme of things. They stick with the chase. They wait for the right time. They know it will come.

As they see it, morality is an exotic dish to be sampled gingerly.

Death is everyday fare in a world where shooters and lives are cheap, and weapons expensive. They are in the firing line every day and the fastest one on the draw is the one still left standing.

And still, a mother holds on to a thread of hope that some day her eldest son will be found. 'He just vanished. We think he may have been murdered for the gold,' says her youngest son, sub-inspector Daya Nayak. 'That is one case I can't solve. Where do I look for my brother? I don't even know where to begin.'

The Bhendibazar Gharana

Suvarnalata Rao

Some time around 1870, three musician brothers Nazir Khan, Chhajju Khan and Khadim Hussain Khan migrated to Bombay from their native place, Bijnaur, in the Moradabad district of Uttar Pradesh. They came to live in the Bhendibazar area of Bombay. In those days, the governor lived there as did several wealthy businessmen and industrialists. Geographically, Bhendibazar was behind the commercial Fort area. Though there was no market of any sort there, the Englishmen identified this area as 'Behind the Bazaar'—the term bazaar obviously meant to denote the important commercial zone. The area came to be known as Bhendibazar because of the colloquial mispronunciation of the English word 'behind'. These brothers chose to live in the Bhendibazar area because their brother, Vilayat Hussain, a merchant, already resided there.

Several historical records maintain that besides receiving training from their father, Dilabar Hussain Khan, the brothers also acquired extensive training from great ustads such as Inayat Hussain Khan of Saheswan and Inayat Khan of the Dagar family. Apart from being accomplished performers, they were able composers. Chhajju Khan alias Amarsha and his son, the celebrated vocalist, Aman Ali Khan, composed hundreds of compositions in several ragas under the pen name 'Amar', creating a rich new repertoire. It was against this background, around 1890, that the three brothers were able to forge a new style, which came to be known as the Bhendibazar gharana, so called because of the musicians' place of residence.

The term gharana, is derived from ghar in Hindi or griha in Sanskrit, meaning home. In India, where the mode of knowledge transfer has been mainly oral, it seems only natural that one family of musicians should hand over its lore to the next generation or to its disciples. Musicians are known by their gharanas and initiated listeners can roughly identify the distinguishing features of prominent gharanas. Names of the gharanas indicate the place of origin of the performing musicians. Many gharanas get their names from the former princely states that lent them feudal patronage. However, after the advent of British rule, musicians were deprived of royal patronage and were forced to move to urban areas.

Several performers of other gharanas also came in search of opportunities to Bombay, but maintained their individual traditions. The Bhendibazar gharana was the only new musical tradition born right here in Mumbai; a product of a colonial environment in which the musicians were left to fend for themselves. The 'Behind the Bazaar' gharana was supported and sustained entirely by the common art lover. In particular, this style was patronized by several upper-class Hindus.

The founding brothers were employed in the music school run by a Parsi organization, the Parsi Gayan Uttejak Mandali. It was established in the year 1870 and was perhaps the first formal music club to have been started in the city. Here, the brothers came to be associated with Vishnu Narayan Bhatkhande (1860-1936), a great visionary and one of the outstanding theorists of the twentieth century. Bhatkhande was engaged in the mammoth mission of compiling hundreds of compositions from various sources and grouping them into ragas. The Bhendibazar brothers participated actively in this project.

The stylistic evolution of the Bhendibazar gharana can be traced in two distinct stages—before Aman Ali Khan and after. The initial style as propagated by Nazir Khan and his brothers was mainly oriented to alaap, the free-flowing melodic prelude. Aman Ali's approach, however, was marked by the emphasis on lilting elements such as layakari, sargam and fast tans. One of the main features of this gharana is the use of merukhand, a technique based on a mathematical formula resulting in a combination of notes that can be performed within the parameters of a raga. But in order to rise above the predictability associated with a dreary mathematical formula, a singer must have complete control over intonation as well as alertness of mind, besides possessing a keen sense of aesthetics. Another peculiarity of the style pioneered by Nazir

Khan is the open-throated singing in slow tempo. This requires a singer to cultivate good breath control, and steady and strong voice production. It is said that the slow legato phrases rendered in such a languorous pace could even challenge an expert player of the rudraveena (a fretted string instrument, presently not in vogue). In order to do justice to each beat of the time cycle, a vocalist also needs to develop command over various ornamental features associated with the intonation of notes. Music critics had lauded the vocalists of this gharana for performances 'marked by delicacy and bewitching inflections'.

Musicians of this gharana have an unusual repertoire of ragas. They include commonly heard ragas such as Yaman, Malkauns, Todi, Jhinjhoti, Rageshri, Jog, as well as somewhat lesser-known ragas including Gunakri, Motakitodi, Hem, Khem, Savanikalyan, Triveni, Kaushibhairavi and Patbihag. Ragas from the Carnatic tradition also figure in this wide-ranging list. This composition-oriented style is known for its emphasis on clear enunciation and posture devoid of unnecessary gestures and facial expressions. The same attitude of purity is also reflected in their lifestyles. By and large, the practitioners of this gharana have steered clear from the negative tendencies such of groupism observed in other gharanas.

Ustad Nazir Khan (d. 1919), one of the pioneering Bhendibazar trio, was known for his extraordinary breath control, a resonating voice and fabulous command over volume dynamics. His disciple, Anjanibai Malpekar (1883-1974), who brought name and fame to this style, was known to have the same ability and could sustain a given note for a whole minute without affecting the quality of the sound. She had the privilege of being trained under all the three masters of this gharana. Special efforts were taken to groom her in all aspects of the Bhendibazar gharana so that she could be a challenge to another lady singer, the famous Chunnabai of the Kirana gharana. With a beautiful resonating voice and a stunning appearance, Anjanibai had an imposing presence on stage. No wonder that the celebrated painter Raja Ravi Verma was so taken in by her stage presence that he once requested her to sit for a life-size portrait for him. Her reply was a firm and courteous, 'No'. It is said that thereafter the painter had to attend her concerts in order to sketch her. Through her performance, the glory of the Bhendibazar gharana spread all over India. At a time when women from 'respectable' families did not give public performances, Anjanibai had a full-fledged performing career. For this, she became the first ever recipient of the prestigious Sangeet Natak Akademi Award in 1958.

Ustad Aman Ali Khan's (1884-1953) name is synonymous with this gharana. During his long performing career, he remoulded the Bhendibazar philosophy by bringing in some additional stylistic features, which made it even more accessible and popular. The present style of the gharana is largely the result of Aman Ali's contribution. A major change was brought in the pace of rendition. It was made a trifle faster because his breath control had been affected by a series of surgical operations. With the increase in tempo, the performances became more lilting. The credit of popularizing some Carnatic ragas among the North Indian musicians rightly goes to Aman Ali. His disciples included noted film playback singer Lata Mangeshkar.

In spite of being born a devout Muslim, Khansaheb was known to be an ardent devotee of Lord Krishna and was closely associated with 'Vallabh Sampraday'—a sect devoted to the worship of Krishna. Many of his compositions are in praise of various Hindu deities. Being of a highly spiritual nature, Khansaheb considered music as a means to communicate with the Supreme Being, so he was not very keen on public performances.

Until the 1960s, the Bhendibazar gharana was feted all over India for its many talented exponents. Other than Aman Ali Khan, there was hardly anybody from his family who took to music, and the gharana was largely patronized by musicians who were 'outsiders' and not connected with this bloodline. Able musicians such as Jhande Khan, Mamman Khan, Shahmir Khan, Chand Khan, Kadar Baksh, and Amir Khan received training from this gharana, but instead of adopting the Bhendibazar style completely, they preferred to adopt some salient features relevant to their own style of music. Furthermore, it was unfortunate that by 1923 Anjanibai Malpekar, the doyenne of the gharana, chose to give up her performing career. Another blow came when the singing career of Aman Ali Khan's illustrious disciples—Shivkumar Shukla and Ramesh Nadkarni—were cut short due to ill health and premature death respectively.

At this juncture, the connoisseurs began to wonder about the future of the 'Behind the Bazaar' gharana. Although, all these masters made efforts to propagate the tradition by teaching, an apparent dearth of performing representatives was a definite setback for the propagation and promotion of the gharana. According to Dr Suhasini Koratkar, suggestions have been made to rename the gharana the 'Moradabad gharana' to overcome the tackiness associated with the Bhendibazar area. Today it is regrettable that a rich musical tradition is fading. Despite its strengths, this gharana hasn't received the recognition it deserves.

For the survival of any gharana it is imperative that the tradition is passed on, uninterrupted. The wider it spreads, the better its chances for survival. The original style of Bhendibazar vocalism seems to have vanished with Anjanibai's departure from the performing scene. Although its basic principles remain strong in the style instituted by Aman Ali, it is appalling that no audio records are available of Anjanibai's music, except in some private collections. From this point of view, a great service is being rendered by the octogenarian T.D. Janorikar, who had the privilege of receiving guidance from both Anjanibai Malpekar and Aman Ali Khan. In his music one can hear the authentic Bhendibazar ideology, a confluence of the original style created by Nazir Khan and his brothers, and the later dimensions added by the creative genius of Aman Ali Khan. It is fortunate that even at this age, he is striving hard to keep this tradition alive by grooming several serious disciples. His senior-most disciple, Dr Suhasini Koratkar, is also active in teaching and spreading awareness about this style.

Now, as we have entered the twenty-first century, let us hope that this gharana stages a comeback from 'behind' to the mainstream, and once again enriches the world of Hindustani khayal tradition.

Never at Home

Shabnam Minwalla

From detergent-blue walls and cluttered cupboard-tops, several generations of Wakrulkars gaze upon a familiar scene of bustling domesticity. A solicitous visitor pops in to ask about seth's health. A daughter-in-law is dispatched to buy a kilo of laddoos. The demanding shriek of the pressure cooker and rapid-fire conversations in Marathi provide the soundtrack for this theatre of the mundane.

But as Mozel Wakrulkar begins to speak, the mid-morning bustle sheds its triviality. The household in Alibag is being dismantled. Soon the laminated uncles and cousins will peer only at dust-covers and nostalgia. 'There is nothing left for us here,' says the grandmother with an air of finality. 'One of my sons is in Israel, the other is planning to move there soon. This very evening my nephew and his family from Pen, totally ten people, are leaving for Israel. My husband suffers from paralysis, but as soon as he can walk we will sell our rice mill and go to Israel. Yahaan sab khaali ho gaya hai.' (Everything has become empty over here.)

Her farewell speech teeters between bravado and regret. The fact that Mrs Wakrulkar has a Star of David painted on her doorway, is married to a man named Moses and figures in the census as a Jew is only part of the story. She also makes a mean fish curry, is happiest gabbing in Marathi and dresses in Indian national costume, both the old and new varieties—the sari and voluminous cotton nighty. 'I'm an Indian,' she declares fiercely. Then she adds an afterthought. 'But it's written in the Bible that we all have to go to Israel one day.'

Mrs Wakrulkar's predicament is felt by all the Bene Israel—the children of Israel—a tiny community of Jews from coastal Maharashtra. Although they have lived in India for over 2000 years, the birth of Israel has prompted waves of migration since the 1950s. Some went because they grew up believing that they would return to the Promised Land, so central to Judaism. Others departed because Israeli passports came with desirable jobs, subsidized housing and social security. Still more got on the plane because, almost like a travelling circus, their entire world had suddenly packed up and shifted base.

When Mrs Wakrulkar arrived at her marital home in Alibag exactly fifty years ago, Israel Street had 200 Jewish families, mezuzah (holy scrolls) at every doorway and an overflowing synagogue. Today only five families remain. Most homes are shuttered or sold, and on the Sabbath, barely a single pew is packed at Magen Aboth. 'Slowly, our maami, kaaki, maushi, (various categories of aunts) everybody left,' says Mrs Wakrulkar. 'Families who didn't have enough to eat over here are today driving cars over there. Of course they miss India, but they visit every year.'

Three minutes down the street at the bright, white synagogue, this observation is echoed by the stooped hazaan baba. Although Saul Telkar serves as a religious caretaker, dutifully kisses the mezuzah every time he hobbles out of his house and wears a white skullcap, he is much happier talking about the Bombay neighbourhood of Mazagaon than menorahs. The Holocaust to him is a vague memory about 'a man named Hitler who killed many people', and the Israel-Palestine conflict is only real because a mullah in a Mumbai mosque mentioned it during a venomous sermon. 'India is not a place that anybody can forget,' says Telkar, who retired from the Bombay Port Trust about fifteen years ago. 'My son is in Israel but I don't like it there. Wahaan ki sanskriti baraabar nahin hai.' (Something is wrong with their culture.)

But his is the minority report. That's why Israel Street continues to empty out into Dimona and Beersheba, and Mrs Wakrulkar experiences the occasional pang. 'The Bene Israel took some customs from here, some from there,' she says about the hybrid culture that flourished amidst the palm and betelnut groves of the Konkan. 'During weddings our brides wear veils like the Catholics. We have a mehendi ceremony like the Muslims. And our bridegrooms wear sehras (floral headgear) just like Maharashtrian Hindus. I wonder how long these customs will remain in place. Already the younger generation in Israel speaks only Hebrew, no Marathi. As more and more of our community moves to Israel and slowly integrates, I wonder how long we will retain a distinct identity.'

*

It takes an hour for our boat, rather ambitiously named Ecstasy, to cover the glittery grey distance between Alibag and the Gateway of India. The spires and rectangular blocks of Bombay glimmer through the haze, as tantalizing and deceptive as an immigrant's idea of home.

Gradually the city skyline clarifies into Afghan Church, the Oberoi and matronly highrises with names like Sunita and Ajanta. But answers to the riddles of Israel Street remain elusive. Even as I replay the words of the plump grandmother and the hunched hazaan baba in my head, other voices fade in and out—somewhat like rappers in a remixed Hindi film song. For the story of the Bene Israel echoes the narratives of so many other displaced communities.

Early in 2000, while the world was still hung-over and cadging passes to get into London's Millennium Dome, I spent three months interviewing members of the Kutchi Leva Patel youth club, a Sikh football team, the AsianDubFoundation band and other groups that have come to make up the British Asian community in the UK. The questions I wanted to resolve were admittedly naive. Did these second-and-third generation immigrants consider themselves Indian or British? How many years would it take for the nostalgia to fade and the 'outsider' label to fall off? Where was home?

I expected answers that would lend themselves to a neat bar chart. What I got instead was a crazy mosaic of unexpected encounters. So there was Asjad Nazir, the twenty-something child of Pakistani parents, who knew the dialogue of every single Shammi Kapoor film by heart and wanted nothing more than to work as an assistant director on a Goregaon set. There was Bally Jagpal, the bhangra heart-throb of Birmingham, who was showered with phone-numbers during every concert but planned to marry a good Punjabi girl from some place like Bhatinda. And there was Harinder Chhokar, an academic who made the trip after years of pining for the India of her parents—only to find that the India of her bedtime stories had no more substance than

Goldilocks and her three hairy chums.

Likewise, the history of the Bene Israel ding-dongs between the curious and the clichéd. During its 2000-year-long sojourn in India, the community gave up its clothes, language and food. But, almost perversely, it held on to homesickness. Families with names like Murudkar and Jhirad continued to light diyas in the general direction of their mythical homeland, and later adopted the practice of hanging a picture of Jerusalem on the western walls of their homes. It seemed natural, then, that when the Promised Land was realized in 1948, many submitted to the tug of nostalgia and religion.

In the realm of fiction, this would have been a perfectly satisfactory ending. But in the real world, it's Chapter I of the sequel. Now that these members of the Jewish diaspora have returned to Israel, they seem to be exhibiting all the classic symptoms of Indian-diasporitis. Mozel Wakrulkar seems destined to live in emotional limbo between two airports. Her sons probably worry that Israel's 'European culture' will spoil their children, who will grow up with sly trips to rave parties, the shriek of the pressure cooker, and the legend of a long-ago shipwreck.

★

Centuries ago, the sea brought with it more than the predictable plastic bags and oil slicks. Around 1000 years ago, it deposited shiploads of refugees from Iran at Sanjan in Gujarat—setting the stage for *patra-ni-machi*, the House of Tatas and 'mad bawa' jokes. A few hundred kilometres to the south, the thriving ports and lush hamlets of the Konkan were abustle with Sidi potentates and Arab traders. Russian merchant Afanasy Nikitin, who landed in Chaul in 1469 and wandered the Maharashtra coast, describes Dabhol as 'a very big harbour, and horses are brought thither from Egypt, Arabia, Khorassan, Turkestan, and Old Hormuz'. He also mentions that the large city attracts 'people from the whole coast of India and Ethiopia'. (In the Dabhol of today, the Ethiopians have been replaced by an Enron electricity plant.)

It was along this golden stretch that the Bene Israel landed in India.

Believed to be a group of refugees from the Kingdom of Israel (either exiled by the Assyrian King Shalmaneser around 700 BC or fleeing the Greek emperor Antioch in 175 BC), they were shipwrecked off the Konkan coast. Legend has it that seven men and seven women survived, and settled down amidst the prosperous wadis of the Konkan. Over the centuries, the Bene Israel became oil pressers, switched to Marathi and found their niche in the caste system.

That they integrated is hardly noteworthy. What was astounding was that they clung to an alien and apparently inexplicable code of conduct. Although their scriptures and holy texts had been lost in the shipwreck, they continued to observe the sabbath and refrained from working on Saturdays, which gained them their distinct identity as 'Shaniwar Telis', the people who did not press oil on Saturday. (Hindus did not work their oil presses on Monday, and so were called 'Somwar Telis'.) They circumcised their sons, ate only kosher food and recited a single Hebrew prayer, the *Shema Yisrael*. Although the Bene Israel retained memories of a lost homeland, their Jewish identity slipped through the gap of centuries.

But like a Bollywood blockbuster in which the two halves of a locket come together in an emotionally charged climax, these lost children of Israel were eventually located. A mysterious figure named David Rahabi—opinion differs on whether he was a tenth century Egyptian Jew or an eighteenth century Cochini Jew—stumbled upon the Bene Israel and was intrigued by their strangely familiar habits. He asked the women to cook him fish and when, in keeping with the rules of kosher, they chose fish with fins and scales he agreed to instruct three families in the tenets of Judaism.

The early chapters of this fragmented story were enacted beneath the generously sloping roofs and ample porches of the Konkan. After all, it was in the town of Navgaon that two mounds were said to mark the graves of those unfortunate ancestors who drowned. Tiny Sagav nearby was home to Eliyahu Hannabi*cha tapaa*—a holy rock upon which Prophet Elijah's chariot is believed to have landed during one of his two trips to the region, leaving behind a deep hoof-mark.

In the late 1700s, Bene Israeli families began to move to the growing city of Bombay. It was here that they encountered members of India's other Jewish communities—the Baghdadis and Cochinis. Many Bene Israelis became masons and carpenters, while others joined the East India Company. Says the Gazetteer of Bombay City and Island, 1909, with decided approval, 'Certain it is that there was hardly an infantry regiment of the Bombay army from 1760 onwards which did not include a certain number of Bene Israel, many of whom rose to the ranks of officers and were present at the great engagements such as the storming of Seringapatam, the siege of Multan, the battle of Kirkee, which laid the foundation of British power in India.'

This was part of a wider religious resurgence, and the worthy *Gazetteer* had reason to administer another pat on the back. 'As a class, the Bene Israel are sober, cleanly and loyal and even in the hurry of modern urban life, which acts unfavourably upon the maintenance of old customs, they never forget the synagogue on the Day of Atonement, the most solemn festival in the Jewish calendar, and offer prayers for the welfare of the Royal family of England and the Governor of Bombay.'

★

Some years ago, a delegation of local merchants demanded that the name of Samuel Street at Masjid Bunder be changed. Never mind that Samuel Divekar's family has been in India for more than two millennia, that the synagogue he built is over 200 years old, or even that his modest house of worship is the masjid that gives the entire neighbourhood its name. In their eyes, he was a foreigner.

In a similar case, a historically challenged municipal corporator claimed to be offended that Khodadad Circle at Dadar was named after 'an Afghani god'. His statement caused an uproar because, as citizens' groups were quick to point out, the name commemorated the architect of Parsi Colony. Khodadad Circle emerged unscathed from this unseemly tussle, but half of Samuel Street was sacrificed. Incidents like these don't just demonstrate ugly ignorance—they indicate that, alongside the temple pillars in Ayodhya, a newer, narrower definition of Indianness is being chiselled. Even in these times of straitjacketed identities, some communities are more liable to be labelled 'foreign' than others. India's Jews certainly are the most vulnerable.

This is partly because Judaism—unlike Islam, Christianity or even Zoroastrianism—never bothered to establish ownership rights in India. Though they are India's tiniest community, the Jews have neglected to acquire official 'minority status' in a country in which dusty tomes of regulations and by-laws play a vital role in everyday life. No Jewish holidays figure on the government calendar. Although the religion arrived in India well before the birth of Christianity and Islam, its adherents are often seen as 'foreigners'—and not just by fundamentalist politicians like L.K. Advani and Narendra Modi.

In Sunny House, the Colaba building in which my grandmother lived, the name-boards announced the presence of families named Grant, D'Souza, Irani and Asundaria. But even amidst this extremely cosmopolitan gathering, Mrs Moses stood out as distinctly foreign. About once a month or so, as we climbed down past the first floor, my mother or an aunt would remark with an air of fresh wonder, 'She's Jewish, you know.'

This surprise was a trifle unwarranted, given that Mrs Moses was hardly the only Jew on our horizon. The nursery school I attended was run by the immaculately coiffed and lavender-rinsed Mrs Shellim. By the time my brother arrived on the scene, Dr Aptekar, the gynaecologist who delivered me, had already departed to spank the tiny bottoms of Joshuas and Hannahs in Israel.

But not even the reality of epidurals can pierce the crust of some perceptions. Judaism remains inextricably linked with Isaac Bashevis Singer and Woody Allen, New York delis and *Fiddler on the Roof*. Kosher meals are about challah bread and sweet noodle kugel, not *pohe* and fish curry. While the fast to commemorate the destruction of the great temple of Israel may be familiar to some of us as Tisha B'Av, nobody has heard of Birdiacha Roja—an occasion that the Bene Israel commemorate not with the customary meal of hard-boiled egg and bread but with a curry made of pulses.

The Bene Israel aren't a political vote bank and they haven't yet inspired a niche restaurant. Their kirtans haven't yet made the 'Spiritual' racks of music stores, and Elijah Hannabicha Oorus, the anniversary of Elijah, doesn't cause traffic snarls. This is possibly why most mentions of Indian Jews meet with blank stares and vague nods. 'Most Indians don't even know there are Jews here,' is the inevitable complaint. 'Usually they think we are Maharashtrians. Or if we are wearing a skullcap, they mistake us for Parsis.' This is inevitably followed by some cynical soul adding, 'What does it matter? Soon all that will be left of us is Jacob Circle and some cemeteries that the municipality will grab.'

★

Dead men may tell no tales, but their resting places certainly do. Mumbai cemeteries, for instance, are particularly articulate about the relationship between the city's various Jewish communities.

For years I had peered at the unkempt tombstones and forgotten vaults that punctuate the Central Railway commute between Byculla and Dadar. But it was only recently that I set out one Sunday morning, notebook in hand, to explore the Jewish cemetery at Chinchpokli. The notebook, it turns out, is a bad idea. I had just started reading the plaque at the gate when a security guard bustled up. 'Do you have permission?' he barks, making it clear that while guests from bahargaam (abroad) were more than welcome, kolhapuri-slipper clad Indians were to be sternly discouraged. 'Are any of your family members buried here? No? Then why do you want to enter?'

It comes as something of a shock that a cemetery could be more exclusive than the Breach Candy Club. But some pleading and persuasion later, I am allowed a brief ramble under the gimlet-gaze of the watchman. This is enough to catch up with Mr Shellim (the husband of my old nursery teacher), Reuben Abraham of Calcutta ('Beloved father of famous filmstars Romilla and Pramilla') and an evocative snapshot of the past. This overgrown patch of land, hemmed in by slums and rattled by Titwala fast trains, is one of the few remaining record of those flamboyant birds of passage, the Baghdadi Jews.

The wealthy Baghdadi Jews started arriving in India in the late eighteenth century, partly to escape religious persecution in their homes in Iraq, Syria, Iran and Yemen, and partly for reasons of commerce. They were careful to cultivate European habits and acquaintances, and were important cogs in the machinery of the British Empire. By the 1940s, there were almost 7000 Baghdadi Jews in India. However, most left the country along with their British associates and today little remains besides 170 individuals and a trail of hospitals, docks and libraries named after the prominent Sassoon family.

The Chinchpokli cemetery was 'Set apart forever by Elias David Sassoon in January 1878 as a Jewish Burial Ground in memory of his beloved son Joseph' who died in Shanghai in 1868. Some of its denizens—such as Sassoon Ezekiel Gubbay, who was born in Baghdad in 1826 and died in Mumbai in 1897—reflect an age when India was a land of immigrants rather than emigrants. Others represent sadder, uglier forces. Many Jews who fled Germany and Austria after Kristallnacht, the night when the Nazis smashed the glass-fronts and windows of Jewish shops and businesses in 1938, opted to wait out troubled times in Bombay and Calcutta. Some of them erected plaques in Chinchpokli to relatives who died in the ovens of Auschwitz and other death camps. Perhaps the most familiar of these latter exiles is the incurably gentle, billiwale pagal (cat-loving loony) protagonist of Anita Desai's *Baumgartner's Bombay*, who surely rests in spirit if not in form in this grassy pocket of Mumbai's mill district.

A ten-minute drive away, the Bene Israel cemetery at Mahalakshmi tells the story of a people relatively untouched by the storms of anti-Semitism. Instead of the elaborately carved memorials to Moses and Esther Ashkenazy are functional tombstones with Marathi inscriptions recalling Elizabethbai Indarpurkar and Hanokh, son of the late Khanbahadur Aaron Bhorapkar.

Solomon Pendkar, the genial, old caretaker points out the oldest graves and introduces us to various upright citizens and members of his family. 'That's my cousin, a very good man,' he says, before pointing to a crowded part of the graveyard. 'There are my parents. But I don't know how many of us will end up here with them. My brother went to Israel fourteen years ago and joined a very good firm. Now his legs have given up and he can't walk, but he still gets a solid pension. I am also thinking of going to Israel. People there get a retirement benefit of Rs 27,000 a month. That is more than we get here doing a full job.'

While the very existence of separate cemeteries for the Baghdadi and Bene Israel communities indicates some dissension, those early differences are symbolized by the ugly wall that defaces the Jewish cemetery in Mazagaon. The Bene Israel, who had never encountered any persecution during their sojourn in India, had their first taste of discrimination from their Jewish brethren in Bombay. The Baghdadi Jews were convinced that the Bene Israel were impure and doctrinally unsound. In Baghdadi synagogues, the Bene Israel were not allowed to hold the holy scroll or blow the shofar. They were not even counted as part of the minyan—the quorum of ten Jewish males required for the prayers. But it was the wall in the Mazagaon cemetery that was the last straw. Like some Yellow Fever quarantine centre at the airport, it huddled the Bene Israel into one clearly demarcated section. Clearly, the gora Baghdadis felt that the Bene Israel were too kala, too impure, even to be buried alongside.

★

A few Sundays later, at the Seventh All India Jewish Conference, the Mazagaon cemetery makes another controversial appearance. Although the official topic is 'Securing a Jewish Future', it's clear that for an aging and dying community, the need of the hour is burial space. 'The Worli Jewish cemetery is filling very fast, and we are encountering serious problems. One option is the Mazagaon cemetery, but I must say the trustees are being very, very uncooperative,' warns David Haeem, a management consultant and one of the first speakers at the seminar. He launches into a complicated story about the Kelly Brothers—not, as their name suggests, Chicago mobsters—but the reclusive trustees of the cemetery in question.

But by this time I have stopped listening, I am overwhelmed by a sense of déjà vu. The issues are spookily similar to those that haunt that other miniscule Mumbai community, the Parsis. In recent years, furious battles have erupted over the Parsi way of death, the practicality of the Tower of Silence and its inability to cope with the huge numbers. As Jewish representatives from Thane, Pune, Cochin and Delhi make their dispiriting presentations, I am transported to those padlocked

Parsi fire temples in the small towns of Gujarat, the endless and poisonous debates about mixed marriages, and the preoccupation with dwindling numbers. The details may be different but the substance is the same—both communities fear assimilation and extinction.

The situation confronting the Bene Israel today is particularly piquant. In Israel, the community is flourishing economically and demographically, but its gentle, bucolic customs are endangered by the dry desert air. In India, the community has shrunk faster than a Fashion Street tee shirt. Around Independence, there were 35,000 Jews in the country. Today there are just 5000.

Little wonder, then, that even as the cemeteries overflow, the synagogues are empty. There have actually been times when Jewish males have had to be paid to make up the quorum for prayers on holy days. 'The Hebrew situation is very bad. Youngsters don't want to attend classes, and one or two people are loaded with all the prayers,' gripes the representative from Pune. Agrees a voluble fellow from the Thane community, 'Our boys are definitely more intelligent than those of other communities. But they are so very busy. Somehow we have to make our youngsters know what is a Jew, what is his identity, his purpose.'

The 1500-strong Thane community is attempting this with the help of marriage bureaus, parties and cookery contests ('so that our traditional dishes are not forgotten'). But this has not really countered the trend of 'intercaste marriages'—as the community refers to marriages outside the faith—which is estimated at about 50 per cent. 'There is a crisis,' admits Rabbi Joshua Koletkar, the lone shepherd of the Mumbai flock. 'We have to learn to deal with the cannibalizing effects of assimilation. Throughout history Jewish people have learnt to integrate without being fully absorbed. But the dangers are greater than ever today.'

★

Beneath the epidermis of peeling buildings and shiny restaurants lies many hidden Mumbais. Sassoon Dock and E. Moses Road may be part of the surface city, but most of Jewish Mumbai runs like a discreet capillary under the skin. As I visit synagogues tucked away amidst plastic bag wholesalers and cemeteries at the feet of glossy skyscrapers I realize that sometimes all it takes to travel to an alien city is a 4 Ltd single-decker.

Few would guess that just minutes beyond Hotel Nagina at Byculla lies a control room from which a serious battle is being waged—not with guns and bombs, but with ballroom dances and Torah classes. In a quiet compound behind two stone lions stands the Rodef Shalom, from where the American Jewish Joint Distribution Committee works to 'keep the flame of Judaism alive in this country'. While Mumbai boasts of over thirty Jewish social organizations and clubs, most are practically defunct. It took American funds and bossiness to yank the community out of its slumber, waggle an admonitory finger at all those sloppy about keeping kosher or observing the sabbath, and link it with world Jewry.

While most Mumbaikars haven't heard of the Rodef Shalom, it is as much of a landmark on the orthodox-Jewish-travel circuit as American Express. Almost every day, a stream of jetlagged Americans and Israelis come for information about kosher guest houses and homes at which they can spend the sabbath. Typical is the young Israeli with a mountainous backpack and even heavier accent who lands up straight from the airport. He is speedily furnished with addresses and a telephone number for the ever-obliging Freddie Sofer, who hosts disoriented travellers over the sabbath. After completing their military training, thousands of Israelis seek to decompress by taking trips to Goa, Himachal Pradesh and even Tibet. 'It's strange,' says Rabbi Joshua Kolet (Koletkar until a few generations ago). 'We go to Israel for religious reasons, and they come here seeking spirituality. As a devout Jew I don't approve, but I suppose it's good for India's foreign exchange.'

Half an hour down the 4 Ltd route, in a workshop space in a Mahim industrial estate is the Evelyn Peters Jewish Community Centre. This is at the heart of the movement to reassert community identity and keep youngsters within the occasionally claustrophobic fold. The crowded notice board offers some clues to the strategies being employed: The Bol Bhai Bol advanced Hebrew class will be kicking off next week; the first-ever official Valentine's Day bash is being held at the centre this year; all those interested in participating in 'The March of the Living' in Poland and Israel should send in an application and an essay on 'What the holocaust means to me'.

At around 6 p.m. on a Wednesday, a largely middle-aged trickle begins. It's time for the Torah class and from the vantage point of his glass-fronted cubicle, Solly Aptekar watches with an anxious expression. 'I feel depressed when I don't see people turning up,' says the young man, who oversees the centre. 'It's very important for Indian Jews to understand their roots and religion. Few of us know who we are. In my ten years at school there was only one line about Jews or Judaism in the syllabus—'Six million Jews were killed in the Holocaust'.' While Aptekar scolds people who call in to say that they will be bunking class, Sharona Ghasulkar organizes her notes to the beat of Radio Mirchi. Recently back from a stint in Israel, the young woman in a neat white headscarf and serious expression is now fulfilling her 'voluntary community service' obligations. Although not very voluble, she thaws a bit when asked about the distinctive Groom Song sung during Bene Israel weddings. Rummaging in her bag she produces a little booklet that she distributed at her own wedding in October. 'According to the Law of Moses and of Israel,' it states, announcing the union of 'Sharon and Sharona'. Inside is the song that even the most tuneless grooms must sing to welcome their bashful brides:

Oh my dove, the radiance of your beauty
Shines like the starry constellations of Orion and Pliedes
And I, for the sake of your love
Shall sing a song about young maids.

In the adjoining room—which triples up as classroom, conference-room and ballroom—fourteen students form a circle, chomp on toasted sandwiches and exchange 'shaloms'. I find myself next to Sophie ('although my name was changed to Jyoti at my marriage, everybody calls me Sophie') Bhingarde, the managing director of Hotel Shalom International at Chiplun, a coastal town half way to Goa. When I ask how she makes the time to attend the Bible Class, the middle-aged woman whispers with a guilty air, 'Our community is hardly 5000 people, so it is very difficult to get a good boy. Actually I had an inter-caste marriage. My husband is a Hindu Maharashtrian. If I am to teach my children about the religion, I need to know first.'

Meanwhile, Sharona has launched into the story of Cain and Abel. Cain is a shetkari (farmer) and Abel gaay-bakri sambhalta (a shepherd), she tells her students, before plunging into the rather ambiguous tale of sibling rivalry. 'Why did the brothers fight?' she asks her class. After much prompting, she gets a few halting responses. 'Cain was jealous of Abel,' someone says. Says another, 'To raagavla.' (He got angry.)

Getting into her stride, the confident Sharona proffers a number of Midrashes, hypothetical stories that attempt to fill in the holes left by the Torah. One suggests that the brothers divided up the world between them and then, like so many industrial families, squabbled over property. Another suggests that both brothers wanted to control the Holy Temple. But it is the third that really grabs the imagination of the class. 'Both Cain and Abel were born with twin sisters, with whom they were supposed to procreate,' reads Sharona. 'Cain desired Abel's twin, who was the more beautiful of the two. So he thought, "Let me kill Abel and have his twin sister to myself." ' 'I don't think that can be possible,' interjects a horrified woman, who looks like she would like to clap her hands over her son's ears. Proving once again that sex sells, the hitherto drowsy class erupts into an excited discussion. It's still underway when I get up to go, back to the 4 Ltd and the crowded Bombay in which I work and live.

★

Sentimentalists wandering Samuel Street and Jacob Circle might encounter the ghosts of Hannukahs past, but it's the ironies of Hannukahs present that are much more in evidence. Bene Israeli families who for centuries lived in Bombay's Israel Mohalla and pined for the lost homeland of Israel today live in the Promised Land in mini-Indias and long for the subcontinent. So they return in their dreams and December holidays, buy Hindi film music CDs and consume chaat with the zeal of pilgrims.

'They are always flying back to visit relatives, they know the latest Hindi songs and wear the latest saris,' says Shalva Weil, an anthropologist with Hebrew University in Jerusalem, who has studied communities like the Cochini Jews and Ethiopian Felashas that make up the rainbow nation of Israel. 'This is no hangover from the past. We are talking about fourteen- and fifteen-year-olds as well. That they are living in Israel and proud to be Jewish doesn't contradict the fact that they are Indian. I have studied many ethnic communities in Israel, but none have retained their ethnic identity like the Bene Israel.'

The British-born academician has tracked the community for thirty years, visiting their derelict synagogues in the Konkan, cataloguing their difficulties with Hebrew and observing their progress in their new homes in Lod and Ramallah. In the course of a morning meeting at Hotel President, Ms Weil describes the paradox of the Bene Israel.

Early though it is, her breakfast is interrupted by constant calls from friends from around the country. The first is from Ahmedabad-based writer Esther David, who in a recent novel wrote about her gradual discovery that 'I did not have to live in Israel to feel more Jewish than I felt in India'. Another call is from a Jewish friend who, after working in the aircraft industry in Israel, returned to Delhi where he set up a massive factory. 'One chappie actually went back to his village in the Konkan,' says Ms Weil, between sips of coffee. 'Some people have come back to India. You can't call it a trend, but it certainly is a phenomenon.'

The 45,000 Bene Israelis who cannot return to their Konkan villages have carted the necessary props back to Israel. Ms Weil describes a life complete with Bollywood fanzines, Marathi chat sessions and saris drying in the balconies. 'My daughter Ilana was born in the community and they had a naming ceremony for her,' she recalls. 'The women dressed me in a sari, tucked coconuts and fruit into my belly and said, "May you have better luck next time, may you have five sons." After that I only had sons, but that is another story. Even today the distinctive *malida* and henna ceremonies are conducted, and the Bene Israel synagogues have retained their liturgy.'

But why have the Bene Israel, more than any community in Israel, retained their links with their motherland? 'Probably because they never suffered anti-Semitism in India,' says Ms Weil. Then, with some reluctance, she admits, 'And possibly because they did suffer discrimination in Israel.'

This is the cruel twist to the 2000-year-long saga. Ever since its formation in 1948, Israel adopted a policy under which anybody with a Jewish parent qualified for citizenship. Most westernized Baghdadi Jews opted to migrate to Britain or Australia. But the few that went to Israel integrated and became Israeli overnight, relegating India to a convenient transit lounge in their history. Somehow, the Bene Israel didn't find it so easy to switch identities.

In the early fifties, some Bene Israelis claimed they were being discriminated against on the grounds of colour, and wrote to David ben Gurion saying they wanted to go back to India. All 137 were sent back, only to find that the India of the fifties had its own share of problems. Jobs and houses were tough to come by, so the group did a quick rethink, another letter was despatched to Ben Gurion, and by 1958 they were all back in Israel.

Just as tempers were cooling and routine was numbing the pain of displacement, another controversy erupted in 1961. This time, Israel's chief rabbi cast aspersions on the purity and practices of the Bene Israel and prohibited other Jews from marrying them. A two-year-long sit-down strike forced the authorities to initiate an anthropological investigation and declare that the Bene Israel were 'full Jews in every respect'. 'The Bene Israel perceived it as a continuation of the discrimination that they had received at the hands of the Baghdadi Jews,' says Ms Weil. The chief rabbi was, indeed, an Iraqi Jew. 'There was a lot of bitterness which is remembered to this day.'

And not just in Israel. At a talk Ms Weil gives one January evening at Bombay's British Council—as on other occasions—many Bene Israel express mixed feelings about the stern Fatherland. Many, like Solly Aptekar, are waiting for 'the situation to settle down' before they make the move. 'It's really nice—just like any European country,' Aptekar says, before quickly assuming a pious expression and adding, 'We love the land of India. But our prayers connect us to Israel.'

Others, however, are not so compelled to make their aliyah—the return to the land of milk, honey and explosives. A housewife looks around conspiratorially before admitting that she is 'terrified of the compulsory military service' that comes as a package deal with a comfy house in Beersheba. 'We are peace-loving people, and we are used to getting along with all castes and communities,' she murmurs. Management consultant David Haeem doesn't even try to hide his distress over the exodus. 'True, Jews all over the world feel the need to go to the Holy Land. But if everybody leaves, what will happen to the synagogues, cemeteries and prayer halls which our forefathers built with such pain?' he says, virtually yelling.

Indeed, decades of neglect by Israel have meant that resentment often elbows aside the seemingly compulsory declaration that 'Israel holds a very special place in our hearts'. As Haeem complains, 'I recently attended a seminar in Israel, and I am sorry to say the demographic chart overlooked Indian Jewry entirely. However small we may be, our forefathers struggled to keep the religion alive and we deserve a mention as much as anybody else.'

However, such omissions are becoming rare. After centuries of rejection and suspicion, the Bene Israel have suddenly been rediscovered and repackaged. Enterprising Israeli travel agents are busy marketing Jewish heritage tours to India—complete with 'Shabbos at leisure', a morning at Sassoon Dock and prayers at the Samuel Street synagogue. Also thrown in is a side-trip to 'quaint' Alibag, during which the tourists will be treated to an ice-cream at the no-frills S. Daniel Soda Company and allowed to 'meet with community elders to understand the unique culture and lifestyle'.

Tourists apart, the Bene Israel have captured the imagination of academicians of the sort who are prone to justifying their six-month stints in India with statements like, 'Our generation will probably witness the extinction of Indian Jewry. This makes study and collecting imperative. There is much to be learnt from an ancient Jewish community that has never experienced persecution.' The outcome is a veritable invasion of sociologists, biologists and anthropologists armed with questions and theories—the Bene Israel are one of the ten lost tribes; the Bene Israel are descendents of Moses' brother Aaron, and so on. Even the normally guarded Rabbi Kolet feels compelled to declare, 'After all these years, suddenly we are being described as exotic.'

★

At the Tiphereth Israel Synagogue at Jacob Circle—also known as Kandlekaranchi Masjid at Saat Rasta—the mood is triumphant. Status-symbol cars disgorge suited occupants. Gaily dressed families enter the airy gabled structure and wave to acquaintances. Video cameras stand at alert.

Somewhere towards the middle of the room, a woman is energetically brushing a man's gums with a little plastic rod. She completes the job and then moves on to another elderly gent. It is only after this mysterious ritual is repeated a few times that I realize that what she is collecting are mouth-swabs, those clinching clues to the mysteries of millennia.

On the podium, flowery welcome speeches are under way. But finally Dr Tudor Parfitt of London's School of Oriental and African Studies and a celebrity in Bene Israel circles begins his eagerly anticipated presentation. The historian has used genetic testing to arrive at conclusions that have generated jubilation among the Bene Israel worldwide.

For 2000 years, the Bene Israel believed that they were children of Israel. But the only supporting evidence they had was admittedly flimsy—a rather over-the-top oral history and a handful of traditions. Little wonder, then, that they were dogged by scepticism over centuries, first from the Baghdadi Jews and later from disbelieving academics and suspicious rabbis. For the first time, they had been furnished with proof, nothing less than a *Times of India* clipping with an unambiguous headline announcing, 'DNA tests confirm India's Jewish community carries unusual Moses gene'.

'In the mid-nineties, when DNA was recognized as a means of verification of identity, an international project was launched in England to study the origins of the Jewish priesthood,' Dr Parfitt tells his rapt audience, which has foregone a lazy Sunday to hear him speak. 'We got thousands of genetic samples from Jewish priests or kohens, and discovered that 52 per cent of them had a unique constellation of DNA which marked them out from others. We believe that they are all descendents of a single individual who lived 3000 years ago, and it is tempting to believe that this was Aaron, the brother of Moses.'

The findings made a huge splash in the often-contradictory worlds of science and religion. 'It provided corroboration of at least one element of the Biblical story, and confirmed that the Jewish priesthood had carried on for 3000 years,' says Dr Parfitt. He undertook to test the Lemba tribe in southern Africa and came up with dramatic results. 'Here were all these black people who claimed a connection with the land of Israel which nobody believed. But we found the same signature in 51 per cent of their priests.'

Next, Dr Parfitt turned his rather disbelieving gaze and mouth-swab-gear to India. 'Once processed, the results were surprising, though not nearly as surprising to you as to me,' he tells his Bene Israeli listeners. 'Your oral tradition had nurtured you, it was of your fibre. But for me the results were unexpected and delightful. They are perfectly, transparently, overpoweringly and unambiguously clear—your community did hail from outside India.'

As Dr Parfitt delivers his extraordinary message, I study the names inscribed in the synagogue over the last century—names like Milkabai Moredebai Talkar and Benjamin Ashtankar, people who had to believe in their identity without the support of science and genetic signatures. How would they have reacted to this stunning vindication? Will the presence of a single hapletyte in the DNA change the way the Bene Israel perceive themselves? Could this finding resolve their persistent dilemma about the geography of home? In this Bombay synagogue, alive with excited teenagers and jabbering matrons, the story of the Bene Israel may have come a full circle, but the questions continue to niggle.

Meanwhile, Dr Parfitt is drawing to a close. 'What this means is that you are as Jewish as any other Jewish community. We each carry within us an encyclopaedia, and the history of our ancestors is written there,' he thunders as deafening, ecstatic applause breaks out. 'In your case, we have only read the first page, but it is clearly stamped: the Bene Israel came from Israel.'

Morning You Play Different, Evening You Play Different

Naresh Fernandes

Their eyes give it away. Chris Perry wears a slick black jacket, the sleeves of his crisp white shirt revealing the glint of dark cuff links. His fingers clasp a gleaming tenor saxophone with a lover's gentleness. Arms crossed coquettishly above her waist, Lorna Cordeiro is chic in a bouffant and a form-fitting gown that shows a flash of ankle. They stare into each other's eyes, mesmerized. Behind them looms a giant camera aperture borrowed from the opening sequence of the Bond films.

You couldn't miss the poster as you sauntered down Jamshetji Tata Road in downtown Bombay. It hung outside the Astoria Hotel, across the street from the octagonal Art Deco turret of Eros cinema, inviting the city to Chris and Lorna's daily shows at the Venice nightclub. It was 1971. India was savouring its newfound place on the world's stage. The country's armed forces had decisively liberated Bangladesh and the idealism of Independence had welled up again. India's middle classes were capturing their polyester memories on Agfa Click IIIs that cost forty-six rupees and fifty paise (taxes extra), aspiring to the lifestyles of 'The Jet Set Air Hostesses' described in the *Illustrated Weekly of India* (price: eighty-five paise), and being encouraged by newspaper ads to 'Go gay with Gaylord fine filter cigarettes.'

As the City of Gold bubbled through its jazz age, Lorna and Chris enthralled Bombay with their shows at Venice each night. Remo Fernandes, who would go on to become the first Indian pop musician to record an album of original English-language tunes, was among those locked in the spell. 'Two artists sometimes ignite a creative chemistry in each other which goes beyond all logical explanation.

Mere mortals can only look and listen in awe,' he rhapsodized. 'In such duos, one plus one does not make two. It makes a number so immeasurable, it defies all laws of calculus.'

But the sparks that flew at Venice gradually built into a roaring conflagration. As Remo put it: 'Hyper-intense, high-temperament artistic relationships often end in emotional disaster, like two comets when they steer too dangerously close. Chris's and Lorna's, as we all know, was no exception.'

Like the myths about the city in which they soared to fame, the tale of Chris and Lorna has gained so much in the re-telling that it's sometimes difficult to thresh the apocrypha from the actual. Thirty years after the two stopped performing together, old-time musicians in the bylanes of Dhobi Talao and Bandra still beg anonymity as they reminisce in sad whispers.

'He was shameless. He left his wife and three small children for that girl.'

'Chris and Lorna were in love. When they fought, they became mortal enemies. He destroyed her and he destroyed himself.'

'She was a very good singer. Beyond that, she was nothing. She got her break with Chris Perry. He made a contract with her. She couldn't sing without his permission. She had no brains, so she signed. Then he went back to his wife.'

'He didn't let her perform with anyone else. He threatened to break the legs of one Hindu fellow who tried to get her to sing with him.'

'She hit the bottle, men. She became an alcoholic and just disappeared.'

Chris Perry—who was born Pereira—died on 25 January 2002, his last years hobbled by Parkinson's disease. Lorna has refused to recount her version of events for publication. But the fidelity of her contralto booming out of our speakers, embroidered with Chris's perfectly crafted sax filigrees, speaks its own truth.

★

Ronnie Monserrate was nineteen when he began to play Sunday gigs at Venice with the Chris Perry band, sitting in for the regular pianist.

Venice had a reputation. It was the jazzman's jazz haunt, the rendezvous for musicians from around the country and occasionally from around the world. Dave Brubeck swung by when he visited Bombay in 1958, as Duke Ellington had when his band set out on their famous world tour of 1963. As Ronnie tells it, the dapper Chris Perry was the musician's musician: 'He had perfect pitch. He was an arranger, a composer, a player.' Chris played both trumpet and saxophone, sometimes switching from one to the other mid-tune, a feat that required elaborate lip control. His trumpet tone was broad and true. He didn't have a flashy technique, but the notes he coaxed out of his horn had a mellowness that kept the fans coming back night after night.

Chris was forty-three at the time, Lorna was twenty-five. No one seems quite sure exactly how they met, but everyone's agreed that he groomed her into one of the Bombay's finest crooners. One version maintains that Lorna got her break when still in school, after she won the Connie Francis soundalike competition at Metro cinema. This prompted a musician named Raymond Albuqerque to invite her to sing in his show at the Bandra Fair. Her rendition of *Underneath the Mango Tree* got the crowds so fired up that Chris Perry, already an established performer, went to her home to audition her. She was just sixteen when she joined Perry's band.

A vocalist in the Shirley Bassey mould, Lorna belted out every tune like it was her last time on stage. 'She had a lot of black feel,' is how Ronnie describes her performances. 'You could see the intensity when she was on stage. She'd give it her best, every time. She was like a magnet. You couldn't help but be attracted to her when she was on stage. And with the Chris Perry band by her side, it was like magic happening. There was incredible attraction. There was a lot of love in the interaction. It was apparent in their body language. They brought out the best in each other. They'd look into each other's eyes and their understanding was so great that there'd be spontaneous combustion.'

Offstage, though, things could get awkward. Any man attempting to talk to Lorna was liable to get a taste of Perry's famously volatile fists. During breaks, the musicians would sit around their table, absolutely silent. 'They were jolly people but they were afraid to laugh around Chris,' Ronnie says. Ronnie was the only exception, perhaps because his youth made him seem unthreatening. Two decades later, he'd find opportunity to call in that bond of trust.

Venice was around the corner from Bombay's swinging jazz strip, Churchgate Street (now Veer Nariman Road). Pianists, trios and quartets were to be heard all the way down the 200-metre thoroughfare as it led off from Churchgate station to the Arabian Sea. First came Berry's, with tandoori butter chicken that was the stuff of Bombay legend and accomplished piano-fronted groups led by Dorothy Jones and Stanley Pinto. Across the fence was Bombelli's, named after its Swiss owner, where a trio held sway as ad men sipped cappuccinos. Then came the Ambassador, where Toni Pinto's quintet encapsulated Bombay's diversity: the group had two Jews—a singer named Ephrim Elias and drummer Abie Cohen, an Anglo-Indian tenor saxophonist named Norman Mobsby, and, in addition to Pinto, another Goan, the bassist Clement Furtado.

Pinto's kingdom was named the Other Room, so called because after the rich and famous had finished drinking at the bar, they'd say, 'Let's go to the other room.' He ruled for sixteen years from 1958, his sharply dressed group spinning out hard-driving bop and light classics, and playing back-up for cabarets and visiting acrobats, magicians and flamenco dancers. The Ambassador was owned by the cigar-chomping Jack Voyantzis, an ebullient Greek who was assisted by his brother, Socrates. The siblings had started their subcontinental journey in Rangoon, opened a cafe in Delhi, and finally found their way to Bombay, where they transformed a hotel known as the Argentinian into the Ambassador. The cream of Bombay society turned out to catch Toni's tightly-rehearsed band. Toni remembers once looking up from his piano to see three of the city's leading editors appreciatively tapping their feet: Rusi Karanjia, editor of the Left-wing tabloid *Blitz*, D.F. Karaka, editor of the rival *Current*, and Frank Moraes, editor of the *Indian Express*, with his American girlfriend. Another time, as the band was going through its routine, Toni realized that someone from the back of the room was playing along on a trumpet. It turned out to be American hornman Eddie Calvert. 'He came for dinner one night even though he was staying at the Ritz,' Toni says, and he asked his drummer, Bobby Hadrian, to go back and get his instrument. Calvert and Toni's band jammed for an hour, playing the tunes the American had made famous: *Cherry Pink, Begin the Beguine* and *Wonderland by Night.*

Elsewhere on Churchgate Street, music spilled out through the doors of the Napoli, The Talk of the Town and Gaylord's. Opposite Venice, there was jazz at the Ritz, while at the Little Hut, Neville Thomas led a group calling itself Three Guys and a Doll. Past Flora Fountain stood Bistro and Volga, home to a quartet led by the grandfatherly baritone saxophonist, Hecke Kingdom.

Dave Brubeck was impressed enough by the local musicians to attempt to make some recordings with them during his visit. But Bombay defeated him. He later recounted the episode to an interviewer: 'The current fluctuated in Bombay in those days and so the tape would speed up and slow down. Like, when you were shaving, the speed of the motor would go up and down. It ruined one of my favourite tapes I've ever made.' Another visiting jazzman, the pianist Hampton Hawes, was overwhelmed by problems that were rather more basic. 'Bombay turned me around,' he wrote. 'I'd never seen poverty before.' Art, he decided, was irrelevant amidst the gnawing deprivation. 'Here I was thinking about making a big splash, a hit record, going home a hero, and I'm walking the streets with motherfuckers who don't even know what a piece of bread is, let along Stravinsky or Charlie Parker. If Bird was alive and played for them they wouldn't be able to hear him because they'd be too damn hungry.'

Admittedly, jazz had always been the preserve of Bombay's elite. But while the audiences were upper crust, the musicians who cooked up the syncopated rhythms were not. Like Toni Pinto, Ronnie Monserrate, Chris and Lorna, the majority were Roman Catholics strivers from the former Portuguese colony of Goa, 550 kilometres south of Bombay. They'd been an important part of the Bombay music scene since the 1920s, when Bombay began to develop its appetite for what was then called 'hot music'. Jazz had made its way from New Orleans in the waxy grooves of phonograph records and travelled over the oceans with touring American bands that played for the administrators of the Raj. Bombay's first jazz concerts were performed at the Bandstand, south of the Oval. Among the earliest jazzmen to play an extended stint in Bombay was Leon Abbey, a violinist from Minnesota, who led an eight-piece band at the Taj during the 1935-36 season. Abbey wore white tails on stage and played the freshest sounds. He told one interviewer, 'I kept up with the latest numbers because someone would always come up to the bandstand and say, 'Old Bean, would you play so and so . . .', because as far as he was concerned, we should know how to play *everything* that had ever been written.' Midway through the trip, the Taj management sent Abbey and saxophonist Art Lanier back to New York to pick up the latest music.

Abbey's outfit was replaced by the Symphonians, fronted by the cornet player, Cricket Smith. Smith had been featured on the seminal recordings made by James Reese Europe's Society Orchestra in 1913 and 1914, capturing jazz at the moment of its transition from the relatively unsophisticated ragtime style. Smith 'signed his contract for a fixed amount of money and two Coronas a day, so every day, the manager would have to bring him his cigars', recalls Luis Moreno, a Spanish trumpet player who lived in Bombay for twenty years. 'He was a character.'

In 1938, pianist Teddy Weatherford, who had played with Louis Armstrong, took the stage with his men. His swinging style and treble voicing had been an important influence on jazz during its formative years. The Taj, it would seem, wasn't quite the genteel venue it now is—not at least from the way Weatherford's occasional bassist, a Russian named 'Innocent Nick', described the gigs to the jazz magazine, *Storyville*. 'Teddy used to play downstairs, in the Tavern of the Taj, for the soldiers, sailors and others, a very rough place,' Nick said. 'Teddy would play for hours without a break. Even with drinks, he would continue one-handed. He had tremendous hands.'

For the African-American musicians, Bombay provided refuge from the apartheid in the US. Men like Weatherford and his sidemen, such as the saxophonist Roy Butler, spent long years shuttling between Europe and the subcontinent, where racial barriers seemed non-existent, at least for them. Butler's years in India as a Weatherford sideman, he told *Storyville*, were among his happiest—the work was relatively easy, the pay and conditions good, he was treated splendidly by both management and clientele, and enjoyed the luxurious life under the British Raj. The Taj management, on its part, honoured Weatherford by naming a dish after him: Poires Glace Weatherford. (The absence of colour prejudice was only to be expected. After all, industrial baron Jamshetji Tata was moved to build the Taj after being prevented, one leisurely Bombay evening, from dining at the Europeans-only Pyrke's Apollo Hotel. Later, he famously hung a notice in the Taj forbidding entry to South Africans and dogs.)

Weatherford's sidemen were an eclectic lot and opened Bombay's ears to a wealth of new sounds, the Cuban drumming of Luis Pedroso and the Spanish brass of Luis Moreno, among them. Butler, who was known as the Reverend in acknowledgement of his abstemious ways, helped Weatherford drill the band. Moreno characterized Butler as the 'gentleman of the orchestra'. Moreno added, 'He never drank in his life and if someone said, "How about a round of drinks?" Roy would say, "I'll have an ice-cream. You enjoy beer, I enjoy ice-cream." ' Butler went on to lead his own band at Greens, located where the Taj Intercontinental now stands.

Both Weatherford (who married an Anglo-Indian woman, before dying of cholera in Calcutta in 1945, aged forty-one) and Butler recruited Goan sidemen, plugging Bombay into the source of jazz. The trumpet player Frank Fernand, who played in Weatherford band with his Goan compatriots, Micky Correa and Josique Menzies, says that his stint with the American taught him to 'play like a negro'. Moreno helped Fernand develop the ability to hit long, high notes, eventually extending his range up to E flat. Butler, it must be noted, was less than thrilled with his Goan employees. 'My short stretch as a bandleader in India was not too earth-shaking,' he told *Storyville*. 'The local musicians were not too familiar with jazz at that time. I understood that there are some very good jazzmen out there now, but the time was too short for anything to develop, good or bad.' For their part, some of the Goan musicians weren't overly impressed with Butler, either. They believed his decision to stay in India was motivated by the fear that he wouldn't find work in the US. As Fernand put it, 'The faltu fellows stayed, the good ones went home.'

But by the forties, Bombay's swing bands had earned a solid

reputation. After listening to Micky Correa and Frank Fernand play their hearts out in the wind section in the outfit fronted by Rudy Cotton (a Parsi who had been born Cawasji Khatau), one contemporary correspondent wrote that 'the band really jumped, just another bunch of righteous boys who helped to prove, if proof were needed, that this jazz of ours has developed into an international language'.

*

Both Lorna and Chris lived on the edges of a precinct of cemeteries known as Sonapur—the City of Gold. Lorna lives to the south of Sonapur, in Guzder House in the Dhobi Talao neighbourhood. When the wind blows east, her starkly furnished room is filled with the aroma of hot mawa cakes and fluffy buns being unloaded from the ovens in Kayani's bakery next door. In the narrow corridors of Guzder House, even whispers carry clear down the hallway, and the mundane details of Lorna's spats with Chris became common knowledge. 'He was a big gambler,' one neighbour recalls. 'He'd come in a car and say, "Lorna, give me 5000 rupees." She'd go to the bank and withdraw it. All her savings were wiped out.'

Chris lived to the north of Sonapur, opposite the church of Sao Francis Xavier in Dabul. Once he got home, he became a strict but caring father. 'He was very religious,' his eldest son Giles told one interviewer. 'We had to recite the Rosary at eight every evening. At twelve noon and at dusk, we had to say the Angelus. If the phone ran during prayers he would say, "Throw the phone out." Miles, another of Chris Perry's sons, described his father's devotion to his art. 'His daily routine when he woke up was to first smoke a cigarette and then blow his trumpet. Only then would he go for a wash.' His son Errol added: 'He always had his favourite instrument close to him. Even while he slept, the trumpet would be on one side and mummy on the other.'

The neighbourhood in which Lorna and Chris lived had long been the focus of Catholic migrants from Goa. The first significant numbers of Goan migrants came to Bombay in 1822, liberal partisans fleeing political persecution in the Portuguese colony for the safety of

British India. More followed in 1835 after a rebellion by mixed-race mestizos deposed Goa's first native-born governor general, Bernardo Peres da Silva. The mestizos launched a two-year reign of terror, forcing da Silva's supporters into exile. As the century progressed, Goan emigration to Bombay swelled. The Portuguese hadn't been especially attentive to developing industries, so the pressure on cultivable land was intense. Adding to this, many Goans chafed under the oppression of the bhatkars, as the feudal landlords were known. By the 1920s, many Goan men were being employed as seamen by such British lines as BI, P&O, Anchor and Clan. They used Bombay as a base between their voyages. Other Goans found work as domestic helpers in British households and social institutions. The early Goan fortune-seekers were almost all male: The arduous overland journey from Goa to Bombay, which took between ten and fifteen days, discouraged women. But the opening of the rail line between territories in April 1881 changed that. By the 1930s, Goans in Bombay had come to be associated with the ABC professions: they were ayahs (maids), butlers and cooks. In a column titled 'Random Jottings', published by the *Anglo-Lusitanian Journal* in 1931, a writer calling himself Atropos noted that of the 37,000 Goan residents in Bombay that year, 14,000 were seamen, 7000 were cooks or waiters and 3000 were ayahs. A full 700 were estimated to be musicians. (At least 7000 Goans were unemployed.)

The neighbourhoods around Sonapur began to fill up with Goan dormitories known as coors, a word that is derived from the Portuguese cuadd or room. These were established by individual villages back in Goa to provide a home away from home for their neighbours who were too poor to maintain two residences, one in the village and the other in the city. By 1958, half of the estimated 80,000 Goans in Bombay lived in such quarters—which were now being called 'clubs', adopting the word used to describe the chummeries many firms had established for their single European employees, writes Olga Valladares in her 1958 thesis titled *The Coor System—a Study of Goan Club Life in Bombay*. As you walk down the narrow lanes of the neighbourhoods around Sonapur today, you can see fading signboards for them everywhere: the Boa Morte Association (Club of Majorda); St. Anne's

Club of Ponda; Fatradicares Club; The Original Grand Club of Pombura; Nossa Senhora dos Milagres, Club of Sangrem. There were 341 Goan clubs in the city in 1958, mainly between Dhobi Talao and Dabul. The seamen who lived in them found it easy to get from there to the docks and the shipping offices, while the cooks and domestics were within walking distance of the produce sellers at Crawford Market, where their chores began before they moved on to their employer's establishments each day.

Life in the clubs was spartan. Residents were allowed minimal baggage, usually just a big trunk. 'Life was lived out of the box and on it,' Valladares says. The club-dweller's box 'is not only the repository of all personal possessions, his wardrobe and his safe, but it is his dining table at mealtimes and his bed at night'. The altar was the centrepiece of the club. In addition to statues of Christ and Mary, they contained icons of the patron saint of the village, decorated with offerings of flowers. Every evening, members were required to gather around the altar to say the Rosary. The highlight of the year was the celebration in exile of the village feast. Collections were taken up and, after Mass, there was an elaborate meal, followed by musical performances.

The music, old-timers recall, was superb. After all, the musical talents of Goans had earned the community a formidable reputation throughout the subcontinent. The Portuguese may have neglected higher education in Goa, but the parochial schools first established in 1545 put into place a solid system of musical training. As early as 1665, a Goan choir performed an oratorio by Giacome Carissimi in seven voices at the Basilica of Bom Jesu. The recital caused such a sensation, it led the Carmelite musician Guiseppe di Santa Maria to declare, 'I feel I am in Rome.' The clash of civilizations in Goa created a whole range of syncretic forms: the Goa sausage was a Portuguese *chorizo* with a tear-inducing splash of Indian spice; cashew feni was drunk in a leisurely Iberian manner after sundown; and the mando—the only harmonized folk musical form on the subcontinent—melded saudade, the nostalgic melancholy that pervades Portuguese fado, with Indian folk melodies. Transgressing subcontinental norms, the mando was the accompaniment for social dancing between the sexes; as the musicians crooned their songs of yearning, couples struck up delicate postures of stylized courtship.

Their musical inclination came in handy when Goans sought work in British India. They soon established themselves as the musicians of the Raj, staffing the orchestras established by British administrators and by Indian maharajahs seeking to appear sophisticated. In Bombay, Goan musicians took over both ends of the music business. The *Times of India* mentions a Goan ensemble playing in the Bombay Philharmonic Orchestra in the Town Hall in 1888. Other Goan groups are said to have displaced the Muslim street bands that played at the weddings of the common folk and other festive occasions. Salvador Pinto, who played the cornet in the Volunteer Corps, is thought to have formed the first proper street band, writes Bombay local historian Dr Teresa Albuquerque. She says that the demand for Goan musicians was so great that one ingenious man named Francisco Menezes trawled through the clubs to find unemployed men to march in the processions, instructing them to inflate their cheeks without blowing a note. Dhobi Talao's Goans were prominent not only as musicians but also in the city's musical instrument trade. L.M. Furtado opened his store in Jer Mahal, around the corner from where Lorna lived, in the 1920s, importing pianos and violins that had been tropicalized to keep them from warping in the Bombay swelter. Marques and Company was nearby.

Goan musicians also conjured up soundscapes for the silent films. Bombay's Watson's Hotel had been host to India's first cinema screening on 7 July 1896, a show that advertised itself as 'living photographic pictures in life-sized reproductions by Messrs Lumiere Brothers'. By New Year's day in 1900, the Tivoli Theatre was screening twenty-five pictures, with music by a string band. A portrait photographer named Harishchandra Sakharam Bhatavdekar became the first Indian to import a motion-picture camera from London and he shot a wrestling match between two well-known musclemen in 1897. Other locally shot films followed, including *Alibaba, Hariraj* and *Buddha* by a Bengali named Hiralal Sen. A creative flashback projects the tantalizing image of Bombay audiences drinking in black-and-white scenes from Indian folktales as a Goan string quartet trots out phrases from Mozart and snatches of mandos, varying the tempo to match the action on screen. Goans have stayed in the picture ever since.

When jazz swung into the subcontinent, Goans seized it as the song of their souls. 'Jazz gave us freedom of expression,' explains Frank Fernand, who played in the Teddy Weatherford band at the Taj. 'You played jazz the way you feel—morning you play different, evening you play different.' New tunes came to India as sheet music, but that sometimes wasn't much help even to accomplished readers: jazz scores contained such unconventional instructions as glissando, mute and attack. 'But when we heard the records, we knew how to play the notes,' Frank says. For a Goan jazzman, the greatest accolade was to be told that he 'played like a negro'. No one seems to have received more praise on this account than Chic Chocolate, who occasionally led a two-trumpet barrage at the Green's Hotel with Chris Perry. Chic— whose name Goans pronounced as if they were talking about a rooster's offspring—was known as the 'Louis Armstrong of India'. His stratospheric trumpet notes and his growly scatting were a tribute to his New Orleans idol. 'He had a negro personality,' Frank Fernand marvels. 'He played everything by heart.' His stage presence was unforgettable. As the band reached a crescendo, Chic would fall on one knee and raise his horn to the stars.

Chic had been born Antonio Xavier Vaz in Aldona in 1916. His mother wanted him to be a mechanic and earn a respectable living, but he dreamt of a life in music. He started out with a group called the Spotlights and, by 1945, his own outfit, Chic and the Music Makers, beat out twelve other bands to win a contract at Green's, which was also owned by the Taj. The pianist Johnny Fernandes, who later married Chic's daughter, Ursula, remembers the stir the trumpet player caused when he played at parties in Dhobi Talao homes. He says, 'People would flock to see him as if he was a (movie) hero.' To have Chic perform at a wedding or a christening was a matter of prestige, but it could bump up the catering expenses. 'You'd have hordes of gatecrashers coming to hear him,' Johnny explains. Chic, his contemporaries say, not only played like a negro, he even looked like one. The swarthiness of some Goan jazz musicians, such as the saxophonist Joe Pereira, came from ancestors with roots in Portugal's

African colonies of Mozambique and Angola. But Chic's dark skin is attributed by one musician to his being a Mahar, a member of an untouchable caste. Many of Bombay's jazzmen, this musician says, were drawn from this caste. As he theorized: 'In Goa, Mahars were grave diggers. They'd also play snare drums and blow conches in funeral bands. When they came to Bombay, they became good jazz drummers and trumpet players.'

They say Chic performed one of his greatest feats of improvisation offstage. 'Chic lived in Marine Lines and had a girlfriend called Catherine, with whom he had a son', a matter that shocked conservative Catholic sensibilities, one musician recalls. 'But then he decided to marry another girl. The wedding was to be at the Wodehouse Road Cathederal in Colaba. But Catherine landed up there with her son, so the wedding was shifted hastily to Gloria church in Byculla, across town.' The befuddled guests waited patiently in the Colaba church, even as Chic said 'I do' in the deserted neo-Gothic nave of Gloria church.

Many early Goan jazzmen were sideman in Micky Correa's band, which played at the Taj from 1939 to 1961. Among them was Ronnie Monserrate's father, Peter, who was known as the 'Harry James of India'. Peter's five sons formed Bombay's second-generation of Goan jazzmen: Joe and Bosco play trumpet and fluegelhorn, Blasco the trombone, Rex the drums and Ronnie the piano. The family lived in Abu Mansion, an apartment block in the textile mill district of Parel. The boys would come home from school at four and begin to practice, each having been allotted a two-hour slot by their father. The music would continue late into the night, then occasionally start again in the wee hours when Peter Monserrate and his gang—violinist Joe Menezes, trombone player Anibal Castro, drummer Leslie Godinho and Chic Chocolate—returned from a drink after work to demand an impromptu performance. As their mother cooked up a meal, the Monserrate boys would go through their paces. Their neighbours, mainly working-class Hindus, tolerated this with fortitude. Ronnie surmises, 'I suppose it's like living next to the railway tracks. After a while, you get immune to the roar of the trains if you want to get any sleep.'

Activity in the Monserrate household would get especially hectic just before the biennale Sound of Surprise talent shows that the Bombay Musicians' Association organized on the Sunday in November closest to the feast of St. Cecilia, the patron saint of musicians. Bombay's hottest swing bands took to the Birla theatre's revolving stage to compete for the Franz Marques award for best original composition. Even though Peter Monserrate rehearsed his band hard in the corridors of Abu Mansion, his group never managed to win the trophy. His friend, Chris Perry, won in 1964, the first year it was given out. Toni Pinto took the award home in 1966 for *Forever True*, a gentle bossa nova tune that leapt out at him late one night as he travelled home in a cab. With only the bulb above the meter for light, he scribbled the theme down on the back of a matchbox.

Goan musicians who didn't play in the nightclubs, mainly worked at weddings, Parsi navjote initiation ceremonies and Catholic funerals. For many, finding a job for the evening meant taking a trip to Alfred's, the Irani restaurant on Princess Street, midway between Chris's home and Lorna's apartment. Tony Cyril, Dennis Vaz, Johnny Rodriges, Johnny Baptist, Mike Machado and Chris Perry—the major bandleaders each had a regular table at which they'd slurp up endless cups of milky chai. 'You'd come there every morning and hang around there as a routine,' says Johnny Fernandes, Chic Chocolate's son-in-law. People who wanted to liven up their parties would land up at Alfred's and approach one or the other leader. The cry would go up: one bass player needed, two trumpets and one piano. 'Once you got your assignment, you'd go home to get your suit and head out to the venue,' Johnny says. It paid to be sharply turned out: in addition to their fifteen-rupee fee, musicians got three extra rupees for dressing up in a white jacket and black trousers.

★

When Bollywood films are beamed through their melodramatic prism of stock characters and broad stereotypes, Catholics emerge as not being quite Indian. They speak a mangled Hindi patois with Anglicized accents. They're dolled up in Western clothes. The men are given to wearing climatically inappropriate jackets and felt hats. Unlike Hindus who knock back the occasional glass of something in bars, Catholic men tipple at home, as their wives and children look on. Still, they're genial drunks, unthreatening sidekicks to the hero. Often, their role as sidemen was literal: The screen musicians, backing the hero as he performs that nightclub sequence that seemed mandatory in every Hindi film shot in the fifties, answer to names like George, Sidney and Michael. As for Catholic women, they never wear saris and their immodest legs show out from under their frocks. Older Catholic women, often called Mrs Sequeira or Mrs D'Souza, are landladies or kindly neighbours who offer the hero consolation when he is temporarily stymied in his pursuit of the loved one. But younger Catholic women (with notable exceptions) are danger incarnate. They smoke. They have boyfriends to whom their parents don't object. They dance in nightclubs and lure men to their doom with their promise of a world in which the sexes interact more freely, in which arranged marriages aren't the norm, in which love isn't taboo. In the end, though, the Catholic characters have only minor roles, a reflection of their lives at the margins of Indian society.

The bit parts in which Catholics found themselves cast on screen weren't an accurate portrayal of the vital role Goans played in the Hindi film industry. Until the eighties, India had no pop music save for Hindi film songs. Millions memorized and hummed the compositions of C. Ramachandra, Shankar and Jaikishan, Laxmikant and Pyrelal and S.D. Burman, whose names rolled by in large letters at the beginning of the movies. But the Sound of India was actually created by Goan musicians, men whose names flickered by in small type under the designation 'arranger'. It's clear: The Hindi film classics that resound across the subcontinent and in Indian homes around the world wouldn't have been made without Goans. Their dominance of the Hindi film world is partly a function of the structural differences between Indian and Western music. Indian classical music is melodic. The ragas that form the basis of Indian music are unilinear, each instrument or vocalist exploring an independent line. To move an audience, film scores must be performed by orchestras, with massed instruments playing in harmony. Only Goans, with their training in

Western music, knew how to produce what was required.

Frank Fernand was among the first Goans in Bollywood and assisted such worthies as Anil Biswas, Hemant Kumar and Kishore Kumar. As he describes it, the men who composed the scores for Hindi films couldn't write music and had no idea of the potential of the orchestras they employed. They would come to the studio and sing a melody to their Goan amanuensis, or pick out the line on a harmonium. The Goan assistant would write it out on sheet paper, then add parts for the banks of strings, the horn sections, the piano and the percussion. But the assistant wasn't merely taking dictation: It was his job to craft the introductions and bridges between verse and chorus. Drawing from their bicultural heritage and their experience in the jazz bands, the Goans gave Bollywood music its promiscuous charm, slipping in slivers of Dixieland stomp, Portuguese fados, Ellingtonesque doodles, cha cha cha, Mozart and Bach themes. Then they would rehearse the orchestras, which were staffed almost entirely by Goans. After all, hardly anyone else knew how to play these Western instruments. To Frank Fernand, the music directors were mere subcontractors, men whose main job was liaising with the financiers. 'We arrangers did all the real work. They'd show off to the directors and producers and try to show that they were indispensable. But to be a music director, salesmanship was more important than musicianship.'

Chic Chocolate spent his mornings assisting C. Ramachandra, who is popularly credited with having introduced swing into Bollywood. But tunes like *Ina mina dika* and *Gori gori* (inspired by the mambo standard *Chico Chico from Puerto Rico*) bear Chic's unmistakable signature. His stamp is also audible on the throbbing Cuban percussion opening of *Shola Jo Bhadke*, a tune from *Albela*. Chic and the Music Makers made a brief appearance in the film to perform the tune, clad in an Indian wardrobe director's frilly Latinesque fantasy. Cawas Lord's conga beats out the introduction and hands clap clave. Chic smiles broadly at the camera in the best Satchmo tradition.

Among the most reputed arrangers in Bollywood was the venerable Sebastian D'Souza, who did his best-known work with the duo of Shankar and Jaikishan between 1952 and 1975. 'His arrangements were so brilliant, composers would take snatches of his background scores and work them into entire tunes,' says Merlin D'Souza, Sebastian's daughter-in-law and a rising Bollywood music assistant herself. Sebastian had a brush with the film world in pre-Partition Lahore, where he led a band at Stiffle's hotel. His earliest arrangements were for Lollywood composers Shyam Sundar and Mohammed Ali, recalls the saxophonist, Joe Pereira. Joe was Sebastian's cousin, and had been adopted as a fourteen-year-old by his older relative. Joe would spend his mornings taking music lessons from Sebastian, then take him his tiffin in the afternoon when Sebastian took a break from rehearsals. After 1947, Sebastian made his way to Bombay, but found that there was a glut of bandleaders in the hotels. He called on his Lollywood contacts and made his way to the film recording studios, where he got a break with O.P. Nayyar. The first tune he arranged was *Pritam aan milo*, which was sung by C.H. Atma in 1955. Merlin, who occasionally accompanied her father-in-law to the studios, remembers him walking around with a pencil tucked behind his ear. He devised a system of notation that incorporated the microtones that characterized Indian melodies. Sebastian was highly regarded by his musicians for his ever-generous nature. He often lent musicians money to buy better instruments or tide over a crisis. His contemporaries also remember him for the patience he showed to even less-than-dexterous musicians. Merlin says that Sebastian was willing to give anyone a break. 'Even if you played the viola haltingly, you'd find a place there, on the back row,' she says.

That proved the lifeline for many Goan musicians, who, by the mid-seventies, were increasingly being thrown out of work as Bombay's nightclub scene went into decay. A more rigorous enforcement of the prohibition act and a crippling tax on establishments featuring live music kept patrons away. Besides, rock and roll was changing musical tastes and Bombay was developing an ear for beat groups. The film studio, which until then had been a source of supplementary income, suddenly became everyone's main job. But the relatively simply Hindi film music Goan musicians were forced to play ate them away. 'Their passion was to play jazz and big band,' Ronnie Monserrate says. 'This was their bread and butter but they didn't enjoy it. They were really frustrated. That's probably why so many of them became alcoholics.' It took only four or five hours to record each tune. Musicians would be paid at the end of each shift, so they'd grab their money and head out for a drink. Few actually cared to see the movies in which they'd performed.

Chris Perry also had a stint in the film studios, assisting Khayyam and working with such names as Lakshmikant and Pyarelal, R.D. Burman and Kalyanji Anandji. He eventually was emboldened to produce his own film. *Bhuirantlo Munis* (The Man from the Caves) was the first colour film to be made in Konkani, the language spoken along the west coast between southern Maharashtra and northern Karnataka, and which is the mother tongue of most Goans. Chris wrote the story, the music and the lyrics. It starred Ivo Almedia, Helen Pereira and C. Alvares, who had gained prominence for their work in *tiatr*, as Goa's satirical musical theatre is known. The film was based on *The Count of Monte Cristo*, a tale that has great resonance in Goa because one of the characters, Abbe Faria, who in the Dumas novel is described as an Italian priest, in real life had been born in Candolim, in Goa, in 1756. Father Jose Custodio de Faria is acknowledged as having been among the earliest protagonists of scientific hypnotism, and a statue of him stands prominently in Goa's capital, Panjim. The priest, who moved to Lisbon, was forced to flee to France in 1787 when a rebellion he had been associated with in Goa was crushed. The *Conjuracao dos Pintos*, the conspiracy of the Pinto family, was the first Asian struggle that aimed to replace European colonial rule with an independent state on the European model. That's how Dumas came to meet the man he knew as 'the black Portuguese'. Abbe Faria threw himself into the vortex of the French Revolution, was imprisoned and died of a stroke in 1819. In the Dumas novel, Abbe Faria takes it upon himself to educate the hero, Dantes, when the two are unjustly imprisoned in the French version of Alcatraz for fourteen years. Dantes escapes, transforms himself into the Count of Monte Cristo and destroys his enemies. When the novel was published in 1844, it earned the Vatican's ire because the tale was seen to propagate the un-Christian impulse of revenge. But as the trumpeter Frank Fernand points out, it seemed like an entirely appropriate subject for Chris Perry, the man whose quick temper was the stuff of popular lore.

★

One April evening in 1966, the Goan pop musician Remo Fernandes, barely a teenager then, strolled down to Panjim's Miramar beach to take the air on the esplanade. All Panjim society, high and low, was there too. 'There, decked up in our over-flared bell bottoms, we checked out the chicks dolled up in what we all thought were mini skirts—after all they did reach a full quarter of an inch above the knee,' Remo recalls. Keeping an eye on the younger folk, clumps of parents sat on the green wooden benches on the esplanade, 'running a commentary on whose son had gone off with whose daughter for a walk along the sea'.

From a kiosk on the beach, a pretty lady named Bertinha played records on the speaker system provided by the Panjim Municipality. She had a weakness for Cliff Richard tunes, Remo says. But that evening, she spun out a song called *Bebdo* (Drunkard). Miramar Beach was hypnotized. 'The Panjim citizenry stopped in its tracks, the sunken sun popped up for another peep, the waves froze in mid-air,' Remo has written. 'What manner of music was this, as hep as hep can be, hitting you with the kick of a mule on steroids? What manner of voice was this, pouncing at you with the feline power of a jungle lioness? And—hold it—no, it couldn't be—yes, it was—no—was it really? Was this amazing song in Konkani?'

Bebdo had been recorded a few months earlier by Chris Perry and Lorna in a Bombay studio and released by HMV. The jacket bore the flirty image that would later hang outside the Venice nightclub. The 45 rpm record had four tracks, opening with the rock-and-rolling *Bebdo* and ending on the flip side with the dreamy ballad, *Sopon*. 'Sophisticated, westernized urban Goa underwent a slow-motion surge of inexplicable emotions: the disbelief, the wonder, the appreciation, and then finally a rising, soaring and bubbling feeling of pride,' Remo says. 'The pride of being Goan. The pride of having a son of the soil produce such music. Of having a daughter of the soil sing it thus. And, most of all, of hearing the language of the soil take its rightful place in popular music after a period of drought. Chris and Lorna had come to stay.'

It isn't as if there hadn't been Konkani records before. HMV released its first Konkani tunes in 1927. The earliest records had been made by Anthony Toloo, Joe Luis, L. Borges, Kid Boxer and Miguel Rod, all of them *cantarists* from the tiatr world. But by the sixties, Konkani song had grown creaky and old fashioned. The melodies often were copied from western songs and the lyrics, for the most, were banal. Konkani songs, Remo says 'were predictable to a fault—you could whistle the next line and anticipate the next chord change on the very first hearing. Add to that a few wrong notes from two inevitable trumpets and modest recording quality'.

Chris Perry's tunes shattered the mould. They married the sophistication of swing with the earthiness of the Goan folk song. 'The songs were sensuous, funny, sexy, sad, sentimental, foot-tapping,' Remo raves. 'His songs are peopled by unforgettable fictional characters whom we have come to picture as real-life acquaintances—*Bebdo, Pisso* (Madman) and *Red Rose* are as palpable as personages created by a skilled novelist or cartoonist. He has taken us on unforgettable journeys to *Lisboa* and *Calangute*,' the Goan beach that was being colonized by hippies around the time Chris was making his landmark recordings. Some of the tunes had been written for the two tiatr shows Perry had produced: *Nouro Mhozo Deunchar* (My Husband, the Devil) and *Tum ani Hanv* (You and Me). *Nouro Mhozo Deunchar* was Goa's introduction to Lorna and the twenty-eight performances were an unqualified success. The crowds were so large, people waited outside the performance tent to hear her voice, one correspondent writes. After the shows, people would surge backstage to shake Lorna's hand. One tune she sang, *Saud* (Peace), became a standard at Goan weddings, and is still sung before the toast is raised.

Chris Perry's heart may have been in Goa, but it was Bombay that made it possible for him to record his classics. His albums crystalized the nostalgia of Bombay's Goan community, giving voice to their rootlessness—and his. Bombay allowed him to soak in jazz and rock and roll, sounds from which he crafted his own template. Besides, his Bombay nightclub stints helped him assemble the tight-knit band that accompanied him to the studio—where his Bollywood experience came in very handy. 'His recording work meant that, unlike the tiatr people, he knew his way around the studio,' notes Ronnie Monserrate. 'He knew about placing microphones to get the best sound, and about mixing.'

Most of all, there was Lorna. Her rich, sassy voice, everyone's agreed, is what alchemized Chris's compositions. Their long years together gave him an acute sense of her potential and he composed especially for her. 'Her nightingale's voice created the magic in rendering the songs effectively,' insists Tomazinho Cardoz, the tiatrist who went on to become the speaker of Goa's legislative assembly. Remo, among others, has no doubts about this. 'Without Chris there would have been no Lorna, and without Lorna there would have been no Chris,' he has written.

*

Lorna stopped performing in 1973 after her relationship with Chris Perry fell apart. The stories about their break up are hazy on the details. In one version, Lorna came home from a vacation to find that the apartment they shared had a new lock on the door. Chris's wife, Lily, is said to have served him an ultimatum and he went home to Dabul. But before the split, he'd made Lorna sign a bond on stamp paper, prohibiting her from singing for twenty years with any other band leader without his permission. He is said to have reasoned that Lorna was his creation, so she had no right to perform without him. Chris is said to have enforced the bond in a muscular fashion. 'Once, Emiliano got her to sing with him when he was performing at the Flamingo. Chris landed up there, chased him all the way down Marine Drive and gave him a black eye,' one musician says. 'Imagine doing that to Emiliano. He's such a harmless bugger.'

Another musician told of how Chris would leap out of his seat at Alfred's restaurant when he saw Lorna go by on her way to the bazaar. She would squirm out of his clutches, but was terrified enough to refuse all offers to perform again.

Chris eventually moved to Dubai with his family in the mid-seventies, and opened the Dubai Music School. The split is said to have left Lorna a wreck. People who knew her say she became an alcoholic. She worked as a secretary in a firm that sold earth-moving equipment for a while, but disappeared from the world of show business. Every afternoon, though, Goa radio would broadcast the tunes she and Chris had recorded and two decades after she'd made her last record, every Goan still knew Lorna's voice. Rumours boiled over: She's emigrated. To Canada. To Australia. No, she's dead.

★

Goans were still discussing Lorna's whereabouts a quarter of a century after Ronnie Monserrate first backed her at Venice. Now a successful record producer and hot film studio sideman with his brothers, Ronnie kept receiving inquiries about Lorna when he toured Goa in 1994 to promote a new album. He decided to take a trip to Guzder House to persuade her to record again.

A woman fresh from the shower with her hair in towel opened the door. She sat him down and asked what he wanted. 'I want to see Lorna,' he explained. She replied, 'That's me.' Ronnie was taken aback. 'She looked like a wreck. I remembered her as she was in 1971—a total bombshell. But since then, she had hit the bottle and become total gone-case.'

It took a while to convince Lorna that he was serious about getting her into the studio again. She told Ronnie that it had been a couple of decades since she'd last performed. 'She was trying to tell me tangentially that anyone who'd tried to get her to sing had got a pasting from Chris Perry,' Ronnie says. But after another visit, Ronnie managed to recruit her mother to his cause and win Lorna over. They began rehearsing in February 1995, knocking the rust off her voice. 'The old power was still there,' Ronnie says. 'I began to feel good about the project.' Ronnie also made a trip to HMV's vaults to dig out the infamous contract. The company's lawyer assured him that it wasn't legally binding. Back in Goa, Ronnie had recruited Gabriel Gomes to write tunes for the album. 'It had been Gabru's dream to have Lorna sing his songs,' Ronnie says. Gabriel set to work in a frenzy of cigarettes, building into such a peak that, after composing just one track, he took ill and had to be taken to hospital. He died shortly thereafter. New composers had to be brought in.

When the recording of *Hello Lorna* finally got underway in a Juhu studio five months later, Ronnie would travel back across town with her after each session. She was still afraid that Chris Perry would accost her.

On 3 December 1996, Lorna performed publicly for the first time in twenty-four years at a tourism festival at Miramar beach. The traffic was snarled up for kilometres as Goans swarmed to catch a glimpse of the legend. State police say that the show drew 3,00,000 people—the biggest crowd since the one that had gathered to celebrate Goa's liberation from Portuguese rule in 1961. At a press conference the day before, Lorna had been mobbed. 'There was mayhem,' Ronnie recalls. 'People ran on to the stage and were hugging her and kissing her. They were so overjoyed that Lorna was back.' Chris Perry landed up at Lorna's hotel in a last-minute attempt to scare her off. She wasn't in, so he left a note. Ronnie intercepted the missive and didn't pass it on.

A few hours later, cheers erupted as Lorna climbed to the stage, looking out over a choppy ocean of heads. When the hubbub subsided, Ronnie's aching piano introduction washed over the audience and Lorna began to belt out the opening tune from her comeback album. '*Aicat mozo tavo,*' she urged. '*Avaz mozo canar tumchea sadonc ishtani ravo portun aicunc mozo tavo.*' Hear my voice. Let the sound linger in your ears, my friend. Hear my voice.

Mumbai

Suketu Mehta

Bombay (now officially Mumbai) is a city with an identity crisis; a city experiencing both a boom and a civic emergency. It's the biggest, fastest, richest city in India. It held twelve million people at the last count—more than Greece—and 38 per cent of the nation's taxes are paid by its citizens. Yet half the population is homeless. In the Bayview Bar of the Oberoi Hotel you can order [a bottle of] Dom Perignon champagne for 20,250 rupees, more than one-and-a-half times the average annual income; this in a city where 40 per cent of the houses are without safe drinking water. In a country where a number of people still die of starvation, Bombay boasts 150 diet clinics. *Urbs prima in Indis*, says the plaque outside the Gateway of India. By the year 2020, it is predicted, Bombay will be the largest city in the world.

Six years ago, this divided metropolis went to war with itself. On 6 December 1992 the Babri Masjid was destroyed by a fanatical Hindu mob. Ayodhya is many hundreds of miles away in Uttar Pradesh, but the rubble from its mosque swiftly provided the foundations for the walls that shot up between Hindus and Muslims in Bombay. A series of riots left 1400 people dead. Four years later, at the end of 1996, I was back in Bombay and was planning a trip with a group of slum women. When I suggested the following Friday, 6 December, there was a silence. The women laughed uneasily, looked at each other. Finally, one said, 'No one will leave the house on that date.'

The riots were a tragedy in three acts. First, there was a spontaneous upheaval involving the police and Muslims. This was followed, in January, by a second wave of more serious rioting, instigated by the Hindu political movement Shiv Sena, in which Muslims were systematically identified and massacred, their houses and shops burnt

A version of this piece appeared in *Himal*, Vol. 2, No.8, August 1998.

and looted. The third stage was the revenge of the Muslims: on 12 March, ten powerful bombs went off all over the city. One exploded in the Stock Exchange, another in the Air India building. There were bombs in cars and scooters. Three hundred and seventeen people died, many of them Muslims.

Yet, many Muslims cheered the perpetrators. It was the old story: the powerful wish of minorities all over the world to be the oppressor rather than the oppressed. Almost every Muslim I spoke to in Bombay agreed that the riots had devastated their sense of self-worth; they were forced to stand by helplessly as they watched their sons slaughtered, their possessions burnt before their eyes. There are 1.6 million Muslims in Bombay: more than 10 per cent of the city's total population. When they rode the commuter trains, they stood with their heads bent down. How could they meet the eyes of the victorious Hindus? Then the bombs went off, and the Hindus were reminded that the Muslims weren't helpless. On the trains, they could hold their heads high again.

Last December, I was taken on a tour of the battlegrounds by a group of Shiv Sena men and Raghav, a private taxi operator, a short, stocky man wearing jeans labelled 'Saviour'. He was not officially a member of Shiv Sena, but he was called upon by the leader of the local branch whenever there was party work to be done. He led me through Jogeshwari, the slum where, on 8 January 1993, the second wave of trouble began. A Hindu family of mill workers had been sleeping in a room in Radhabai Chawl, in the Muslim area. Someone locked their door from the outside and threw a petrol bomb in through the window. The family died screaming, clawing at the door. One of them was a handicapped teenage girl.

Raghav and a couple of the others took me into the slums through passages so narrow that two people cannot walk abreast. They were cautious, at first. But as we passed a mosque, Raghav laughed. 'This is where we shat in the Masjid,' he said. One of his companions shot him a warning look. Only later did I learn what he meant. The Sena zealots had burnt down this mosque; it was one of the high points of the war for them, and they recalled it with glee. One man had taken a cylinder of cooking gas, opened the valve, lit a match and rolled it inside. He then joined the police force, where he remains to this day.

We were discussing all this not in some back room, in whispers, but in the middle of the street, in the morning, with hundreds of people coming and going. Raghav was completely open, neither bragging nor playing down what he had done; just telling it as it happened. The Sena men—the sainiks—were comfortable; this was their turf. They pointed out the sole remaining shop owned by a Muslim: a textile shop that used to be called Ghafoor's. During the riots some of the boys wanted to kill him, but others who had grown up with him protected him, and he got away with merely having his stock burnt. Now it has reopened, under the name Maharashtra Mattress. Raghav pointed to the store next to it. 'I looted that battery shop,' he said.

He led me to an open patch of ground by the train sheds. There was a vast garbage dump on one side, with groups of people hacking at the ground with picks, a crowd of boys playing cricket, sewers running at our feet, train tracks in sheds in the middle distance, and a series of concrete tower blocks beyond. A week ago, I had been standing on the far side with a Muslim man, who pointed towards where I now stood, saying, 'That is where the Hindus came from.'

Raghav remembered. This was where he and his friends had caught two Muslims. 'We burnt them,' he said. 'We poured kerosene over them and set them on fire.'

'Did they scream?'

'No, because we beat them a lot before burning them. Their bodies lay here in the ditch, rotting, for ten days. Crows were eating them. Dogs were eating them. The police wouldn't take the bodies away because the Jogeshwari police said it was in the Goregaon police's jurisdiction, and the Goregaon police said it was the railway police's jurisdiction.'

Raghav also recalled an old Muslim man who was throwing hot water on the Sena boys. They broke down his door, dragged him out, took a neighbour's blanket, wrapped him in it and set him alight. 'It was like a movie,' he said. 'Silent, empty, someone burning somewhere, and us hiding, and the army. Sometimes I couldn't sleep, thinking that just as I had burnt someone, so somebody could burn me.'

I asked him, as we looked over the waste land, if the Muslims they burnt had begged for their lives.

'Yes. They would say, 'Have mercy on us!' But we were filled with such hate, and we had Radhabai Chawl on our minds. And even if there was one of us who said, let him go, there would be ten others saying no, kill him. And so we had to kill him.'

'But what if he was innocent?'

Raghav looked at me. 'He was Muslim,' he said.

★

A few days later I met Sunil, deputy leader of the Jogeshwari shakha, or branch, of the Shiv Sena. He came with two other Sena boys to drink with me in my friend's apartment. They all looked around appreciatively. We were on the sixth floor, on a hill, and the highway throbbed with traffic below us. Sunil looked out of the window. 'It's a good place to shoot people from,' he said, making the rat-tat-tat motion of firing a sub-machine gun. I had not thought of the apartment this way.

Sunil was one of the favourites to be pramukh, the leader, of the entire shakha one day. He first joined the Shiv Sena when he needed a blood transfusion, and the Sena boys gave their blood, an act which touched him deeply—his political comrades were, literally, his blood brothers. He was in his twenties now, helpful, generous and likeable. He has a wide range of contacts with Muslims, from taking his daughter to a Muslim holy man to be exorcized, to buying chickens in Mohammedali Road during the riots for resale to Hindus at a good profit. But what preyed on his mind now was the conviction that the handicapped girl who died in the fire in Radhabai Chawl had been raped by her Muslim assailants. There was no evidence of this; the police report did not mention it. But that didn't matter. It was a powerful, catalytic image: a disabled girl on the ground with a line of leering Muslim men waiting their turn to abuse her, while her parents matched her screams with their own as their bodies caught the flames.

Sunil insisted on referring to the riots as a 'war'. Certainly, at the J.J. Hospital, he had witnessed scenes typical of wartime: corpses identifiable only by numbered tags. And at Cooper Hospital, where

Hindus and Muslims were placed next to each other in the same ward, fights would break out; wounded men would rip saline drips out of their arms and hurl them at their enemies. During the riots, the government sent tankers of milk to the Muslim areas. Sunil, with three of his fellow sainiks dressed as Muslims, put a deadly insecticide in one of the containers: the Muslims smelt it and refused all the milk. Sunil's men also shut off the water supply to the Muslim quarter. After six days, he said, the Muslims were forced to come out to the big chowk in the centre of the quarter. 'That's when we got them,' he recalled.

I asked him: 'What does a man look like when he's on fire?'

The other Shiv Sena men looked at each other. They didn't trust me yet. 'We weren't there,' they said. 'The Sena didn't have anything to do with the rioting.'

But Sunil would have none of this. 'I'll tell you. I was there,' he said. He looked directly at me. 'A man on fire gets up, falls, runs for his life, falls, gets up, runs. It is horror. Oil drips from his body, his eyes become huge, huge, the white shows, white, white, you touch his arm like this'—he flicked his arm—'the white shows, it shows especially on the nose.' He rubbed his nose with two fingers, as if scraping off the skin. 'Oil drips from him, water drips from him, white, white all over.

'Those were not days for thought,' he continued. 'We five people burnt one Mussalman. At four in the morning, after we heard about the Radhabai Chawl massacre, a mob assembled, the like of which I'd never seen. Ladies, gents. They picked up any weapon they could. Then we marched to the Muslim side. We met a paowala on the highway, on a bicycle. I knew him, he used to sell me bread every day. I set him on fire. We poured petrol over him and set light to him. All I thought was that he was a Muslim. He was shaking. He was crying, "I have children, I have children." I said: "When your Muslims were killing the Radhabai Chawl people, did you think of your children?" That day we showed them what Hindu dharma is.'

★

'We used to roller skate down Teen Batti,' an architect said to me. He used the past imperfect tense; he meant that he used to *be able* to roller skate down Teen Batti. Teen Batti is at the top of the road that winds up from the sea; the Ridge Road leads from there up Malabar Hill. The area is now a shabby high-rise ghetto where the cars leave no room for the juvenile traffic of roller skates and bicycles. What he said stuck with me because I used to roller skate down Teen Batti and cycle around there too. I cannot imagine a twelve-year-old boy doing so now.

The sounds, colours and moods of the sea lent heft and weight to my childhood. From my uncle's apartment I can still see the rocks where the boys from our building would catch little fish trapped in the hollows when the tide went out. We sat down there and watched the whole progress of the sunset, from light to dark, and planned our lives—who would become the police inspector, who the astronaut. Gradually, a colony of hutments took over these rocks, and when we walked on them we would sometimes slip and fall on shit. The rocks are now a public latrine, full of strange smells. There are two million people in Bombay who have to defecate in any space they can find. The sea air sometimes wafts the stench over the skyscrapers of the rich, nudging them, reminding them.

We lived in Bombay and never had much to do with Mumbai. Mumbai was what Maharashtrians called the city; and Bombay was the capital of Maharashtra. But so far as we Gujaratis—migrants, like so many in Bombay—were concerned, Mumbai meant the people who came to wash our clothes or look at our electricity meters. We had a term for them—ghatis: people from the ghats—meaning someone coarse, poor. There were whole worlds in the city which were as foreign to me as the ice fields of the Arctic or the deserts of Arabia. I was eight years old when Marathi, the language of Maharashtra, became compulsory in our school. How we groaned. It was a servants' language, we said.

I moved to New York when I was fourteen. When I went back I found that the city had grown in wild and strange ways. In front of my uncle's building, for instance, was a monstrous skyscraper, its skeleton completed more than a decade before, lying vacant. Several such buildings dot the city. The flats have been bought for huge sums but are empty because they violate municipal height limits. The builders knew they would not get planning consent but went ahead anyway. The first priority was to put up the concrete reality; they could deal with the extraneous issues—municipal clearances, legal papers, bribes—later. But the city corporation put its foot down, and the fate of the building entered the courts. While the most expensive, most desirable real estate in Bombay lies vacant, half the population sleeps on the pavement.

Land is to Bombay what politics is to Delhi: the reigning obsession, the fetish, the raison d'être and the topic around which conversations, business, newspapers and dreams revolve. Property is the mania of island dwellers all over the world, and Bombay is washed by water on three sides. It regards the rest of India much as Manhattan looks on the rest of America: as a place distant, unfamiliar and inferior. The lament I kept hearing—from both Hindus and Muslims—was that the riots were an ungentle reminder that Bombay was part of India.

In 1994 a survey revealed that real-estate prices in Bombay were the highest in the world. There was general jubilation in the city. It confirmed something that Bombayites had long felt: that this was where the action was, not New York or London. Here, if you wanted a flat in a new building shooting up from the narrow strip of land behind the National Centre for the Performing Arts in Nariman Point, you would need three million dollars.

*

The manager of Bombay's suburban railway system was recently asked when the system would improve to a point where it could carry its five million daily passengers in comfort. 'Not in my lifetime,' he answered. Certainly, if you commute into Bombay, you are made aware of the precise temperature of the human body as it curls around you on all sides, adjusting itself to every curve of your own. A lover's embrace was never so close.

One morning I took the rush hour train to Jogeshwari. There was a crush of passengers, and I could only get halfway into the carriage. As the train gathered speed, I hung on to the top of the open door. I feared I would be pushed out, but someone reassured me: 'Don't worry, if they push you out they also pull you in.'

Asad Bin Saif is a scholar of the slums, moving tirelessly among the sewers, cataloguing numberless communal flare-ups and riots, seeing first-hand the slow destruction of the social fabric of the city. He is from Bhagalpur, in Bihar, site not only of some of the worst rioting in the nation, but also of a famous incident in 1980, in which the police blinded a group of criminals with knitting needles and acid. Asad, of all people, has seen humanity at its worst. I asked him if he felt pessimistic about the human race.

'Not at all,' he replied. 'Look at the hands from the trains.'

If you are late for work in Bombay, and reach the station just as the train is leaving the platform, you can run up to the packed compartments and you will find many hands stretching out to grab you on board, unfolding outward from the train like petals. As you run alongside you will be picked up, and some tiny space will be made for your feet on the edge of the open doorway. The rest is up to you; you will probably have to hang on to the door frame with your fingertips, being careful not to lean out too far lest you get decapitated by a pole placed close to the tracks. But consider what has happened: your fellow passengers, already packed tighter than cattle are legally allowed to be, their shirts drenched with sweat in the badly ventilated compartment, having stood like this for hours, retain an empathy for you, know that your boss might yell at you or cut your pay if you miss this train and will make space where none exists to take one more person with them. And at the moment of contact, they do not know if the hand that is reaching for theirs belongs to a Hindu or Muslim or Christian or Brahmin or untouchable or whether you were born in this city or arrived only this morning or whether you live in Malabar Hill or Jogeshwari; whether you're from Bombay or Mumbai or New York. All they know is that you're trying to get to the city of gold, and that's enough. Come on board, they say. We'll adjust.

Bombay Meri Hai

Music: Mina Kava
Lyrics: Naju Kava
First recorded in 1969 by Uma Pocha and
Chorus with Mina Kava and his Music Makers

---

*Long before Indi-pop became fashionable, Mina Kava (born
Kavarana) mixed up shehnais and saxophones to present Bombay
with a bilingual yowl that truly reflected its mongrel origins. The tune
still is a favourite at Christian and Parsi wedding celebrations.*

—Eds

Verse
Come from England, come from Scotland, come from
Ireland
Come from Holland, come from Poland, come from any
land,
If you're looking out for a pleasant holiday,
Come to Bombay, come to Bombay, Bombay meri hai.

Chorus
Bom bom bom bom
Bombay meri hai
Bom bom bom bom
Bombay meri hai
Our ladies are nice, they are so full of spice
Come to Bombay, come to Bombay
Bombay meri hai.
Wear a dhoti, put a topi and a small coatie
Mini or bikini is so good for you honey

If you ain't so gay then you can live the sadhu way
Come to Bombay, come to Bombay
Bombay meri hai.

Verse
Puri bhaji, bhelpuri you can try and tell
Idli dosa, hot samosa you will like it well
Once you come to stay then you won't like to go away
Come to Bombay, come to Bombay
Bombay meri hai.

Notes on Contributors

Khwaja Ahmad Abbas was a socialist and a man of letters. He was the filmmaker Raj Kapoor's conscience and helped craft some of the early classics of RK Studios. He was also a journalist and above all a Bombay man.

Neera Adarkar is an award-winning architect and activist involved with urban issues, gender issues, environmentalism and secularism. She is a visiting lecturer at the Academy of Architecture and Rizvi College of Architecture.

Salim Ali, also known as 'The Birdman of India', was the face of ornithology in India until his death in 1985. He received numerous awards including the J. Paul Getty International Award, The Golden Ark of the International Union for Conservation of Nature and the Padma Vibhushan from the Indian government. He was nominated to the Rajya Sabha in 1985. His *Book of Indian Birds* is still a classic.

Chirodeep Chaudhuri makes photographs. He has worked with a newspaper, a magazine and a website. His photographs have been published in many recent important books on Mumbai. He has mounted two solo exhibitions, The Clocks of Bombay and Portfolio, and has participated in several group shows. His work can be viewed at www.chirodeep.com

Dilip Chitre is a poet, fiction-writer, playwright, painter and film-maker. He has won the Sahitya Akademi Award for his book of Marathi poems, *Ekoon Kavita-1*, and the Sahitya Akademi Translation Prize for *Says Tuka*, his English translation of the poetry of the seventeenth century Marathi poet-saint, Tukaram.

Behram Contractor, born and brought up in Mumbai, was a Bombay man to the core. His journalistic career spanned over forty-two years. He worked with the *Free Press Journal*, the *Times of India* and *Mid-day*, from where he left as executive editor to launch his own paper, the *Afternoon Despatch & Courier* in 1985. His column 'Round and About' which he wrote under the pseudonym of Busybee, had a large fan following. He was awarded the Padma Shri in 1990 and the B.D. Goenka Award for Excellence in Journalism in 1996.

J. Gerson da Cunha was Vice President of the Bombay branch of the Royal Asiatic Society, Knight Commander of the Literary and Scientific Order of St. James of Portugal and a member of the I.R. Zoological and Botanical Society of Vienna, among other affiliations. He has also written books about Bassein and Chaul, and about Konkani literature. He died as the last sheets of *The Origin of Bombay* were being printed in 1900.

Farrukh Dhondy's books include *East End at Your Feet* and *Come to Mecca* (both winners of the Other Award), *Poona Company* and a short story collection, *Trip Trap. Bombay Duck* was shortlisted for the 1990 Whitbread Award for the best first novel.

Duke Ellington was arguably the most influential jazz composer ever.

Nissim Ezekiel is best known as a poet although he has worn many hats. He has been editor, art critic, professor and cultural organizer. His books of poetry include *A Time to Change, The Unfinished Man, The Exact Name* and *Hymns in Darkness*.

Sunil Gavaskar is among cricket's greatest batsmen. He ended his career with thirty-four Test centuries.

Aldous Huxley, the English novelist and essayist, established his reputation with his first novel, *Crome Yellow*. His other books include *Eyeless in Gaza, The Doors of Perception* and *Heaven and Hell*. His most celebrated work, *Brave New World*, is a satiric account of an inhumane society controlled by technology.

Pico Iyer is the author of six books, most recently of *Abandon*, a novel. His previous works include classics of travel writing like *Video Night in Kathmandu, The Global Soul* and *Falling Off The Map*. He lives in suburban Japan.

Dosebai Cowasjee Jessawalla's autobiography, *The Story of My Life*, was published in 1911.

Adil Jussawalla is a poet, critic and essayist. His two books of poetry are *Land's End* and *Missing Person*. He also compiled and edited *New Writing in India*.

Mina Kava and **Naju Kava** were lyricists and musicians.

Sameera Khan is a Mumbai-based freelance writer, researcher and journalist. A former Assistant Editor with the *Times of India*, she has an MS in Journalism from the Columbia University Graduate School of Journalism, New York. An executive member of the Bombay Local History Society, she is also an active founder-member of the Network of Women in Media, India. She is researching and writing a book on the old Muslim neighbourhoods of Mumbai.

Rudyard Kipling, the English author with a firm belief in shouldering the White Man's Burden, was born in Mumbai. Educated in England, Kipling returned to India in 1882 and worked as an editor on a Lahore paper. His works include *The Jungle Book*, *The Second Jungle Book, Kim* and *Stalky and Co.* He won the Nobel Prize for literature in 1907.

Arun Kolatkar is a poet. He was born in Kolhapur and works in Mumbai as a graphic artist. His first book of poetry in English, *Jejuri,* was awarded the Commonwealth Poetry Prize in 1977. He also writes in Marathi.

André Malraux, the French writer, spent some time in Asia, where he helped organize the Young Annam League in Indo-China and founded the newspaper *Indochina in Chains*. His books include *The Temptation of the West, The Conquerors, The Psychology of Art* and *The Voices of Silence*.

Saadat Hasan Manto's literary, journalistic, radio-scripting and film-writing career spreads over more than two decades. He produced around 250 stories, scores of plays and a large number of essays and is widely regarded as the greatest short-story writer in Urdu. He also wrote over a dozen films, including *Eight Days*, *Chal Chal Re Navjawan* and *Mirza Ghalib*.

Nina Martyris, who works with the *Times of India*, grew up in the industrial town of Jamshedpur. She came to Mumbai ten years ago as a student and stayed on. An alumna of Sophia College, she has been a journalist for the past seven years.

Suketu Mehta is a novelist and journalist who grew up in Mumbai and lives in New York. He has won the Whiting Writers Award, the O. Henry Prize, and a New York Foundation for the Arts Fellowship in fiction. His work has appeared in *Granta, Harpers Magazine, Time,* the *New York Times*, and *Civil Lines*. His non-fiction book, *Maximum City: Bombay Stories,* will be published in 2003.

Meena Menon has been working with the textile workers movement in

Mumbai city since 1991, with an independent organization called Girni Kamgar Sangharsh Samiti, which organizes around the issues of unemployment and job losses in the textile and other industries. She is also with the Focus on the Global South, a research and advocacy organization.

Shabnam Minwalla is a journalist with the *Times of India*. She studied at St. Xavier's College in Mumbai and then at the University of Southern California in Los Angeles. She chose to return to Mumbai because home is where the Colaba Causeway is.

Cyrus Mistry published his first short story in 1976, when he was twenty. Since then, he has gone on to publish fiction and journalistic writing in several magazines and newspapers. He has also written screenplays, collaborating with Saeed Mirza for the film *Arvind Desai ki Ajeeb Dastaan*, and with wife Jill Misquitta for *Percy*, which won a National Award for Best Gujarati Film of 1990 and the Special Jury Award at the Mannheim Film Festival the same year. *Doongaji House* won the Sultan Padamsee Award in 1978.

Hemant Morparia is a radiologist and cartoonist. His work appears daily in *Mid-day*, among other publications. His first collection, *Fanatics and Their Antics*, was published in 2002.

Kiran Nagarkar has written three novels, two in English (*Ravan and Eddie* and *Cuckold*) and one in Marathi (*Saat Sakkam Trechalis*, translated into English under the title *Seven Sixes are Forty-Three*). He is also a playwright.

V.S. Naipaul was born in Trinidad in 1932. He went to England on a scholarship in 1950. After four years at Oxford he began to write, and he has followed no other profession. He has published more than twenty books of fiction and non-fiction, including *A House for Mr Biswas*, *An Area of Darkness*, *A Bend in the River*, *Among the Believers*, and *The Enigma of Arrival*. He won the Nobel Prize for Literature in 2001.

Daya Pawar, writer and poet, shook Marathi society with his book *Baluta*, an autobiographical account of life as a Dalit. The response to the book encouraged Pawar to write another book in which he explained how his life had been altered by the Dalits' negative response to *Baluta*. He died in 1996.

Nikhil Rao is completing his PhD dissertation at the University of Chicago. His work deals with the processes of urbanization in Mumbai in the late 19th and 20th centuries. He has taught courses in modern South Asian history and social theory.

Suvarnalata Rao is a sitar player and a musicologist. She has been a visiting faculty for various institutions at home and abroad. Her areas of studies include computational musicology, organology and stylistic analysis of music. Currently, she is a research scientist and music coordinator at the National Centre for the Performing Arts, Mumbai.

Salman Rushdie is the author of eight novels (many of which travel through Mumbai), a collection of short stories titled *East, West* and three works of non-fiction. His numerous awards include the European Union's Aristeion Prize for Literature. He is a fellow of the Royal Society of Literature and Commandeur des Arts et des Lettres. His novel *Midnight's Children* won the Booker Prize in 1981, and in 1993 it was judged the Booker of Bookers, the best novel to have won the Booker Prize in its first twenty-five years.

Vilas Sarang writes in English and Marathi. He holds PhDs in English from Mumbai University and in Comparative Literature from Indiana University. He has taught at the University of Basra in Iraq, Mumbai University and now teaches at Kuwait University. His books include *A Kind of Silence, Fair Tree of the Void* and *In the Land of Enki*.

Jeremy Seabrook is a journalist and campaigner based in London. He has written widely on aspects of social injustice, from housing to workers in the sex trade. His books include *Freedom Unfinished: Fundamentalism and Popular Resistance in Bangladesh Today, Children of Other Worlds*, and *Travels in the Skin Trade: Tourism and the Sex Industry*.

Manjula Sen is an independent journalist and researcher based in Mumbai. Formerly with the *Business Standard* and the *Times of India*, she contributes to *Man's World, Verve* and *Elle*.

Khushwant Singh was founder-editor of *Yojana*, and editor of the *Illustrated Weekly of India*, the *National Herald* and the *Hindustan Times*. Among his published works are the classic two-volume *A History of the Sikhs*, several works of fiction—including the novels *Train to Pakistan* (winner of the Grove Press Award for the best work of fiction in 1954), *I Shall Not Hear the Nightingale, Delhi* and *The Company of Women*—and a number of translated works and non-fiction books on Delhi, nature and current affairs. His autobiography, *Truth, Love & a Little Malice* was published in 2002.

Rahul Srivastava works at PUKAR, Partners for Urban Knowledge, Action and Research, Mumbai—a research institute with a focus on urban issues. He coordinates the Neighbourhood Project, which encourages students to document narratives about the city's various localities. He has studied anthropology and has written on tribal issues, popular culture and the environment.

Arundhathi Subramaniam is a poet. Her first book of poems was *On Cleaning Bookshelves* (Allied). Her poems have been published in national and international journals, and in an anthology of Indian English women's poetry. They have also been translated into Italian. Subramaniam is also a freelance journalist who has written extensively on theatre and dance. She heads Chauraha, an interactive interdisciplinary arts forum at the National Centre for the Performing Arts, Mumbai.

Paul Theroux, the American writer, has authored several highly praised fiction and travel books. His canon includes *Picture Place*, which won the Whitbread Literary Award in 1978; *The Mosquito Coast*, which was made into a film; *Riding the Iron Rooster*, which won the 1988 Thomas Cook Travel Book Award; *The Great Railway Bazaar*; and *Kowloon Tong*.

Gillian Tindall is a novelist and short-story writer who lives in London. Her novels include *Fly Away Home*, which won the Somerset Maugham Award, and *The Intruder*. Her novella *The China Egg*, is set in Mumbai. Her non-fiction works include *City of Gold* and *The Fields Beneath: The History of One London Village*.

Paromita Vohra is a filmmaker and writer. She has directed *Unlimited Girls, A Woman's Place, A Short Film About Time* and *Annapurna*, and written *Skin Deep, Veru* and *A Few Things I Know About Her*. She lives in Mumbai where she also teaches and is a PUKAR Associate.

About the editors:

Jerry Pinto is a poet and journalist. His first book, *Surviving Women*, was published by Penguin India, and his first poetry collection, *Asylum*, by Allied Publishers.

Naresh Fernandes has worked with the *Times of India* in Mumbai. He has previously worked in New York with the *Wall Street Journal*, and in Mumbai with the Associated Press and on the *First Edition*, a television news programme produced by Asia-Pacific Communication Associates. His pieces have appeared in *Transition, Man's World*, the *Los Angeles Times* and *Letras Libres*.

Acknowledgements

The editors would like to acknowledge the following people:

Adil Jussawalla, who, were he a professional acknowledgee, would be a rich man. Adil opened his library to our ransacking paws and dug out piles of stuff for us;

Lalitha Luke, who typed the manuscript which was twice as long as this and did not complain when we changed selections mid-stream;

The Bombay University Library at the Fort Campus, which made available its rich collection;

Our parents, friends, siblings and suchlike who listened to us burble on about inclusions, exclusions, deadlines and other disasters. In that wonderfully useful American phrase, you guys know who you are.

Copyright Acknowledgements

Grateful acknowledgement is made to the following for permission to reprint copyright material:

Oxford University Press India, New Delhi for 'Island' from *Collected Poems* by Nissim Ezekiel and for the extract from *The Fall of a Sparrow* by Salim Ali;

Pico Iyer for the extract from *Tropical Classical*;

Vilas Sarang for the extract from *Fair Tree of the Void*;

The Random House Group Limited for the extract from *Jesting Pilate* by Aldous Huxley, originally published by Chatto & Windus, copyright © the Estate of Mrs Laura Huxley;

Penguin Books India and Kiran Nagarkar for the extract from *Ravan and Eddie*;

Gillon Aitken Associates for the extract from *An Area of Darkness* by V.S. Naipaul, published by Andre Deutsch;

Jonathan Cape Ltd for the extract from *Bombay Duck* by Farrukh Dhondy;

Random House Group Limited for the extract from *The Ground Beneath Her Feet* by Salman Rushdie published by Jonathan Cape;

Rupa & Co. for the extract from *Sunny Days* by Sunil Gavaskar;

Curtis Brown for the extract from *City of Gold* by Gillian Tindall, published by Penguin Books India;

Penguin Books India and Khalid Hasan for the extract from *Stars from Another Sky* by Saadat Hasan Manto;

Farzana Contractor for 'Temples of Desire' by Busybee;

Penguin Books Ltd for the extract from *The Great Eastern Railway Bazaar* by Paul Theroux;

India Book House Pvt. Ltd for the extract from *The Story of the Freedom Struggle* (*Amar Chitra Katha*, Jumper Issue No. 10);

Doubleday, a division of Random House, Inc. for the extract from *Music Is My Mistress* by Duke Ellington, copyright © 1973 by Duke Ellington, Inc.;

Dilip Chitre for 'The View from Chinchpokli' from *Travelling in a Cage*, published by Clearing House;

Editions Gallimard and Penguin Books Ltd for the extract from *Antimemoirs* by André Malraux © Editions Gallimard, Paris, 1972, translated by Terence Kilmartin;

Professor Dinaz Kavarna for 'Bombay Meri Hai' by Uma Pocha and Chorus with Mina Kava and his Music Makers;

Cyrus Mistry for the extract from *Doongaji House*, published by Praxis;

Ravi Dayal Publisher and Penguin Books India for the extract from *Truth, Love & a Little Malice* by Khushwant Singh;

Arun Kolatkar for 'Fire' from *The Literary Endeavour*;

Jeremy Seabrook for the extract from *Life and Labour in a Bombay Slum*;

Urvashi Jain for the extract from *Bombay, My Bombay: The Love Story of the City* by K.A. Abbas;

Man's World for 'Hoops, Hunger, and the City' by Nikhil Rao;

Suketu Mehta for 'Mumbai'.

While every effort has been made to trace copyright holders and obtain permission, this has not been possible in all cases; any omissions brought to our attention will be remedied in future editions.